T0338774

Big Data Processing With Hadoop

T. Revathi
Mepco Schlenk Engineering College, India

K. Muneeswaran
Mepco Schlenk Engineering College, India

M. Blessa Binolin Pepsi
Mepco Schlenk Engineering College, India

A volume in the Advances in Data
Mining and Database Management
(ADMDM) Book Series

Published in the United States of America by
  IGI Global
  Engineering Science Reference (an imprint of IGI Global)
  701 E. Chocolate Avenue
  Hershey PA, USA 17033
  Tel: 717-533-8845
  Fax: 717-533-8661
  E-mail: cust@igi-global.com
  Web site: http://www.igi-global.com

Library of Congress Cataloging-in-Publication Data

Names: Revathi, T., 1965- author. | Muneeswaran, K., author. | Pepsi, M.
  Blessa Binolin, 1990- author.
Title: Big data processing with Hadoop / by T. Revathi, K. Muneeswaran, and
  M. Blessa Binolin Pepsi.
Description: Hershey, PA : Engineering Science Reference, [2018] | Includes
  bibliographical references.
Identifiers: LCCN 2017022368| ISBN 9781522537908 (hardcover) | ISBN
  9781522537915 (ebook)
Subjects: LCSH: Big data. | Apache Hadoop.
Classification: LCC QA76.9.B45 R485 2018 | DDC 005.7--dc23 LC record available at https://lccn.
loc.gov/2017022368

This book is published in the IGI Global book series Advances in Data Mining and Database Management (ADMDM) (ISSN: 2327-1981; eISSN: 2327-199X)

British Cataloguing in Publication Data
A Cataloguing in Publication record for this book is available from the British Library.

All work contributed to this book is new, previously-unpublished material.
The views expressed in this book are those of the authors, but not necessarily of the publisher.

For electronic access to this publication, please contact: eresources@igi-global.com.

Advances in Data Mining and Database Management (ADMDM) Book Series

ISSN:2327-1981
EISSN:2327-199X

Editor-in-Chief: David Taniar, Monash University, Australia

MISSION

With the large amounts of information available to organizations in today's digital world, there is a need for continual research surrounding emerging methods and tools for collecting, analyzing, and storing data.

The **Advances in Data Mining & Database Management (ADMDM)** series aims to bring together research in information retrieval, data analysis, data warehousing, and related areas in order to become an ideal resource for those working and studying in these fields. IT professionals, software engineers, academicians and upper-level students will find titles within the ADMDM book series particularly useful for staying up-to-date on emerging research, theories, and applications in the fields of data mining and database management.

COVERAGE

- Quantitative Structure–Activity Relationship
- Neural Networks
- Data Warehousing
- Data Mining
- Customer Analytics
- Predictive analysis
- Web Mining
- Data quality
- Database Testing
- Text mining

IGI Global is currently accepting manuscripts for publication within this series. To submit a proposal for a volume in this series, please contact our Acquisition Editors at Acquisitions@igi-global.com or visit: http://www.igi-global.com/publish/.

Titles in this Series

For a list of additional titles in this series, please visit:
https://www.igi-global.com/book-series/advances-data-mining-database-management/37146

Data Clustering and Image Segmentation Through Genetic Algorithms Emerging Research...
S. Dash (North Orissa University, India) and B.K. Tripathy (VIT University, India)
Engineering Science Reference • ©2019 • 160pp • H/C (ISBN: 9781522563198) • US $165.00

Optimization Techniques for Problem Solving in Uncertainty
Surafel Luleseged Tilahun (University of Zululand, South Africa) and Jean Medard T. Ngnotchouye (University of KwaZulu-Natal, South Africa)
Engineering Science Reference • ©2018 • 313pp • H/C (ISBN: 9781522550914) • US $195.00

Predictive Analysis on Large Data for Actionable Knowledge Emerging Research ...
Muhammad Usman (Shaheed Zulfikar Ali Bhutto Institute of Science and Technology, Pakistan) and M. Usman (Pakistan Scientific and Technological Information Center (PASTIC), Pakistan)
Information Science Reference • ©2018 • 177pp • H/C (ISBN: 9781522550297) • US $135.00

Handbook of Research on Big Data Storage and Visualization Techniques
Richard S. Segall (Arkansas State University, USA) and Jeffrey S. Cook (Independent Researcher, USA)
Engineering Science Reference • ©2018 • 917pp • H/C (ISBN: 9781522531425) • US $565.00

Bridging Relational and NoSQL Databases
Drazena Gaspar (University of Mostar, Bosnia and Herzegovina) and Ivica Coric (Hera Software Company, Bosnia and Herzegovina)
Information Science Reference • ©2018 • 338pp • H/C (ISBN: 9781522533856) • US $185.00

Advancements in Applied Metaheuristic Computing
Nilanjan Dey (Techno India College of Technology, India)
Engineering Science Reference • ©2018 • 335pp • H/C (ISBN: 9781522541516) • US $225.00

For an entire list of titles in this series, please visit:
https://www.igi-global.com/book-series/advances-data-mining-database-management/37146

701 East Chocolate Avenue, Hershey, PA 17033, USA
Tel: 717-533-8845 x100 • Fax: 717-533-8661
E-Mail: cust@igi-global.com • www.igi-global.com

Table of Contents

Preface

INTRODUCTION

Information is the oil of 21ˢᵗ century and analytics is the combustion engine.
– Peter Sondergaard, Gartner Research

Due to advent of the availability of the Internet services at very affordable ways, the number of users is increasing in a tremendous way covering a wider range of multimedia-based applications. This causes the heavy traffic in the network, need of heavy storage space, high computational needs. The large data and the requirement of the analyzing the data leads to data science. The data science is not new. However, it has gone through different paradigm of processing such as Data, Information, Knowledge and Intelligent processing. In the last few decades, the people have spent much of their efforts in information processing. Due to the many sensors and their production of the events in the form of varieties of data, coming at fast rate (velocity) and at high volume of data, the processing becomes a challenging task. Data mining techniques have evolved over the period of time for the grouping of data, classification of data and linking one set of data with other for various business analytic purposes.

Millions of users working with variety of applications throwing their data and expecting fast turnaround response have called for new challenges for the service providers using the web technologies. Data is transformed into information and leads to the management of knowledge in the organization. Knowledge is being built in an organization that is modeled from varieties of data sources and their attached labels for each data or event.

Still, the knowledge-based processing moves in the direction of intelligent processing. High storage, high computational needs dictated the technologies to take care of it. Hadoop, which is based on Map-Reduce concept, distributes the tasks across many low-cost commodity machines to store and process the data in a distributed manner. Hence it motivates to write this book which addresses the many of the real-world challenges regarding the dealing of the Big Data. The book is organized as ten different chapters.

ORGANIZATION OF THE BOOK

Chapter 1 outlines the overview of the Big data. This chapter describes the rate of growth of the data identifying the attributes of the data. The data is characterized by Volume, Velocity, Variety, Veracity and Value. Also it outlines the data types such as existing structured data, semi structured and unstructured data, which is the need of the day for processing. The sources of such Big Data are outlined, which includes the sensor data, web data, social networking data etc. The concept of data analytics and its application in a variety of ways such as semantic web, recommendation system, business analytics is outlined.

Chapter 2 presents the big data components organized as four layers such as: Big data sources, Data massaging and store layer, Analysis layer, and Consumption layer. The sources of data are either internal or external. The internal data sources include: Transactional data, Customer relationship management system, Internal documents, Other business applications, Device sensors. The variety of external data includes: Social network profiles, Social influencers, Activity-generated data/Smart Devices, Data management systems/Legacy documents, Data store, Publicly Available Data, Geographical information, Human-generated content. Also, the topics in the chapter include: Data Preparation, Managing Missing Values, Noise Handling, Data Reduction. In addition, this chapter addresses the issues in the storage layer in terms of storage infrastructure. Analytic layer of this chapter deals with varieties of data analysis types and techniques, addressing the need for Big Data Analysis Requirements. Following this, the consumption layer, covering Transaction Capture, Business Process, Real Time Observation, Generation of reports, Recommender System, and Visualization is outlined. The Big Data Consumption from Financial Body, Retail Marketing, Public Sector, Media and Entertainment is outlined. The features affecting the components of logical layer such as: Quality of service, Information integration, Big data governance, Structure Organization are covered.

Chapter 3 gives an overview about Hadoop. It is a distributed processing framework that supports large volume of data. It is an open source. The Hadoop cluster can be formed with commodity hardware. Hence it is cheaper and can be easily configured. How Hadoop has been developed and the different versions of Hadoop are explained in this chapter. Also this chapter explains the architecture of Hadoop in detail.

Chapter 4 explains how Hadoop environment can be setup with commodity machines. The Hadoop is a cluster of machines for implementing big data. It can be run in three different modes – single node, pseudo cluster, distributed cluster. The various steps in setting all modes are explained. These steps clearly show how to implement Hadoop. This chapter gives novice users a practical knowledge to setup Hadoop environment and use it.

Chapter 5 explains the file system used in Hadoop framework called "Hadoop Distributed File System (HDFS)". The main two parts of Hadoop are HDFS and MapReduce. Each Hadoop cluster is made up of one NameNode and number of DataNodes. The functions of DataNodes and NameNode are explained with lucid pictures. To ensure reliability, the data are replicated in different nodes. Also a standby NameNode is maintained so that when the active NameNode fails, the standby NameNode will take over the work. The procedure for replica and standby NameNode are explained. The necessary commands for handling HDFS are explained with syntax and hence the readers can work with HDFS easily.

Chapter 6 deals with YARN. It is Yet Another Resource Negotiator. From Hadoop 2.0 onwards, resource management layer is separately available. ResourceManager is the master daemon that communicates with clients, tracks resources on the cluster and settles it among applications. It has two components – Scheduler and ApplicationsManager. The functions of both are explained in this chapter.

Chapter 7 explains how to do programming using MapReduce. For implementing tasks to be executed in parallel, we have to write map and reduce functions. The different built-in classes available and the various functions in MapReduce are explained in a detailed manner. After reading this chapter, the reader can write map and reduce functions in an efficient manner. This chapter is more helpful for implementation.

Chapter 8 handles MapReduce and YARN API. The MapReduce Application Master API's allow users to get status on the running MapReduce application master. The information includes running job particulars, counters, configuration, number of attempts, etc. The application master should be accessed via the proxy. How it can be accessed and what are the various operations possible everything is explained. The YARN REST API's are set of URI resources that give access to cluster, nodes, applications, etc. The various API's are explained so that the users can use it for practical purposes.

Chapter 9 explains the various Hadoop tools available. The tools are available for Hadoop streaming, Hadoop archives, Scheduler load simulator, etc. Hadoop streaming is used for running jobs with any executable or script as the mapper/reducer. Hadoop archives is used to create archive files. The scheduler load simulator simulates large-scale Yarn clusters and application loads in a single machine. The user can check how different schedulers would work. The detailed steps are given for using all the tools.

Chapter 10 outlines the features of the security services in terms of the requirements and the issues in the business services. Also this chapter deals with little background about the services in the cloud and the interaction between clients and services in the cloud emphasizing the security services. The authentication procedure with the authentication protocol, Kerberos SPNEGO which is offered as a security services in Hadoop is introduced. The configuration details in a typical browser (Mozilla Firefox) are detailed. The usage of the Linux command *curl* is introduced in this chapter. The command to key distribution center 'kinit' is outlined. Also the procedure for accessing the server within the Java code is given. A section on server side configuration speaks about the Maven repository which holds all the necessary library Jar files organized as local, central, and remote. The explanation for the configuration is given with a typical XML file. Also the usage of Simple Logging Facade for Java is introduced. The configuration has many parameters with its values and they are tabulated for better perception.

CONCLUSION

This book gives a detailed knowledge of Hadoop platform. After reading this book, even the novice user can work in the Hadoop environment with confidence. We hope this book will be useful to all readers. Happy reading!

Chapter 1
Big Data Overview

ABSTRACT

Big data is now a reality. Data is created constantly. Data from mobile phones, social media, GIS, imaging technologies for medical diagnosis, etc., all these must be stored for some purpose. Also, this data needs to be stored and processed in real time. The challenging task here is to store this vast amount of data and to manage it with meaningful patterns and traditional data structures for processing. Data sources are expanding to grow into 50X in the next 10 years. An International Data Corporation (IDC) forecast sees that big data technology and services market at a compound annual growth rate (CAGR) of 23.1% over 2014-19 period with annual spending may reach $48.6 billion in 2019. The digital universe is expected to double the data size in next two years and by 2020 we may reach 44 zettabytes (10^{21}) or 44 trillion gigabytes. The zettabyte is a multiple of the unit byte for digital information. There is a need to design new data architecture with new analytical sandboxes and methods with an integration of multiple skills for a data scientist to operate on such large data.

INTRODUCTION

Andrew Brust (2012) stated, "We can safely say that Big Data is about the technologies and practice of handling data sets so large that conventional database management systems cannot handle them efficiently, and sometimes cannot handle them at all". The attributes to be dealt for such big data stands out to be:

DOI: 10.4018/978-1-5225-3790-8.ch001

- Huge volume
- Complexity of types and structures
- Speed of new data growth and its processing

How a big data is differentiated from other data? It is not only voluminous. There are 3 'V's to characterize this data (Viceconti, Hunter, & Hose, 2015). They are:

- **Volume:** It refers to the size of big data, which is definitely huge. Most organizations are struggling to manage the size of their databases and it has become overwhelming. From 2010 to 2020, data increases from 1.2 ZetaBytes (ZB) to 35.2 ZB.
- **Velocity:** It includes the speed of data input and output i.e. given based on the aspects of throughput of data and latency. Here the machine generated data explodes even in milliseconds. For example, Communication Service Provider CSP that generates GPS data, data streaming from websites etc. The challenging fact is to embed analytics for data-in-motion with reduced latency (www.turn.com conducts analytics for online advertisement in 10 milliseconds).
- **Variety:** It refers to various types of data which cannot be easily managed by traditional database. The data in warehouse was compiled from variety of sources and transformed using ELT (Extract, Load and Transform) but this is restricted for structured content. Here, this includes data expanded across horizons which comprises of textual, geo-spatial, mobile, video, weblogs, social media data, and transaction data etc...

Nowadays two more V's are added for big data: 1) veracity; 2) value.

- **Veracity**: It refers to the trustworthiness of data. Some data may have ambiguity. For example, all the posts in Twitter cannot be trusted. The volume may be responsible for lack of accuracy.
- **Value:** It refers to the value/quality usage of data. It is nothing but how far the data is useful to that particular organization.

Figure 1. Raise of Data Evolution Sources

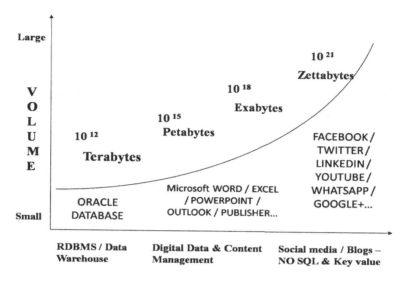

STRUCTURE OF BIG DATA

Billions of rows cannot be stored on a single storage array and it is too large to be processed. Big data can be divided into three types: Structured, semi-structured and unstructured data.

Structured Data

Structured data has a defined type and format but it is not the case for unstructured. For example, CSP records the customer support information from a call centre. Structured data is identifiable and present in an organized manner. Spreadsheets and databases are typical structured data with rows and columns. The data used for storage, retrieval is normally structured and is managed by technology that allows for fast query access. It paves good data management and metadata. The data stored at back end uses SQL server and the data is structured which includes date, time, customer name, problem type etc. This can be entered by a support help desk even as GUI.

Unstructured Data

Unstructured data is in any format that includes media objects like image, audio/video files. In addition the textual data like body of an email too doesn't have a proper type or format with conceptual definition. The same CSP application mentioned in the previous case can also store call log information or phone call description which is unstructured.

Semi-Structured Data

Semi-structured data are intermediate between structured and unstructured. This is a schema less data. It even includes the textual data files from discernable patterns like XML data files which are self describing.

BIG DATA SOURCES AND DRIVERS

Sources and drivers behind big data can't be restricted to a limited system. The main drivers for the sources of big data are given by customers, automation and monetization. Increased automation, offers big data creation and consumption opportunities to the customer and the monetization process provides an efficient market place for big data.

Some of the big data sources which can be automated and monetized are:

- Mouse click on a weblink can be captured as log files and analyzed to identify and understand behavior of the consumer in shopping and to influence their shopping by dynamically recommending products.
- Social media like Facebook and Twitter generate more comments, posts and tweets. This data can be obtained and analyzed using sentiment/ semantic analysis to understand the views behind people (Immonen, 2015).
- General Blog comments can be combined to motivate customers. For example, the meters continuously stream data about electricity, water, or gas consumption that can be shared with customers and combined with pricing plans.
- Tremendous amount of geospatial data that is GPS/GIS information created by cell phones for monitoring weather conditions. The GPS data can be used by applications like Four Square to help you know

the locations of friends and to receive offers from nearby stores and restaurants.

- Image, audio data can be analyzed for applications such as facial recognition systems in security systems.
- Microsoft Azure Marketplace, World Bank, Wikipedia etc. provides data which is publicly available on the web. This data can be taken for any analysis.

BIG DATA ANALYTICS

Stored data does not generate any business value which is of traditional databases, data warehouses, and the new technologies for storing big data. So, once the data is available, it is to be processed further using some data analytics technologies.

Data analysis is the process of extracting some useful information out of available data and hence making some conclusions. It uses statistical methods, questioning, selecting or discarding some subsets, examining, comparing and confirming, etc.

One step further to analysis is data analytics. Data analytics is the process of building predictive models and discovering patterns from data. The evolution of data analytics proceeded from Decision support systems (DSS) to Business Intelligence (BI) and the data analytics. DSS was used as a description for an application and an academic discipline. Over time, decision support applications included online analytical processing (OLAP), and dashboards which became popular. Then, Business Intelligence, broad category for analyzing and processing the gathered data to help business users to make better decisions. Data analytics combines BI and DSS along

Figure 2. Sources of Data Deluge

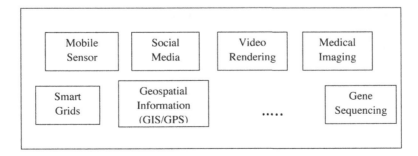

5

with analysis on large amount of data using the techniques to get data in(into data mart), out(query reply) and to analyze with various algorithms(machine learning, neural networks etc.)

The analytic sandboxes are referred to as workspaces which are designed to explore many datasets and for enterprise level for sales dashboards. Analytic sandboxes enable high-performance computing using in-database processing that is analytics done within the storage area.

This big data tsunami requires a massively parallel processing platform (MPP) as a high performance shared service to perform computing. This parallel integration platform should include:

- Database partitioning to optimize storage
- Define partitions like Snippet Processing Units (SPU) within each process
- Support a symmetric multiprocessing (SMP) shared memory server configurations

This entire shared service implementation is a success when the working provides a straight through processing (STP) model which provides dynamic allocation, flexibility and scale-up (Brock & Habib, 2017).

Biggest boost of data analytics is to improve the business vision. Such is predictive analytics which shows what will occur in the future. The methods for predictive analytics include regression analysis, machine learning, and neural networks. But nowadays, software products have been built to perform real time analytics. One such enabling technology is IBM Infosphere Streams, it deals with real time analytics and decision making, including RFID tags, weather data prediction etc. Marketing has become the main target for many predictive analytics application to understand the customer and their needs and preferences.

We can say:

Data analytics = Data analysis + machine intelligence.

The differences between analysis and analytics is listed in Table 1.

Table 1. Data Analysis vs. Data Analytics

Sl. No.	Data Analysis	Data Analytics
1.	It is the process of organizing data into informational summaries.	It is the process of exploring data and extracting meaningful insights.
2.	It pulls particular data.	It extracts what is hidden inside data.
3.	It shows what is happening.	It explains why it is happening and how the user can act on it.
4.	Activities are questioning, examining, comparing, etc.	Activities are interpreting, predicting, discovering patterns, etc.
5.	Examples are 1. What is the standard deviation of sales in the last year? 2. Is there any improvement in the progress of students last month? 3. Is the product No.5 profitable?	Examples are 1. What will be the sales in the next year? 2. What may be the likely population in a city next year? 3. Will the introduction of new product be profitable?

BIG DATA ANALYTICS APPLICATIONS

Social Media Data

It combines the automated search and display of customer feedback expressed publicly on the social media. The customer feedback can be summarized as positive or negative sentiments based on analysis. This big data analytics can be used to monitor social media for feedback on product, price and also helps to automate actions in response to the feedback in turn.

Customer Analytics and Marketing

Sensors can be used to collect data of a customer with the behavioral patterns for analytics. Early usage of market segmentation was based on geographic characteristics of consumer. Now, micro segments is emphasized which is a specific market for a unique customer based on analytics driven parameters. Next Best Action for a customer is to recommend an activity based on his latest experience with the product/or any item bought. Hence big data analytics provides this opportunity to collect myriads of behavioral information and analyze and display an online advertisement related to customer based on micro segmentation information and purchase history.

Web Data Analytics

Web analytics deals with the collection, analysis and generating a report of web data which can be used to measure web traffic, also can be used to improve business and to assess the success of website. This helps to bring on the popularity trends of market research through advertisement campaign.

Market Basket Analytics

Level of analysis is a data driven approach that is the science of shopping can be guessed based on insights retrieved through the customer behavior. Adding up, customer's location is noticed to define their own demographic groups for marketing. The application areas of market basket analysis include, telephone pattern analysis, telecom service purchase, credit card purchase, identification of fraudulent claims, etc.

Recommender System

The system predicts the rating or preference of any user for a product or book or article or movie. The recommendation can either be based on their past behavior i.e. collaborative filtering or utilize discrete characteristics of an item in order to recommend with similar properties i.e. content-based filtering.

REFERENCES

Brock & Habib. (2017). Big data analytics: does organizational factor matters impact technology acceptance? *Journal for Big Data.*

Brust, A. (2012, March 1). *Big data: Defining its definition.* Retrieved from https://www.zdnet.com/article/big-data-defining-its-definition/

Earley. (2014). Big Data and Predictive Analytics: What's New? *IEEE Computer Society Magazine.*

Immonen, A., Paakkonen, P., & Ovaska, E. (2015). Evaluating the Quality of Social Media Data in Big Data Architecture. *IEEE Access: Practical Innovations, Open Solutions, 3,* 2028–2043. doi:10.1109/ACCESS.2015.2490723

Mehmood. (2014). Protection of Big Data Privacy. *IEEE Access.*

Viceconti, M., Hunter, P., & Hose, R. (2015). Big Data, Big Knowledge: Big Data for Personalized Healthcare. *IEEE Journal of Biomedical and Health Informatics, 19*(4), 1209–1215. doi:10.1109/JBHI.2015.2406883 PMID:26218867

Chapter 2
Big Data Architecture Components

ABSTRACT

The previous chapter overviewed big data including its types, sources, analytic techniques, and applications. This chapter briefly discusses the architecture components dealing with the huge volume of data. The complexity of big data types defines a logical architecture with layers and high-level components to obtain a big data solution that includes data sources with the relation to atomic patterns. The dimensions of the approach include volume, variety, velocity, veracity, and governance. The diverse layers of the architecture are big data sources, data massaging and store layer, analysis layer, and consumption layer. Big data sources are data collected from various sources to perform analytics by data scientists. Data can be from internal and external sources. Internal sources comprise transactional data, device sensors, business documents, internal files, etc. External sources can be from social network profiles, geographical data, data stores, etc. Data massage is the process of extracting data by preprocessing like removal of missing values, dimensionality reduction, and noise removal to attain a useful format to be stored. Analysis layer is to provide insight with preferred analytics techniques and tools. The analytics methods, issues to be considered, requirements, and tools are widely mentioned. Consumption layer being the result of business insight can be outsourced to sources like retail marketing, public sector, financial body, and media. Finally, a case study of architectural drivers is applied on a retail industry application and its challenges and usecases are discussed.

DOI: 10.4018/978-1-5225-3790-8.ch002

INTRODUCTION

Long time ago the research and development on infrastructure services included High speed networking for data intensive applications with collaborative systems like grids with dynamic provisioned security (Williams, 2016). Currently this is provided by software defined collaborative systems that is intercloud and Big Data technologies. There requires an architecture to be defined since the data exceeded the processing capacity of conventional systems. Hence, an alternative architecture is to be needed for processing to gain value from this data. (Sathic, 2013). The architecture framework stated to be cost-effective with innovative forms of processing for better insight to perform decision making is done.

BACKGROUND

Big Data can be stored, retrieved, processed and analysed in various ways. This includes many dimensions and requires a high computation model with security and governance. The choice of such an architecture pattern is a challenging task across huge factors. The complexity of Big Data types defines a logical architecture with layers and high level components to obtain a Big Data solution. The logical architecture includes a set of data sources and is relation with atomic patterns by focusing on each aspect for a Big Data solution.

With the beginning of Big Data technologies, organizations started querying, "What kind of insight are possible for business, governance if Big Data technologies comes into existence?" A structured approach is defined based on the dimensions to assess the feasibility of Big Data solution. The dimensions in this approach may include:

- Volume of the data
- Variety of data sources, types, and formats
- Velocity at which the data is generated, i.e. the speed
- Veracity which is uncertainty or trustworthiness of the data
- Business value from analyzing the data
- Governance for the new sources of data and its usage

Figure 1. Dimensions of Big Data viability

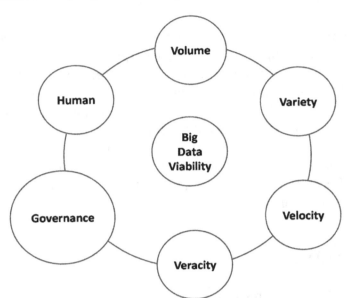

BIG DATA ARCHITECTURE

Big Data architecture is for developing reliable, scalable, completely automated data pipelines (Azarmi, 2016). The developed component needs to define several layers in the stack comprises data sources, storage, functional, non-functional requirements for business, analytics engine cluster design etc. as a Big Data solution for any business case (Mysore, Khupat, & Jain, 2013). These set of layers are the critical components for the defining the process from data acquisition to analytics via business/human insight.

The layers define an approach to organize the components with specific functions. Its highly logical and so functions related does not mean that it runs on separate processes. The layers can be given as

- Big Data sources
- Data massaging and store layer
- Analysis layer
- Consumption layer

BIG DATA SOURCES

Data is ubiquitous but it's hard to discover as required. Data can be collected from all channels for analysis. Many organizations collect data as required and data scientists analyse it for further analytics. The data can vary in various ways of format, origin etc. This defines:

- Format can be structured, semi-structured or unstructured.
- Velocity deals with the pace at which data flows across networks even with human interaction like mobile. The streaming real time data flow is massive and continuous to provide valuable decisions.
- Volume implies huge or enormous data created by machines, networks or human intervention like social media posting etc. Volume requires a proper storage and management capability.
- Data collection can be in real time or batch mode. Processing data with hardware and software requirement is based on the mode. Data can be from direct source (original) or from indirect source (third party).
- Location information of data source can be through global information systems. In some cases the access of data location can be restricted for security purposes.

Two main classifications of data sources can be internal or external. Internal data reflect those under the control of a particular business or organization or customer. Hence it includes all sorts of details owned by its organization environment stored in computer systems or cloud environments. These are easy to collect and process.

Some examples of internal data are:

- **Transactional Data:** Includes firm's financial documents, billing operations.
- **Customer Relationship Management System:** Information like clients' affiliations, location geographical details and its relation with company.
- **Internal Documents:** Copy of emails, Word documents, PDF, XML.
- **Other Business Applications:** Details which include sources for project management, marketing, productivity, enterprise resource management, etc.

- **Device Sensors:** Since Internet of Things develops in this fast moving world, the data from sensors can be an additional unique data for analysis.

External data is the one generated outside the environment and not owned by any company. The data is mostly unstructured and public data gathered from various channels like,

- **Social Network Profiles:** User profiles from Facebook, LinkedIn, Yahoo, and social or travel sites, to gather individuals' user interest based on profiles and demographic information. These data can be gathered from social network API's integration.
- **Social Influencers:** Analysis of data from user forums, Twitter, Blog comments, Facebook requires natural language processing, sentiment and semantic analysis to evaluate the nature of comment as positive/ negative and to derive meaning of it.
- **Activity-Generated Data/ Smart Devices:** Capable of capturing data through smart devices like mobiles, body sensors. Log files which include web site track, application logs, sensor data like check-ins, location tracking etc. are also added. Parsing of these data is to be done being semi-structured. They do real time analytics in certain cases.
- **Data Management Systems /Legacy Documents:** They store legal data, policies, and other kinds of documents in the form of spreadsheets, word documents. Archive of statements like insurance forms, medical records are an added resource.
- **Data Store:** Data store include data warehouses like IBM Netezza, and transactional databases available for analysis.
- **Publicly Available Data:** In Microsoft Azure Data Market, The World Bank, Wikipedia, etc. the data is publicly available on the Web.
- **Geographical Information:** Maps, Regional details, Location details, Mining details.
- **Human-Generated Content:** Social media, Email, Blogs.

Data Massaging and Store Layer

Data Massage

Normally, the process of transferring data is given by "ETL" which means "Extract, Transform and Load". In this, the term "Transform" is given by data massaging which describes the process of extracting data by removing unwanted information or data cleansing to retrieve a useful format. In general, data massage implies that it fixes or smooth out the problems like change of formats from source to target system expectation, replace missing values, filter records not required, check validity of records, normalize values etc... Thereby organizes data into a meaningful structure.

This layer acquires the data from different sources using the data source layer and converts it into a format as required for the process of analysis. The layer should be capable of reading data at different size, format, rate and communication channels. Data digest is a component which involves transformation logic or any complex statistical algorithms to convert source data. This analytics engines identifies the target format and converts it. The big challenge is the conversion of unstructured format like images, audio and video.

Since the data generation rates are at high speed with huge size, data can be imperfect with redundancy or inconsistency. This data need proper mechanisms to analyze it. Before analysis, the basic requirement is to adapt the data to acceptable format for processing or the analysis process becomes unfeasible. The techniques which can be suggested for data massaging includes data preparation and reduction techniques. Data preparation defines the process of data transformation, cleaning, integration and normalization and data reduction includes feature selection, reduction and discretization techniques to minimize the complexity.

- **Data Preparation:** The real-world data can be noisy or incomplete. There are two methods stated for noise filtering and filling up of missing values
  - **Missing Values Reproach:** With missing values, the data seems to be incomplete and it cannot be avoided for analysis since it may cause loss of efficiency. The decisive works on data missing can include statistics. Probability functions can be modeled using maximum likelihood procedures

Figure 2. Data massage: data preparation

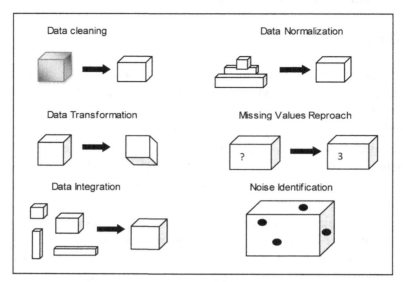

○ **Noise Handling:** The quality of data analysis depends on data so tackling noise is obligatory. This can be handled using data polishing or noise filtering methods.

● **Data Reduction:** When data includes more instances, the computational complexity may rise. It can be handled by removing irrelevant information i.e. a subset can be generated. The techniques involved are stated below:

○ **Feature Selection:** The main goal is to attain a subset from original data as required. The redundant and irrelevant features can be eliminated by defining the correlation factor in machine learning algorithms. Hence, it reduces the search space and makes learning fast with less memory consumption. It's easy to interpret.

○ **Space Transformation:** Instead of reducing the data, this generate a whole new set by joining original ones. The approaches like factor analysis and Principal Component Analysis can be utilized. In order to exploit non linear relations, space transformation procedures like LLE, ISOMAP and its derivatives can be defined.

○ **Discretization:** It's the process to transfer the continuous data into discrete equivalent parts based on any separability measures.

Figure 3. Data Massage: Data Reduction

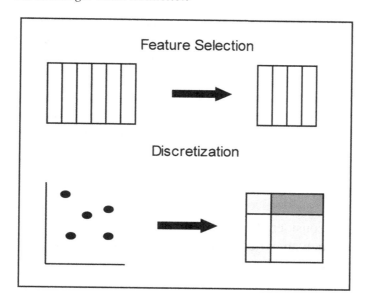

Data Storage

Data store is liable to store the data from different data sources and communication channels. The data being huge, this layer requires a distributed environment for storage. Hence the system can utilize cloud or any distributed file system. The choice of Big Data platform should include a scale-out Network Attached Storage (NAS) so that it can help in storing large amount of data. NAS is a like file access with multiple storage nodes in parallel that scale to billions and petabytes of capacity. Some major NAS products of Big Data include: EMC Isilon, Hitachi Cloudera Hadoop distribution cluster reference architecture, hScaler Hadoop NAS, NetApp etc...The streaming data can utilize high performance SSD's for storage.

Another approach to handle large amount of data is object storage. This replaces the traditional storage tree structures with unique IDs. This includes a flat data structure i.e. files are located using unique ID just like Domain Name System in internet. Object storage products like Dell DX,EMC's ATMOS platform provides the ability to work in Big Data analytics environment.

Object based and scale-out file systems both can handle the Big Data storage architecture but not same. Scale-out system is a global namespace which provides a simple platform for network attached storage whereas object storage uses metadata for good performance of large sets of files.

Traditional warehousing operations use homogenous data sets and so support monolithic storage infrastructures than today's requirement. Industries including financial services use data warehousing techniques to process very large data but it is not the case today for Big Data. The difference is that Big Data includes unstructured data and allows for extracting data from variety of types like blogs, mails, business transactions, images and others. The big applications mostly require real time responses. So the storage methodology should reflect high performance and lower cost for its application with usage pattern.

Storage Infrastructure Factors

The factors to be considered for Big Data storage architecture include frequency and speed at which analytical processing can deliver final result. There are hyperscale compute storage architectures used mainly in Facebook, Google etc. They use simple commodity hardware with multiple nodes to compute with Direct Attached Storage (DAS). This is supported by an environment known as Hadoop. This hyperscale handles workload failure over to another node by building redundancy of data and that new node is replaced in that failure node.

In recognition, EMC's VIPR is a scale-out object storage technology to enable the disparate hardware to Big Data infrastructure. Hybrid storage arrays with SSD, hard disk or PCIe flash with internal or direct attached disk are recommended to attain high speed for data analysis results.

Analysis Layer

The analysis attains the data from data massaging and storage layer for next processing. In certain cases, this layer can acquire the data directly from data source if structured with right type and format. Data analysis is to derive proper insight with desired analytics technique and tools to perform it. The layer includes:

- **Entity Identification:** Is the process to identify or populate the contextual entities. This requires high performance processing.
- **Analysis Engine and Model:** Includes the techniques and tools with algorithms to process the Big Data in parallel. Statistical model and workflow should be defined for verifying and validating the model to be accurate.

The various data analysis types can be as stated as follows:

- **Basic Analytics for Insight:** Slicing of data, simple statistics and visualizations, monitoring large amounts of disparate data
- **Advanced Analytics for Insight:** Complex analysis on structured or unstructured data includes machine learning, neural networks etc. to find patterns for predictive modeling, patter matching etc...
- **Operational Analytics:** Part of business process. For example, model that predicts the likelihood of a claim with a high probability being fraudulent in a company etc...
- **Monetized Analytics:** Make the most of revenue i.e. optimize a business for better decisions to drive bottom and top line revenue.

The classification between traditional business analytics and Big Data analytics are stated as in Table 1.

Techniques for Analyzing Big Data

Big Data analysis is making sense of the huge data model to define its context. The issues to be considered are:

- **Discovery:** What and how different data sets relate to each other.
- **Iteration:** Uncovering insights require iterative process to obtain results that we seek. Many projects are learnt from iteration and so can move to next idea of inquiry.
- **Capacity:** Due to iterative process, it need more resources to solve.
- **Mining and Prediction:** Mine the data to discover patterns and predictive analytics that yield insight.

Table 1. Traditional analytics vs. Big Data Analytics

	Traditional Analytics	Big Data Analytics
Focus	• Descriptive Analytics • Diagnosis Analytics	• Predictive Analytics • Data Science
Data	• Limited • Structured data • Simple model	• Large scale data • Data of more types • Complex model
Support	• Action of something	• Correlation & Insight

- **Decision:** Considering volume and velocity, identify the process to automate and optimize implementation of action.
- **Data Quality Grading and Assurance:** To extend the existing methodologies for merging data from multiple sources and to suggest robust techniques for automated data quality.
- **Identify Unusual Segments:** Methods like ICmetrics to be defined to alert researchers that specific data segments are unusual and requires further analysis to discover the potential issues with unwanted data manipulation and integrity violations.
- **Confidentiality:** Some data includes sensitive information. The researcher should identify the best technique to aggregate or transform that data for the analysis including any privacy preserving or data perturbation algorithms.
- **Text Data Mining:** Textual data has rich information and need to be mined properly by correlations. A set of analysis methodology is to be developed for identifying the relations, opinions and to support semantic indexing, visualization etc...
- **Tracking Interactions:** The interaction between users online provide a wealth of information regarding business, government and any predictive issues. So, methods to identify the context of interaction and individual users are to be framed for improving service delivery.

Big Data Analysis Requirements

To discover hidden relationships in Big Data the significant requirements needed are:

- **Reduce Data Movement:** It's to conserve computing resources. The time required for ETL and movement from one source to another takes more time. So, it makes sense to store and process at same environment and location.
- **Process Skill:** With new real time data, the need is to acquire new skills for analysis. Combination of existing and new tools can be addressed. For example, some people may feel SQL querying to analyze data is familiar than Hive in hadoop but the need is to adapt to new skill for accessing large data.

Figure 4. Big Data Analysis and its Insight

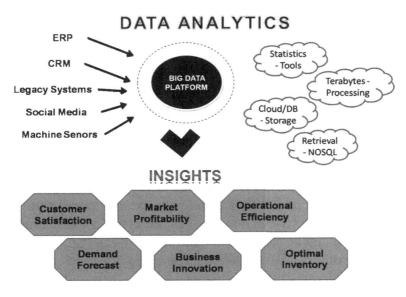

- **Data Security:** It's vital with corporate applications. This often lacks with unstructured data source and open source tools. High attention should be paid for security and data governance when analysis is done and also tools should accommodate the basic requirements on security.

Tools for Data Analysis

The broad five areas to analyze Big Data and to generate insight is given by,

- **Discovery Tools:** Used for fast, perceptive exploration and analysis of data from different combination of structured and unstructured data sources. Helps users to draw new insights with meaningful decisions and conclusion quickly.
- **Business Intelligence Tools:** For analysis and reporting on transactional database, production information system, ad-hoc analysis, enterprise platform etc… To attain business intelligence on a integrated platform.
- **In-Database Analytics:** Range of techniques to discover patterns and relationship on data available within the database and also can restrict data to and from other servers.
- **Predictive Analytics:** includes predictive modeling across multiple channels maximizing the value of real time decision process.

Consumption Layer

The layer uses the result of the business insight derived through analysis layer and the end consumer that can be business outsource, services, human or visualization. The consumers can be various users in and out of organization including customers, vendor, suppliers etc... The main approach is to target customers for product offers. As an example, the insight from analysis layer can be used by a company to obtain customer preference data with location. This can exploit resources to deliver personalized offers to customers while they pass by the store.

This perception from analysis layer can also be used to detect fraud by correlating the transactions in real time with the data previously stored in enterprise. So that corrective actions can be notified to customer immediately regarding the fraudulent transaction. Automated steps can be triggered to process the new order if customer has accepted an offer and also credit card can be blocked automatically if a customer was reported a deceit.

The result of the data analysis layer can be used by a recommendation engine to identify the products customer may like. The recommendation engine or recommender system is a tool to analyze the data to predict what a user interest will be i.e. algorithm developed to discover products for every individual. This play a great part in websites like Facebook, Amazon, Youtube etc... Recommendation system is based on the properties of items user likes or it can rely on other users' interest. From this, the similarity index is computed between users and recommended items.

This consumption layer also provides the ability for internal users to realize, find and navigate the merged data in and out of the enterprise. The internal consumers can build reports for business users which help the stakeholders to create decisions and strategies. In order to look up the operational effectiveness, real time business alerts can be produced with key performance indicators as listed below:

- **Transaction Capture:** The high volume transaction occurring in real time should be converted to suitable format so that it can be stated by the analysis layer for processing. This transaction interceptor has the capability to integrate the data from different Big Data sources like sensors, GPS's, etc... Different API's are worn to connect the data sources, from which streaming analytics, social media analytics, sentiment analysis, etc... can be simplified.

- **Business Process:** This includes the determination of business process execution language or other API's from analysis layer to process the data for obtaining a business value. The value is further utilized to automate the function for IT application, people or other processing

- **Real Time Intelligence:** The alerts can be made from data analysis in real time. This can be sent to user's smart devices based on interest. Also data can be made available to people from different sources to monitor health or to measure success of campaign etc…

- **Business Report:** Scheduled news or weather reports or any query analysis can be created based on the insight derived from analysis layer. This can be similar to business intelligence reports.

- **Recommender System:** Real time, relevant information filtering system used to predict the rating or the preference a user may give to a product. This plays a vital role in today's world in variety of areas like movies. Social tags, products, news, books, tourist place etc… This increases the average value of orders in e-commerce transaction. Hence this engine processes the data in real time with the data stored for registered customers and social media profiles for non registered customers. The result is responded dynamically to users. The approaches include collaborative and content based filtering. Collaborative filtering collects and analyze huge amount of information including users' behavior, preferences to predict the users interest based on similarity to other users. The basic algorithms used are Pearson Correlation and k-nearest neighbor approach. Contest Based filtering is based on description of an item and profile of users' preference. Here, algorithms are framed in such a way that it recommend items based on what the user liked in past.

- **Visualization:** The data after analysis is to be visualized and provided to users irrespective of content and format. This facilitates the organizations to combine the enterprise content with social media content like tweets and blogs into a sole user interface.

Big Data Consumption

Business houses have been reliable on data to analyze the trends, behavior of users, their impacts, and profits to attain some predictions. This computing has now gone from simple spreadsheets to huge data. Besides, Big Data

Figure 5. Big Data Consumption

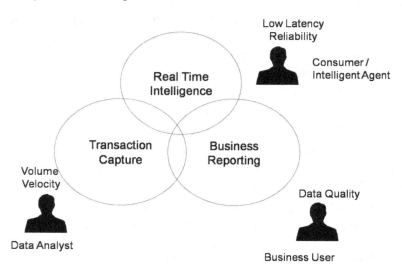

enables more analysis to keep a profitable business as a pathway to growth. The variety of Big Data consumption sources includes the following:

- **Financial Body:** Dealing with money, industries need to refer back the previous trends to make predictions. Earlier data was small so predictions attained a higher margin of risk but now it's reduced due to more data. Share markets and other financial organization checks the spending to evolve some sort of equation that helps to retain maximum profits.
- **Retail Marketing:** Process to promote knowledge and interest of goods and services to consumers for generating profit in sales. It deals with various approaches to improve products i.e. goods and its type's usage. In addition it can also figure out the abilities and techniques for client conversion rate and client retention.
- **Public Sector:** The missions and projects of government sector can be tracked to identify the productivity through analysis of data across people. This can also define better methods for improving the performance. There are still benefits to track information regarding healthcare, employment etc…
- **Media and Entertainment:** Main focus is to compare the customer retention with acquisition. Big Data analysis helps to identify the media interests of users and also to develop the types based on it. Internet

marketing agencies make real time decisions on analysis based on users' behavior and interest according to age groups for advertisements. With this Big Data analysis is able to predict results.

Vertical Layers

The features that affect the components of logical layer are covered in vertical layer. The vertical layer includes:

- Quality of service
- Information integration
- Big Data governance
- Structure Organization

Quality of Service

The layer is meant to define the data quality, privacy issues, rate and size at which data arrives, filters etc…

- **Data Quality:** It is a perception that data serves its purpose according to the context. The aspects include completeness, relevance, consistency, accuracy and accessibility. The data quality is essential for transactional process and has high reliability in case of business analytics. This quality is based on data type or format stored and managed. The process of verifying with inconsistencies or anomalies and effectiveness of data is known as data quality assurance. The data quality solutions are highly reliable for making decisions to identify revenue opportunities, meet compliance prerequisite and respond to customer needs in time. In general, data quality defines:
  - Completeness and Timeliness of data to be identified and provided
  - Data accuracy verification
  - Adhere to common business language
  - Data consistency from various sources
  - Data specification and architecture
- **Privacy and Security:** Data acquired from external agencies may include sensitive data which should be protected using some policies. The sensitive data can be contact information like passwords, address or product pricing information. Data access policies should consider data criticality, data sharing/publish, data authenticity, data provider

constraint etc… One solution to data privacy can be data obfuscation process. The privately identifiable information (PII) i.e. unique identifiable information of each individual can be hidden or destroyed before sending to marketers for security related issues in obfuscation process. Under "opt in" the PII can be released to few as long as it is protected. Furthermore data masking algorithms are used for privacy and it's quite interesting. The algorithm removes or randomizes the PII but not destroyed.

Information Integration

Big Data is acquired from various origins or sources, providers and data storage system like HDFS, NOSQL. This layer is responsible to connect component with sources for processing like data acquisition, digest, management etc… Integrating the information requires characteristics like quality connectors, adapters and protocols. Even accelerator can be used to connect social media data and weather updates since both include a real time processing. Many APIs are made available to store and retrieve back the data from data stores for processing.

Big Data Governance

Governance generally deal with providing right decisions about the data for enterprises. This operates with the complexities of volume, velocity and variety of data coming from internal and external agencies. This frames a set of guidelines to monitor, preprocess, store and secure the data for processing and then again its archived for further analysis. Additionally, unstructured data in variety of formats require models to preprocess before performing analytics. Policy and regulations are to be framed for external data regarding its retention and usage. Replication of data and security encryption principles should be structured.

Structure Organization

Organization of systems in Big Data is highly crucial since it involves a distributed environment across clusters in an enterprise.(Paakokonen & Pakkala, 2015). Examining the overall ecosystem includes:

- Manage the storage and capacity
- Put up with the service level agreements
- Managing system log, applications and its link with other devices
- Reports and analysis of the systems in cluster
- System Recovery, cluster and network management
- Policies to monitor real time alerts, logs and notifications etc…

Case Study: Big Data Application

Big Data case studies deal with the extension from traditional architectural drivers to reference architectures along with analytics methods and challenges in real world applications (Batarseh & Latif, 2016). The reference architecture is termed as extendible non-relational architecture. The major components of an architecture composes data source with integration methodologies, storage, analytics methods etc… and their sub components of the model are defined in the Figure 7.

Figure 6. Big Data Architecture Layers

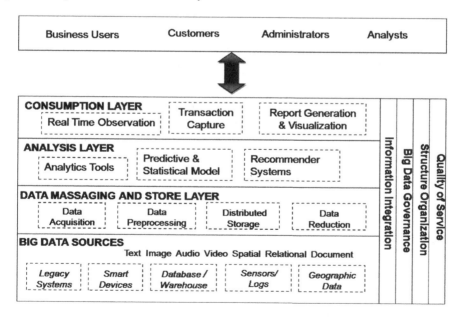

Figure 7. Extended non relational architecture

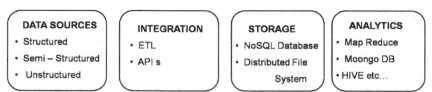

Big Data in Retail Industry

Retail industry future is based on Big Data analytics in the upcoming technological era (Akter & Wamba, 2016). So, the industry needs to adapt itself to the data centric technology for boosting their sales. It has been tested that sales has reached higher 73% where predictive analytics is done by retailers. Therefore retailers identify Big Data solutions to improve their profit and win entrants by personalizing online products.

Data analytics can improve market efficiency by heaving the profits in retail. This industry is competitive since it has numerous companies moving forward to find new purchase trends by observing customer behavior passively. For example, this kind of market based analytics provides preferences for customers to purchase products together based on their interest i.e. the result of customer behavior analytics. This is normally done by recommendation systems, a popular technique in analytics.

As per retail technology survey by Gartner in April 2016, 30% of retailers indicate that their IT budget have increased more than 5%. Their spending priority includes EMV payments (card with chips), social media analytics, product purchase history analysis, and personalization, shopper tracking capability, mobile devices and multiple channels customer behavior analysis. Overall the retailers plan for unified commerce. The analytics on Big Data performs deeper analysis on all data to come across meaningful pattern and hidden insights.

Challenges

Imagine 10,000 customers per month buying products at a frequency of 5 minutes. Then there exist a large number of unique records nearly 5, 00, 00,000. In addition to product details, the data should also include age, gender, and geographic information, time etc... so as to learn customer behavior for retail must handle numerous challenges.

- It is a difficult task for predicting the customer behavior. Since the technology should concentrate with retailers having access to more information about customers and on other hand customer can make a choice of any option. This equally increases the risks in change of customer habits
- Process to analyze the changing trends is tricky without retail analytics, since retail trends change at rapid pace due to communication, consumer tastes etc...
- It's important for retailers to make use of sentiment analysis as customers prediction may spread across. A negative impact on a product may spread viral across the web mostly through social media platforms

USE CASES IN RETAIL INDUSTRY

Retail Analytics in Fraud Detection and Prevention

Data intrusion increases rapidly week by week. That's why fraud detection has become a serious issue to avoid loss and to maintain the trust of customers. Common retail frauds are return of purchased products, stolen financial information etc... Big Data analytics tools like Hadoop and Spark can perform on 50 petabytes of data to predict the risks. Amazon has designed a fraud detection tool in predictive analysis without financial transactions details. Also, it keeps track of browser information, IP address and other technical details of users that can help to detect fraudulent activities.

Retail Analytics in Personalization

Personalization depends on demographics and purchase behavior of customer. The analytics approach includes behavior target, price optimization, site selection, product purchase etc... Amazon offers recommendations to customers based on purchase history, cookies and wish list.

Retail Analytics in Pricing

Transparency in price is must for customers. Real time pricing platform in retail analytics can power millions of pricing decisions in the midst of good retailers. This can attain the intelligence between internal profit and external competitor. Internal profit comprises the cost at which goods sold, shipping, charge, and vendor rate at unit level whereas external includes prices of a product across multiple websites. In present period, retail websites update the price of products every 2 to 5 minutes depending on analytics if required.

CONCLUSION

The architectural layers of Big Data categorize the functions to attain a Big Data solution by suggesting various aspects to address those functions. The logical layers help business users to derive insights from Big Data and its analytics combines the enterprise data with other relevant information to create predictive models of trends. Vertical layer characterizes the concepts that affect the logical layer. Adding up to the architectural layer, atomic patterns define the mechanism to process, store and consume Big Data for users. Case study elucidates that top retailers use Big Data to gain competitive advantage. As well, real time analytics help retailers to synchronize prices hourly with demand and inventory.

REFERENCES

Akter & Wamba. (2016). Big Data analytics in e-commerce: A systematic review and agenda for future research. *Electron Markets, 26*, 173-194.

Azarmi, B. (2016). *Scalable Big Data Architecture: A practitioners guide to choosing relevant Big Data architecture*. Apress. doi:10.1007/978-1-4842-1326-1

Batarseh & Abdel Latif. (2016). Assessing the Quality of Service Using Big Data Analytics: With Application to Healthcare. *Big Data Research, 4*, 13-24.

Mysore, D., Khupat, S., & Jain, S. (2013). *Big Data architecture and patterns*. IBM Developer Works.

Paakkonen & Pakkala. (2015). Reference Architecture and Classification of Technologies, Products and Services for Big Data Systems. *Big Data Research, 2*(4), 166-186.

Sathic, A. (2013). *Big Data Analytics: Disruptive Technologies for Changing the Game*. Mc Press.

Williams, S. (2016). *Business Intelligence Strategy and Big Data Analytics*. Morgan Kaufmann.

Chapter 3
Hadoop History and Architecture

ABSTRACT

As the name indicates, this chapter explains the evolution of Hadoop. Doug Cutting started a text search library called Lucene. After joining Apache Software Foundation, he modified it into a web crawler called Apache Nutch. Then Google File System was taken as reference and modified as Nutch Distributed File System. Then Google's MapReduce features were also integrated and Hadoop was framed. The whole path from Lucene to Apache Hadoop is illustrated in this chapter. Also, the different versions of Hadoop are explained. The procedure to download the software is explained. The mechanism to verify the downloaded software is shown. Then the architecture of Hadoop is detailed. The Hadoop cluster is a set of commodity machines grouped together. The arrangement of Hadoop machines in different racks is shown. After reading this chapter, the reader will understand how Hadoop has evolved and its entire architecture.

INTRODUCTION

Hadoop is an open source framework used for storing and processing big data. It is developed by Apache Software Foundation. Hadoop environment can be setup with commodity hardware alone. It is a framework that supports distributed environment with cluster of commodity machines. It can work with single server or can scale up including thousands of commodity machines.

DOI: 10.4018/978-1-5225-3790-8.ch003

Hadoop has undergone number of revisions also. This chapter gives the novice users an idea about how Hadoop was initiated and what are the major revisions of it. Also this chapter describes in detail the architecture of Hadoop.

BACKGROUND

The most acute information management challenges stem from organizations (e.g., enterprises, government agencies, libraries, "smart" homes) relying on a large number of diverse, interrelated data sources, but having no way to manage their *dataspaces* (Franklin, Halevy, & Maier, 2005) in a convenient, integrated, or principled fashion. Michael Franklin et.al, (2005) highlighted the need for storage systems to accept all data formats and to provide APIs for data access that evolve based on the storage system's understanding of the data.

In the past years, (Dean & Ghemawat, 2004) at Google have implemented hundreds of special- purpose computations that process large amounts of raw data, such as crawled documents, web request logs, etc., to compute various kinds of derived data, such as inverted indices, various representations of the graph structure of web documents, summaries of the number of pages crawled per host, the set of most frequent queries in a given day, etc. Most such computations are conceptually straightforward. However, the input data is usually large and the computations have to be distributed across hundreds or thousands of machines in order to finish in a reasonable amount of time.

Robert Kallman et.al, (2008) developed H-Store, a next-generation OLTP system that operates on a distributed cluster of shared-nothing machines where the data resides entirely in main memory. But it needs a separate database design for the attributes- Table replication and Data partitioning. To solve the above problems, (Chang, Dean, Ghemawat, Hsieh, Wallach, Burrows... Gruber, 2008) developed BigTable which is distributed storage system for maintaining structured data of petabytes size across thousands of commodity servers. Later an open source equivalent to BigTable was created and it was called "Hadoop". Hadoop is an open source platform that brings the ability to cheaply process large amounts of data and it is more suitable for storing voluminous unstructured data.

HADOOP HISTORY

Doug Cutting started writing the first version of Lucene in 1997. Lucene is a full text search library. In 2000, he open sourced Lucene under GPL license. Many people started using Lucene. In the next year (ie, 2001), Lucene was moved to Apache Software Foundation. By the end of 2001, Doug Cutting started indexing web pages. University of Washington student Mike Cafarella also joined in his work. The new product developed is called "Apache Nutch". Nutch is a web crawler going from page to page. Nutch uses Lucene to index the contents of page to make it searchable. It was achieving an index rate of 100 pages per second when installed on a single machine. To improve the performance of Nutch, Doug Cutting and Mike Carfarella used four machines. Space allocation and data exchange between these four machines had to be done manually. Really it was very complex to do all these jobs manually.

They tried further to build a scalable search engine with reliability, fault tolerant and schema less design. In 2003, Google published a paper on their Google File System (GFS) which is a scalable search engine. Taking GFS as reference, Cutting and Carfarella started implementation using Java. They named the new file system as Nutch Distributed File System (NDFS). NDFS focuses on cluster of nodes and single reliable file system making operational complexity transparent to users. Also it handles failures of systems without user intervention.

(Dean & Ghemawat, 2004) from Google published a paper about Mapreduce which is more suitable for data processing on large clusters. Considering its simplicity and powerfulness, Cutting integrated Mapreduce into Nutch in 2005. In February 2006, Cuting pulled out NDFS and Mapreduce from Nutch and started a new project under Lucene. He named the new system as Hadoop and made it as Open Source.

At the same time Yahoo! also started improving their search engine written in C++. Analyzing the features of Hadoop, after a lengthy debate, scientist in Yahoo! decided to move their code to Java. In January 2006, Yahoo! employed Cutting to make the transition. Later many companies like Facebook, Twitter, etc. started working on Hadoop and contributed tools and frameworks to Hadoop open source system.

In 2008, many projects like HBase, Zookeeper, etc. were added to the Hadoop system.

HADOOP RELEASES

Apache Hadoop Releases (2018) gives the latest versions of Hadoop in Table 1.

DOWNLOADING HADOOP

Hadoop is released as source code tarballs as well as binary tarballs. The downloads are distributed via mirror sites also. The recent releases can be downloaded using the following link:

http://hadoop.apache.org/releases.html.

VERIFYING HADOOP RELEASES

The downloads should be checked for tampering using GPG (GNU Privacy Guard) or SHA-256 (Secure Hash Algorithm with hash value of 256 bits).

Verifying Using GPG

1.   Download the release hadoop-X.Y.Z-src.tar.gz.
2.   Download the signature file hadoop-X.Y.Z-src.tar.gz.asc from Apache.
3.   Download the Hadoop KEYS file.
4.   gpg --import KEYS
5.   gpg --verify hadoop-X.Y.Z-src.tar.gz.asc

Table 1.

Sl. No.	Version	Release Date
1.	3.0.3	31 May 2018
2.	3.0.0-alpha2	25 January 2017
3.	3.0.0-alpha1	03 September 2016
4.	2.8.0	22 March 2017
5.	2.7.3	25 August 2016
6.	2.6.5	08 October 2016
7.	2.5.2	19 November 2014

Verifying Using SHA-256

1. Download the release hadoop-X.Y.Z-src.tar.gz
2. Download the checksum hadoop-X.Y.Z-src.tar.gz.mds from Apache.
3. Shasum -a 256 hadoop-X.Y.Z-src.tar.gz

HADOOP ARCHITECTURE

The Hadoop architecture is shown in Figure 1.

The set of connected computers which works together is called "cluster". The individual computers are called "nodes". The Hadoop clusters are called "Shared Nothing systems" because they do not share anything except the network used for communication. Example: Yahoo! is having 32,000 nodes cluster. If there are large number of nodes, those nodes may be arranged in racks also. The structure of racks is shown in Figure 2.

MODULES OF HADOOP

The major modules of Apache Hadoop are:

- **Hadoop Common:** Common utilities that support other modules.

Figure 1. Hadoop Architecture

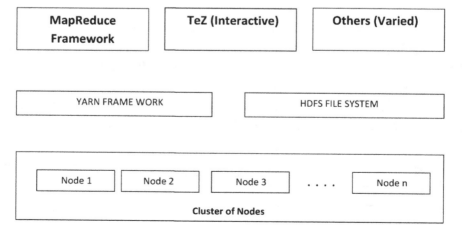

Figure 2. Hadoop racks

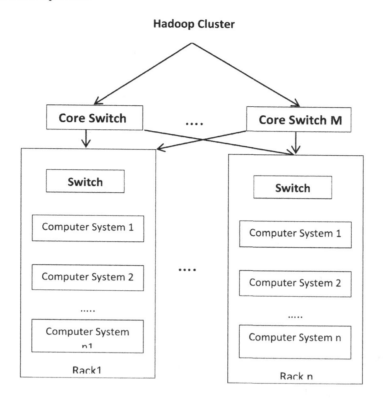

- **Hadoop Distributed File System (HDFS):** File system that provides high throughput access.
- **Hadoop YARN:** Framework for resource management and job scheduling.
- **Hadoop Mapreduce:** YARN based system for parallel processing.

Hadoop Common

Hadoop common is collection of common utilities and libraries that supports all Hadoop modules. It is also known as Hadoop Core. It is the base of the Hadoop framework. The main functionalities of Hadoop Common are:

- Providing essential services
- Providing basic processes – abstraction of operating system, abstraction of file system, etc.

- Maintaining Java Archive files (JARs) and scripts required to start Hadoop

Hadoop Distributed File System (HDFS)

HDFS is a distributed file system designed to run on commodity machines. It was originally developed as part of Apache Nutch web search engine project. The differences of HDFS from other distributed file systems are:

- Highly fault tolerant
- Designed to operate on low cost commodity machines
- Provides high throughput access to application data
- Suitable for handling large data sets
- Enables streaming access to file system data

Goals of HDFS

The main goals of HDFS are:

1. **Hardware Failure Recovery:** Hundreds or thousands of machines may be connected in Hadoop cluster. Hence the probability of failure of a node is more. The detection of faults and faster automatic recovery are core architectural goals of HDFS.
2. **Large Data Sets:** Typical file size is from gigabytes to terabytes. HDFS should handle large number of nodes in the cluster also. It should handle large number of files in a single instance.
3. **Streaming Data Access:** HDFS is designed more for batch processing than interactive applications. It should provide high throughput of data access ie. Latency should be reduced.
4. **Moving Computation:** If the data set is huge, computation will be more efficient if it is executed near the data under operation. Hence it is better to migrate the computation to the location where data is available. HDFS provides interfaces to the applications for moving computation.
5. **Portability:** HDFS is deigned to be easily portable from one platform to another platform.
6. **Simple Coherency Model:** HDFS supports write-once-read-many access for files. A file once created, written and closed need not be modified. This assumption gives high throughput data access.

Name Node and Data Nodes

HDFS supports master-slave architecture. Each cluster consists of single name node (master node) and number of data nodes (slave nodes). The data nodes are normally one per each node in the cluster. The master node manages file system namespace and controls access of files. The data nodes manage the storage effectively.

Hadoop YARN (Yet Another Resource Negotiator)

YARN is the architectural center of Hadoop. It was introduced from Hadoop 2.x versions. The main idea of YARN is to separate resource management and job scheduling. There is a global Resource Manager (RM) and per-application Application Master (AM). The Resource Manager arbitrates resources(CPU, memory, disk, network) among all applications. The per-application Application Master negotiates resources from Resource Manager and executes and monitors tasks. YARN provides:

1. A central platform to deliver consistent operations across cluster and security.
2. Data governance tools.
3. Dynamic resource management and hence better cluster utilization.
4. Independent Software Vendors (ISVs) and developers a consistent framework.
5. Support to multiple data processing engines such as streaming, batch processing, SQL, etc. It is called "multi-tenancy."
6. Effective scheduling and hence scalability.
7. Compatibility with lower versions.

The architecture diagram of YARN is shown in Figure 3.

Hadoop MapReduce

Mapreduce is a software framework for handling large data sets on clusters. It is highly scalable. It supports multiple programming languages such as C,C++, Java, etc. It has two parts:

Figure 3. YARN architecture

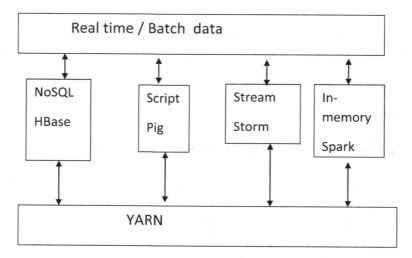

1. A MapReduce *job* usually splits the input data-set into independent chunks which are processed by the *map tasks* in a completely parallel manner.
2. The framework sorts the outputs of the maps, which are then input to the *reduce tasks*. Typically both the input and the output of the job are stored in a file-system. The framework takes care of scheduling tasks, monitoring them and re-executes the failed tasks.

The major advantages of Mapreduce are:

*   Fault tolerance.
*   Framework takes care of scheduling tasks, monitoring them and re-executes the failed tasks.

CONCLUSION

In this chapter a brief history of Hadoop was discussed. The different releases of Hadoop and its installation procedures are outlined. Also the basic architecture of Hadoop along with constituent components are described

REFERENCES

Apache Hadoop Releases. (2018). Retrieved from http://hadoop.apache.org/release

Chang, F., Dean, J., Ghemawat, S., Hsieh, W. C., Wallach, D. A., Burrows, M., ... Gruber, R. E. (2008). BigTable: A Distributed Storage System for Structured Data. *ACM Transactions on Computer Systems*, *26*(2), 2. doi:10.1145/1365815.1365816

Dean, J., & Ghemawat, S. (2004). MapReduce: Simplified Data Processing on Large Clusters. *USENIX Association OSDI '04: 6th Symposium on Operating Systems Design and Implementation*, 137-149.

Franklin, M., Halevy, A., & Maier, D. (2005). From Databases to Dataspaces: A New Abstraction for Information Management. *SIGMOD Record*, *34*(4), 27–33. doi:10.1145/1107499.1107502

Kallman, Kimura, Natkins, Pavlo, Rasin, Zdonik, ... Abadi. (2008). HStore: A High Performance, Distributed Main Memory Transaction Processing System. *ACM VLDB '08*.

APPENDIX: EXERCISES

1. Which of the following are correct in Hadoop?
    a. Open Source
    b. Distributed Processing Framework
    c. Distributed Storing Framework
    d. None of the above
2. The metadata in the Hadoop is:
    a. Data stored by user
    b. Information about the user
    c. Information stored about the data
    d. All of the above
3. In Hadoop we can:
    a. Add 15000 nodes in the cluster on the fly
    b. Loose data if one node fsils
    c. Specify the schema before storing data
    d. Process the data first on Master node and then on Slave node
4. Which of the following is not a goal of HDFS?
    a. Fault detection and recovery
    b. Handle large dataset
    c. Prevent deletion of data
    d. Provide high network bandwidth for data movement
5. All slave nodes in Hadoop:
    a. Should have same configuration
    b. Can have different configuration
    c. Configuration is not a matter
    d. None of the above
6. Hadoop is inspired by which of the following Google project?
    a. GFS
    b. MapReduce
    c. BigTable
    d. None of the above
7. Which one of the following stores data?
    a. Name node
    b. Data node
    c. Master node
    d. None of these

8. How does Hadoop process large volumes of data?
   a. Hadoop uses a lot of machines in parallel. This optimizes data processing
   b. Hadoop was specifically designed to process large amount of data by taking advantage of MPP hardware
   c. Hadoop ships the code to the data instead of sending the data to the code
   d. Hadoop uses sophisticated caching techniques on name node to speed processing of data

9. The following describes Hadoop wxcept:
   a. Open resource
   b. Real time
   c. Distributed computing approach
   d. Java based

10. Hadoop was written in:
    a. Java
    b. C
    c. Perl
    d. Python

11. The core components of Hadoop are:
    a. GFS, BigTable
    b. HDFS, MapReduce
    c. MapReduce alone
    d. Pig, Hive

12. Which one is TRUE for Hadoop?
    a. It works in Master-Slave mode
    b. It works in all equal level
    c. It works in Standalone mode
    d. None of the above

13. The nature of hardware for the NameNode should be:
    a. Superior than commodity grade
    b. commodity grade
    c. does not matter
    d. Just have more Ram than each of data nodes

14. All of the following accurately describe Hadoop, EXCEPT:
    a. Open source
    b. Real time
    c. Java based
    d. Distributed computing approach

15. True or false? MapReduce can best be described as a programming model used to develop Hadoop-based applications that can process massive amounts of unstructured data.
    a. True
    b. False

Chapter 4
Hadoop Setup

ABSTRACT

Apache Hadoop is an open source framework for storage and processing massive amounts of data. The skeleton of Hadoop can be viewed as distributed computing across a cluster of computers. This chapter deals with the single node, multinode setup of Hadoop environment along with the Hadoop user commands and administration commands. Hadoop processes the data on a cluster of machines with commodity hardware. It has two components, Hadoop Distributed File System for storage and Map Reduce/YARN for processing. Single node processing can be done through standalone or pseudo-distributed mode whereas multinode is through cluster mode. The execution procedure for each environment is briefly stated. Then the chapter explores the Hadoop user commands for operations like copying to and from files in distributed file systems, running jar, creating archive, setting version, classpath, etc. Further, Hadoop administration manages the configuration including functions like cluster balance, running the dfs, MapReduce admin, namenode, secondary namenode, etc.

INTRODUCTION

Apache Hadoop being an open source framework provides the utility for storage and large scale processing of data on cluster of machines with commodity hardware. This also uses a simple programming model. The framework includes a distributed storage with cluster of computers for computation. Some modules of this hadoop include an environment as hadoop common with

DOI: 10.4018/978-1-5225-3790-8.ch004

mapreduce and hadoop distributed file system (Jain, 2017). Hadoop common has the java libraries with filesystem and OS supportive level abstractions that contain necessary files to build hadoop. Hadoop Distributed File System has a high throughput for storing the application data. Hadoop mapreduce further named as YARN provides a structure for job scheduling and cluster resource management to work in parallel. This as an environment includes various architecture components and models to work with. The node setup for the hadoop architecture is as follows in the chapter

BACKGROUND

As already discussed in previous chapter, primary components at the core of Apache Hadoop high level architecture includes HDFS and Map reduce layer (Lublinsky et al., 2015). The HDFS is a portable file system written in Java, uses TCP/IP layer for communication. As stated, cluster of datanodes handle the block of data over the network. It is highly reliable since the data stored is replicated thrice with two on same rack and one in other. YARN being a framework builds with jobtracker and task tracker that handle the processing. Job tracker schedules the nodes to task tracker for performing the map or reduce task (Moorthy, 2014). Further the working environment of hadoop can be stated as follows: A user can submit a job by specifying the location of input and output file in the distributed system. Java classes in jar file implements the mapreduce processing. For the above given process, job configuration can be in a single node or cluster node by modifying the different parameters to be specified in the chapter below.

SINGLE NODE SETUP

The steps for setting up a single node hadoop should be backed up by HDFS and YARN running on a Linux environment (White, 2015).

The basic requirements behind the installation of hadoop include Java. Check in command prompt to verify if Java is already installed using:

```
$ java - version
```

In case of recent version released, then the Java runtime environment will support hadoop. If not, we have to install the java into the system. To make the environment local set the java path to ~/.bashrc file by including the following lines.

```
export JAVA_HOME = /usr/local/jdk1.7.0
export PATH=$PATH:$JAVA_HOME/bin
```

Now, can apply the changes to the current system working environment by

```
$ source ~/.bashrc
```

The second step of basic requirement is to configure SSH. SSH setup is used for starting and stopping the distributed daemon shell operations. SSH requires to be setup to allow password-less login for hadoop machines connected in the cluster. This is achieved through public/private key pair to authenticate different users and the public key will be shared across the cluster. Hadoop needs this SSH access to manage between cluster of nodes. Initially check if ssh is mapped to localhost without a passphrase by:

```
$ ssh localhost
```

Without passphrase ssh to localhost allows to generate a key value pair using the following command.

```
$ ssh-keygen -t rsa -P '' -f ~/.ssh/id_rsa
```

To enable SSH access to machine with a new key is done using the command,

```
$ cat ~/.ssh/id_rsa.pub >> ~/.ssh/authorized_keys
$ chmod 0600 ~/.ssh/authorized_keys
```

Finally the SSH server configuration can be checked in the file /etc/ssh/sshd_config

Hadoop Operation Modes

Hadoop cluster can be in one of the three modes:

- **Standalone Mode:** By default, works in this mode by configuring the execution as a single java process.
- **Pseudo Distributed Mode:** Distributed simulation like processing is developed on a single machine. Hadoop daemon with hdfs, mapreduce runs like separate java process.
- **Fully Distributed/Cluster Mode:** Fully distributed with a minimum of two machines running as a cluster. The machines works as a master slave architecture which will be explained below.

Setup Configuration Files

After installation, the complete hadoop setup is done by modifying the following list of files. They are:

- ~/.bashrc
- /home/hadoop/etc/hadoop/hadoop-env.sh
- /home/hadoop/etc/hadoop/core-site.xml
- /home/hadoop/etc/hadoop/mapred-site.xml
- /home/hadoop/etc/hadoop/hdfs-site.xml

~/.bashrc

The java home path and hadoop path can be set by editing the .bashrc file in the home directory.

```
export JAVA_HOME = /home/lib/jvm/java-7-openjdk-amd64
export HADOOP_HOME = /home/Hadoop
```

Hadoop-env.sh

The java home path is to be set in the hadoop environment shell file and so the file is to be edited by adding the below statement.

```
export JAVA_HOME = /home/lib/jvm/java-7-openjdk-amd64
```

Core-site.xml

This includes the configuration properties that Hadoop requires to start with. Already existing default settings can be overridden based on setup mode i.e standalone, pseudo distributed or multi-node. The value tag of default name of filesystem in the xml file has the URI of the namenode which can be modified as per the hadoop mode. The value tag of the temporary directory specifies the path to HDFS:

```
<configuration>
<property>
        <name> hadoop.tmp.dir</name>
        <value>/home/hadoop/hdfsdata </value>
        <description> Temporary Directory </description>
</property>
<property>
        <name> fs.default.name </name>
        <value>hdfs://localhost:9000</value>
        <description> Default filesystem </description>
</property>
</configuration>
```

Mapred-site.xml

The contents of the file mapred-site.xml.template present in the same location are to be copied to the file mapred-site.xml. This file specifies the framework for mapreduce usage. The value tag of default job tracker in the xml file is to be modified as per the mode i.e standalone, pseudo distributed or multi-node from localhost to the respective host IP address with port.

```
<configuration>
<property>
        <name> mapred.job.tracker</name>
        <value>locahost:9000</value>
        <description> Single map and reduce task</description>
</property>
</configuration>
```

Hdfs-site.xml

This file needs to be configured for every host in the cluster. The file specifies the path of directories where namenode and datanode should be in that host. Editing the file is a must to mention the number of datanodes to replicate the data blocks.

```
<configuration>
<property>
        <name>dfs.replication</name>
        <value>1</value>
        <description> Default Block Replication</description>
</property>
<property>
        <name>dfs.namenode.name.dir</name>
        <value>/home/hadoop/hadoopdata/hdfs/namenode</value>
        <description> Namenode Directory</description>
</property>
<property>
<name>dfs.datanode.data.dir</name>
        <value>/home/hadoop/hadoopdata/hdfs/datanode</value>
        <description> Datanode Directory</description>
</property>
</configuration>
```

Format the Hadoop Filesystem

Hadoop filesystem needs to be formatted before the job is submitted into the environment. The command should be present with write permission as it creates a current directory with fsimage files in the /home/hadoop/hadoopdata/ hdfs/namenode folder as mentioned in hdfs-site.xml:

```
$ hadoop namenode -format
```

Start and Shut Down Hadoop

In a new Hadoop environment, the commands to begin start-dfs.sh and start-yarn.sh (or start-all.sh) are to be used for running the HDFS and Mapreduce environment. The nodes in execution are checked using jps command.

```
$ start-dfs.sh
$ jps
Namenode
Secondary Namenode
Datanode
$start-yarn.sh
$jps
Resource Manager
NodeManager
```

Similarly, stop-dfs.sh and stop-yarn.sh (or stop-all.sh) is to be used to shut down the hadoop environment. Once nodes shutdown, it can be checked using jps command.

Hadoop's component HDFS is highly fault tolerant which is deployed on commodity hardware. This provides high throughput access to data and so good for large data applications. HDFS comprises DataNode and NameNode. DataNode has the actual data in filesystem, in case of more than one datanode the data is replicated across nodes to overcome loss of data. Namenode includes the directory of all files in the filesystem in the form of tree structure i.e tracks where the data is stored. Secondary namenode acts as checkpoint and a failover for namenode.

In Yarn infrastructure, the daemons are Resource Manager and Node Manager. Resource Manager is one per cluster and it does the following functions, resource scheduling, event handling, and monitoring the live presence of application master and node manager. Node Manager is used for executing the job.

Standalone Operation

Hadoop though designed as a distributed environment working on commodity of machines, this can work as single node in standalone mode. It runs a single monolithic java process. Mostly this mode is used for debugging a mapreduce application on a small data which needs to be applied for a cluster of computers with big data.

As stated above, the two basic requirements of Java environment and SSH configuration is to be initialised. The next step is to install the hadoop environment as standalone architecture with no daemons running mapreduce in a single system. The development and execution is easy for testing and debugging.

Set hadoop home using the command:

```
export HADOOP_HOME = /usr/local/hadoop
```

Further the steps for execution is given by:

- Open terminal and change the directory to using "cd hadoop".
- Then enter the commands, sbin/start-dfs.sh- for starting the Namenode, Datanode, SecondaryNamenode.
- Enter command jps - Displays all the started nodes.
- Browse the web interface http://localhost:50070 for namenode daemon
- sbin/start-yarn.sh- for starting the node manager and resource manager.
- Check with jps command.
- Enter command mapred classpath - for mapping the mapreduce classpath to hdfs.
- export CLASSPATH=" " for exporting the classpath into dfs.
- javac filename.java - for executing our mapreduce program.
- jar -cvf <jarname.jar >-C <foldername>/ . -For creating a jar file for our code.
- hdfs dfs -mkdir /<directory _name> - To create a directory in hadoop distributed file system.
- hdfs dfs -put <input.txt> /<input directory name> - To place the input in the createddirectory.
- hdfs dfs -ls /<directory_name> - To view the files in created directory.
- hadoop jar <jarname.jar > mainclassname /<input directory name> /<Output directory name> -For execution of mapreduce job.
- hdfs dfs -cat /<output directory name>/part-* -To retrieve the job result from HDFS.

Hadoop Web Interface

Hadoop has several web interfaces by default given in conf/hadoop-default.xml:

```
http://localhost:50070 - Namenode
http://localhost:50030 - Resource Manager(Job Tracker)
http://localhost:50060 - Node Manager(Task Tracker)
```

The namenode web UI shows a cluster summary that includes total capacity, live, dead and decommisioned nodes. The HDFS namespace along with the contents of its files can be viewed. Access to local Hadoop's log files is provided.

Resource Manager web User Interface includes job statistics of hadoop cluster, along with running/finished/failed/killed jobs and history log file. Also it can access local machine log files. Node Manager allows to view the running jobs along with log files.

Example

Given a WordCount mapreduce program to execute on a large text data, apart from config files the execution steps with results are given below:

- **//To set classpath**

```
hadoop@IT-PGL010 ~/hadoop-2.7.3 $ mapred classpath
hadoop@IT-PGL010 ~/hadoop-2.7.3 $ export CLASSPATH="/home/
hadoop/hadoop-2.7.3/etc .................../hadoop/hadoop-2.7.3/
share/hadoop/mapreduce/lib/snappy-java-1.0.4.1.jar:/home/
hadoop/hadoop-2.7.3/share/hadoop/mapreduce/lib/xz-1.0.jar:/
home/hadoop/hadoop-2.7.3/modules/*.jar"
```

- **//Program Compilation**

```
hadoop@IT-PGL010 ~/hadoop-2.7.3 $ javac WordCount.java
```

- **//Create Jar file named "wc.jar" with 3 classes placed into the folder "wc"**

```
hadoop@IT-PGL010 ~/hadoop-2.7.3 $ jar -cvf wc.jar -C wc/ .
added manifest
adding: WordCount$IntSumReducer.class(in = 1739) (out= 739)
(deflated 57%)
adding: WordCount$TokenizerMapper.class(in = 1736) (out= 753)
(deflated 56%)
adding: WordCount.class(in = 1501) (out= 811)(deflated 45%)
```

- **//Create a input directory and place the input file "data.txt" into the HDFS**

```
hadoop@IT-PGL010 ~/hadoop-2.7.3 $ hdfs dfs - mkdir /input
hadoop@IT-PGL010 ~/hadoop-2.7.3 $ hdfs dfs - put /home/hadoop/
data.txt /input
```

- **//To list and check if input file is placed inside the HDFS directory**

```
hadoop@IT-PGL010 ~/hadoop-2.7.3 $ hdfs dfs - ls /input
```

- **//Running the job with main class name "WordCount", Input file is in directory input and output is to be placed in output directory**

```
hadoop@IT-PGL010 ~/hadoop-2.7.3 $ hadoop jar wc.jar WordCount /
input/data.txt /output
```

- **//View the result in part-r-00000 file present under output directory**

```
hadoop@IT-PGL010 ~/hadoop-2.7.3 $ hdfs dfs -cat /output/part-*
After          6
Context           10
Data       11
Dealing           15
Each       3
```

Pseudo Distributed Operation

Hadoop can run in a single node with pseudo distributed mode where hadoop daemons will run as separate java process i.e. NameNode, DataNode, Secondary namenode, Resource Manager and Node Manager all run on a single machine. The configurations to be specified are declared as:

In etc/hadoop/core-site.xml

```
<configuration>
    <property>
        <name>fs.defaultFS</name>
        <value>hdfs://localhost:9000</value>
    </property>
</configuration>
```

In etc/hadoop/hdfs-site.xml specify the replication along with the temporary directory for HDFS:

```
<configuration>
    <property>
        <name>dfs.replication</name>
        <value>1</value>
    </property>
```

```
    <property>
        <name>hadoop.tmp.dir </name>
        <value>/home/hadoop/hdfs</value>
    </property>
</configuration>
```

Mapreduce job on YARN in a pseudo distributed mode requires few parameters along with NodeManager and ResourceManager similar to Task and Job tracker in Hadoop 1.2 versions.

The configurations to be specified further includes:

In etc/hadoop/mapred-site.xml:

```
<configuration>
    <property>
        <name>mapreduce.framework.name</name>
        <value>yarn</value>
    </property>
</configuration>
```

In etc/hadoop/yarn-site.xml:

```
<configuration>
    <property>
        <name>yarn.nodemanager.aux-services</name>
        <value>mapreduce_shuffle</value>
    </property>
</configuration>
```

Further, one can start resource manager and node manager daemon using:

```
$ sbin/start-yarn.sh
```

The web interface for the resource manager daemon can be checked in http://localhost:8088

HADOOP CLUSTER SETUP

Configuring Hadoop Cluster

From two single-node clusters to a multi-node cluster is configuring and testing a "local" Hadoop setup to "merge" the two single-node clusters into one multi-node cluster in which one will become the designated master which also act as a slave with regard to data storage and processing and the other will be only as slave. It's much easier to track down any problems you might encounter due to the reduced complexity of doing a single-node cluster setup first on each machine. Typically one machine in the cluster is designated as the NameNode, Secondary Namenode and JobTracker, exclusively. This is optional as it can also be run on separate nodes. These are the actual "master nodes". The rest of the machines in the cluster will act as both DataNode and TaskTracker. These are the slaves or "worker nodes."

The configurations to be made in the cluster nodes are stated below:

- Move to superuser login for admin rights and redirect to etc directory
- Edit the hosts file in etc folder using the command:
  - gedit hosts
- Add master and slave machine IP & name these files as master and slave. For example,
  - 192.168.118.149 master
  - 192.168.118.151 slave

More number of slave nodes can be added as required in the hosts file by including the host IPs.

- Move to home/hadoop/etc/hadoop in master and slaves machine and update the configuration files
- Select "core-site.xml" directory
  - Update the filesystem properties tag in the xml file from localhost to master or IP address.

```
<property>
<name>fs.defaultFS</name>
<value>hdfs://master:9000 </value>
</property>
```

- In the "hdfs_site.xml", mention the replication value for blocks in value tag under property of dfs replication

```
<property>
    <name>dfs.replication</name>
    <value>1</value>
</property>
```

- In the "slaves" file, edit the localhost to the names of the machines which behaves as datanodes. Here both the master and slave machines are made as datanodes so its specified as:

```
Master
Slave
```

- Now start the nodes again using sbin/start-dfs.sh and sbin/start-yarn.sh in both master and slaves nodes
- To execute mapreduce program, follow the same steps as in hadoop standalone environment
- Enter command mapred classpath - for mapping the mapreduce classpath to hdfs.
- export CLASSPATH=" " for exporting the classpath into dfs
- javac filename.java - for executing our mapreduce program
- jar -cvf <jarname.jar >-C <foldername>/ . -For creating a jar file for our code
- hdfs dfs -mkdir /<directory _name> - To create a directory in hadoop distributed file system
- hdfs dfs -put <input.txt> /<input directory name> - To place the input in the createddirectory
- hdfs dfs -ls /<directory_name> - To view the files in created directory
- hadoop jar <jarname.jar > mainclassname /<input directory name> /<Output directory name> -For execution of mapreduce job
- hdfs dfs -cat /<output directory name>/part-* -To retrieve the job result from HDFS

After the execution of job, the cluster summary with the live nodes connected can be viewed through the web interface as http://master:50070 instead of localhost. Additionaly the jobs submitted/running/finished/killed can be seen through the web user interface http://master:8088.

Operating Hadoop Cluster

Once the entire necessary configuration is complete, distribute the files to the HADOOP_CONF_DIR directory on all the machines. This should be the same directory on all machines. In general, it is optional that HDFS and YARN run as separate users. In the majority of installations, HDFS processes execute as 'hdfs' and YARN as 'yarn' account.

To start a Hadoop cluster you will need to start both the HDFS and YARN cluster.

Format a new distributed filesystem as *hdfs*:

```
$HADOOP/bin/hdfs namenode -format <cluster_name>
```

If etc/hadoop/slaves and ssh trusted access is configured, then HDFS and YARN processes can be started with a utility script.

```
$HADOOP/sbin/start-dfs.sh
$HADOOP/sbin/start-yarn.sh
```

Similarly all of the HDFS and YARN processes may be stopped with a utility script

```
$HADOOP/sbin/stop-dfs.sh
$HADOOP/sbin/stop-yarn.sh
```

HADOOP USER COMMANDS

- Archive:

```
Syntax: hadoop archive -archiveName NAME <source>*
<destination>
```

Creates a hadoop archive

- Distcp:

```
Syntax: hadoop distcp <Source URL> <Destination URL>
```

Copy file or directories recursively

- Fs:

```
Syntax: hadoop fs [GENERIC_OPTIONS] [COMMAND_OPTIONS]
```

Runs as a generic filesystem for the user client.

- Fsck:

```
Syntax: hadoop fsck [GENERIC_OPTIONS] <path> [-move | -delete |
-openforwrite] [-files [-blocks [-locations | -racks]]]
```

Runs a HDFS filesystem checking utility

- Jar:

```
Syntax: hadoop jar <jar> [mainClass] arguments
```

Runs a jar file. Users can bundle their Map Reduce code in a jar file and execute it using this command

- Version:

```
Syntax: hadoop version
```

Prints the version of hadoop environment.

- ClassName:

```
Syntax: hadoop CLASS1
```

Hadoop script can be used to invoke any class. Runs the class named CLASS1.

- Classpath:

```
Syntax: hadoop classpath
```

Prints the class path needed to get the Hadoop jar and the required libraries.

- appendToFile:

```
Syntax: hdfs dfs -appendToFile <localsource> ... <destination
source>
```

Append single src, or multiple srcs from local file system to the destination file system.
Also reads input from stdin and appends to destination file system.

- Chown:

```
Syntax: hdfs dfs -chown [-R] [OWNER][:[GROUP]] URI [URI ]
```

Change the owner of files. The user must be a super-user

- CopyFromLocal:

```
Syntax: hdfs dfs -copyFromLocal <localsrc> URI
```

Copy the file from local system to HDFS distributed filesystem and similar to put, the source is restricted to local file reference.

- CopyToLocal:

```
Syntax: hdfs dfs -copyToLocal [-ignorecrc] [-crc] URI
<localdst>
```

Copy a file from HDFS distributed filesystem to local filesystem environment and similar to get command, the destination is restricted to a local file reference

- Count:

```
Syntax: hdfs dfs -count [-q] [-h] <paths>
```

Count the number of directories, files and bytes under the paths that match the specified file pattern

HADOOP ADMINISTRATION COMMANDS

- Balancer:

```
Syntax: hadoop balancer [-threshold <threshold>]
```

To attain the cluster balancing utility value that is threshold. An administrator can simply press Ctrl-C to stop the rebalancing process

- Daemonlog:

```
Syntax: hadoop daemonlog -getlevel <host:port> <name> Usage:
hadoop daemonlog -setlevel <host:port> <name> <level>
```

Get/Set the log level for each daemon.

- Dfsadmin:

```
Syntax: hadoop dfsadmin [GENERIC_OPTIONS] [-report] [-safemode
enter | leave | get | wait] [-refreshNodes] [-finalizeUpgrade]
[-upgradeProgress status | details | force] [-metasave
filename] [-setQuota <quota> <dirname>...<dirname>] [-clrQuota
<dirname>...<dirname>] [-restoreFailedStorage true|false|check]
[-help [cmd]]
```

To run as HDFS dfsadmin client.

- Mradmin:

```
Syntax: hadoop mradmin [ GENERIC_OPTIONS ] [-refreshQueueAcls]
```

To run as MR admin client

- Jobtracker:

```
Syntax: hadoop jobtracker [-dumpConfiguration]
```

To run as the MapReduce job Tracker node.

- Namenode:

```
Syntax: hadoop namenode [-format] | [-upgrade] | [-rollback] |
[-finalize] | [-importCheckpoint]
```

Runs the namenode with various options to format/ upgrade/ rollback etc..

- Secondary Namenode:

```
Syntax: hadoop secondarynamenode [-checkpoint [force]] |
[-geteditsize]
```

Runs the HDFS secondary namenode as checkpoint and to retrieve the size

CONCLUSION

The chapter concludes our coverage of the history and rationale for HADOOP with HDFS and YARN. The hadoop setup environment for various modes along with the configuration files are briefly defined in the chapter. Hence the design and architectural decisions with the different modes deal in a unique perspective.

REFERENCES

Jain, V. K. (2017). *Big Data and Hadoop*. New Delhi: Khanna Publishing.

Lublinsky, Smith, & Yakubovich. (2015). *Professional Hadoop Solutions*. John Wiley & Sons Publication.

Moorthy, A. C. (2014). *Apache YARN Moving beyond Mapreduce and Batch Processing with Apache Hadoop-2*. Addison Wesley Publications.

White, T. (2015). *Hadoop the definitive guide*. O'Reilly Publication.

Chapter 5
Hadoop Distributed File System (HDFS)

ABSTRACT

Hadoop Distributed File System, which is popularly known as HDFS, is a Java-based distributed file system running on commodity machines. HDFS is basically meant for storing Big Data over distributed commodity machines and getting the work done at a faster rate due to the processing of data in a distributed manner. Basically, HDFS has one name node (master node) and cluster of data nodes (slave nodes). The HDFS files are divided into blocks. The block is the minimum amount of data (64 MB) that can be read or written. The functions of the name node are to master the slave nodes, to maintain the file system, to control client access, and to have control of the replications. To ensure the availability of the name node, a standby name node is deployed by failover control and fencing is done to avoid the activation of the primary name node during failover. The functions of the data nodes are to store the data, serve the read and write requests, replicate the blocks, maintain the liveness of the node, ensure the storage policy, and maintain the block cache size. Also, it ensures the availability of data.

DOI: 10.4018/978-1-5225-3790-8.ch005

INTRODUCTION

HDFS is a Java based distributed file system running on commodity machines. It holds very large amount of data. In order to store large data, the files are split into smaller blocks and stored across multiple machines. This allows parallel processing. For example, if India wants to store aadhar card details of all people in its country, the names starting with 'A' can be stored in one server, the names starting with 'B' can be stored in server2, etc. HDFS demonstrated 200 PB of storage and a single cluster of 4500 servers. This chapter explains the architecture of HDFS. Also the salient features of HDFS are explained so that any reader can easily understand the architecture and use it.

BACKGROUND

Hortonworks (Hortonworks, 2017) stated, "HDFS is a scalable, fault-tolerant, distributed storage system that works closely with a wide variety of concurrent data access applications, coordinated by YARN".

Cloudera (Cloudera Inc, 2017) supported Hadoop by stating:

HDFS is a fault-tolerant and self-healing distributed filesystem designed to turn a cluster of industry-standard servers into a massively scalable pool of storage. Developed specifically for large-scale data processing workloads where scalability, flexibility, and throughput are critical, HDFS accepts data in any format regardless of schema, optimizes for high-bandwidth streaming, and scales to proven deployments of 100PB and beyond.

Vangie Beal (Webopedia 2017) stated, "The primary objective of HDFS is to store data reliably even in the presence of failures including NameNode failures, DataNode failures and network partitions. ".

TechTarget (TechTarget, 2013) stated "Hadoop Distributed file system is designed to be highly fault-tolerant, facilitating the rapid transfer of data between compute nodes".

ARCHITECTURE OF HDFS

HDFS cluster consists of:

1. **One NameNode (Master Server):** That manages file system namespace and regulates file access to clients.
2. **Number of DataNodes (Slave):** One per each node in the cluster – which manages storage in its node.

The architecture is shown in Figure 1.

The NameNode and DataNode are software running on commodity machines using GNU/Linux operating system. Machines with Java can run NameNode and DataNode. Each node can run a single DataNode. But rarely a node can run multiple DataNodes also. Since the data are available on nodes where calculations have to be done, highest read performance is achieved. There is no shared bus between the nodes in the cluster. Point-to-point SAS (Serial Attached SCSI) or SATA (Serial Advanced Technology Attachment) disks are used. Hence highest performance is achieved.

Figure 1. HDFS architecture

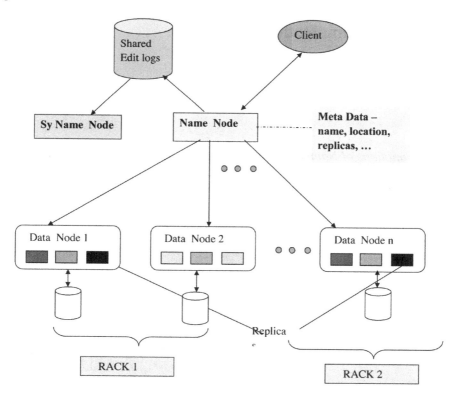

Data Blocks

HDFS supports very large files. It supports write once – read many semantics on files. HDFS files are divided into blocks. The block is the minimum amount of data that can be read or written. The block size used by HDFS is 64 MB. The normal disk block size is 512 bytes. Compared to this 512 bytes, the block size used by HDFS is very larger. Hence seek time is minimized and HDFS operations are faster. These blocks simplify storage management and eliminate metadata.

Every HDFS file is chopped into 64 MB chunks. These chunks are normally stored in different data nodes. All blocks or chunks of a file are of same size except the last one. Hadoop optimizes for full blocks until the last block.

If HDFS block size is smaller, then:

- Metadata would be more and hence larger in size
- Memory requirement on NameNode would be very high
- There would be limitation in storage in HDFS cluster

Functions of NameNode

The working of NameNode is shown in Figure 2.
The features and functions of NameNode are:

Figure 2. Functions of NameNode

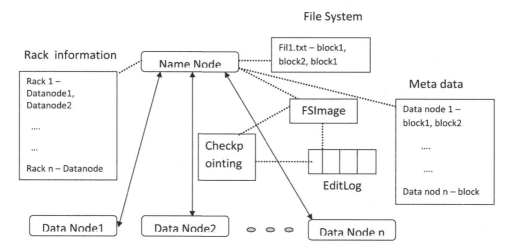

- Master node and hence Single Point of Failure (SPoF)
- Maintains file system tree
- Controls client access
- Maintains all metadata (namespace tree and where data blocks stored in DataNodes) in the file FSImage
- Changes after last checkpoint are logged separately in transaction log called "EditLog"
- Both files are stored in NameNode's local file system
- Redundant copies of both files are available at NAS (Network Attached Storage) or other servers
- Reads EditLog to update FSImage
- Maps FSImage into memory and then EditLog can be truncated
- Knows DataNodes on which blocks of a file are stored
- Piggybacks its instructions in reply to DataNode's Heartbeat
- Stores replication factor (number of replicas) for each file (indicated by application)
- Removes block replicas if load is more (called load balancing)
- User data never flows through NameNode
- Does not call DataNodes directly

Functions of DataNodes or WorkerNodes

The working of DataNodes is shown in Figure 3.
    The features and functions of DataNode are

- Stores actual data
- Serves read and write requests of clients
- Performs block creation, block replication and block deletion after getting instructions fom NameNode
- Stores each block of HDFS data in a separate file in its local file system
- It uses a heuristic to determine the number of files in each directory and creates subdirectories accordingly
- Block replica is made up of two files on the local file system of DataNode:
    ◦ Data itself
    ◦ Block metadata (checksum and generation timestamp)
- At startup, DataNode connects to NameNode and performs handshake to verify ID and version:

Figure 3. Functions of datanodes

The working of DataNodes is shown in Figure3.

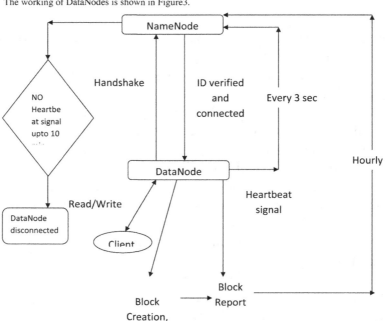

- ○ If any of them does not match, the client node will be shutdown. This is done to prevent corruption by unknown members
- Also it sends a block report to the NameNode hourly
- The block report contains information about all blocks it contains
- At every 3 secs interval, it sends a heartbeat signal to NameNode
- NameNode replies with its storage allocation and load balancing algorithm
- If the hearbeat signal from a DataNode does not come within 10 minutes, then:
  - ○ That particular DataNode is removed by NameNode
  - ○ The replicas of blocks in that particular DataNode are rescheduled to be stored on other DataNodes

DATA REPLICATION

The blocks of a file are replicated at different DataNodes for having fault tolerance. The data replication of a file is shown in Figure 4.

The block size and replication factor can be configured for each file. The application can specify these values. The default replication factor is three. At the time of file creation, replication factor can be configured and it can be changed later also. The NameNode makes decisions regarding replication of files. The location of replicas can change over time.

Replica Placement

HDFS optimizes the placement of replicas. The replica placement policy is to improve data availability, reliability and network bandwidth utilization. The NameNode can determine the rack number for each DataNode using "resolve" API (called "rack awareness"). The chance of rack failure is less than that of node failure.

Figure 4. Data replication

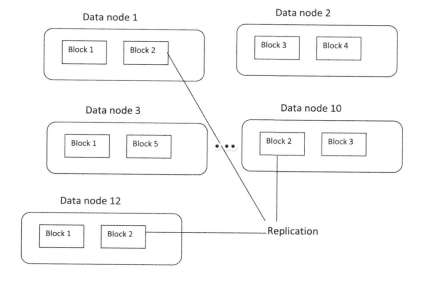

Based on these, the replica placement policy is as follows:

- One replica is placed in one node in the local rack
- Another replica is placed in one node in a different remote rack
- Last replica is placed in another node in the same remote rack

This policy reduces inter-rack write traffic and hence write performance is improved.

If the replication factor is greater than 3, the placement of 4th and remaining replicas is done randomly with the restriction that the number of replicas per rack must be less than

(replicas-1)/racks+2.

Storage Types and Storage Policies

The different storage types supported by HDFS are:

- Archive
- Disk
- SSD (Solid State Drive or Solid State Disk)
- RAM_DISK

Archive has high storage density in terms of petabytes but with little computing power. It is mainly used for archival storage. Disk is the default storage type, RAM_DISK is for supporting single replica files in memory.

The different storage policies supported by HDFS are:

- **Hot:** It is used for both storage and compute. The popular data and which are still being used will use this policy. For Hot blocks, all replicas are stored in disk.
- **Cold:** It is used only for storage with limited compute. The data which is no longer needed for processing or the data which is to be archived is moved from hot storage to cold storage. For cold block, all replicas are stored in ARCHIVE.
- **Warm:** It is partially hot and partially cold. For Warm blocks, some replicas are stored in DISK and the remaining replicas are stored in ARCHIVE.

- **All_SSD:** All replicas are stored in SSD
- **One_SSD:** One replica is stored in SSD and the remaining replicas are stored in DISK.
- **Lazy_Persist:** The replica is first written in RAM_DISK and then later written into DISK.

For implementing the storage policy also, the NameNode:

- First chooses nodes based on rack awareness.
- Checks if the node has storage required by the associated storage policy.
- If it has storage, then the NameNode selects that node.
- Else, the NameNode looks for another node.
- If enough number of replica nodes cannot be found in the first phase, the NameNode looks for fallback storage types in the second phase.

Re-Replication

If there is no hearbeat signal from a DataNode for more than 10 mins, then that DataNode is considered to be dead. Due to this dead DataNode, replication factor for some files may get affected. The NameNode constantly checks this replication factor and finds out which data block needs to be replicated once again. It initiates the re-replication. This re-replication case arises due to:

1. DataNode becomes unavailable
2. Hard disk on DataNode fails
3. A replica gets corrupted
4. Replication factor of a file may be increased

Replica Selection

HDFS tries to satisfy a read request from a node that is closer to reader node. The following policy is applied:

- If there is a replica on the same rack as the reader node, then that replica is used.
- If HDFS cluster includes multiple data centers, then the replica on the same data center is used.

BLOCK CACHE

The frequently used blocks can be cached in an off-heap space called "Block cache". Job schedulers can run job on DataNode where "Block cache" of needed data is available. Normally "block cache" is cached in one DataNode 's memory only. But the number of DataNodes where block cache is available can be configured for each file. For managing cache permissions, "Cache pool" can be formed. The Cache pool is shown in Figure 5. Different cache directives can be added to Cache pool. Applications can specify which files can be cached and how long it can be maintained in cache directive.

HDFS FILE READ OPERATION

The various steps in File read operation are indicated in Figure 6.

1.   Client opens the required file using open() on FileSystem object. This object is an instance of DistributedFileSystem.
2.   This open() initiates the HDFS Client (software) for read operation.
3.   DistributedFileSystem asks NameNode the location information for all the blocks of that particular file.
4.   The location information of all blocks are stored in Metadata in NameNode. Using the Metadata, the NameNode returns the addresses of all DataNodes that have the copy of blocks. These addresses are sorted based on the nearness of DataNode from NameNode.

Figure 5. Cache pool

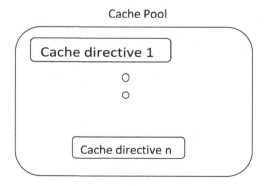

Figure 6. File read operations

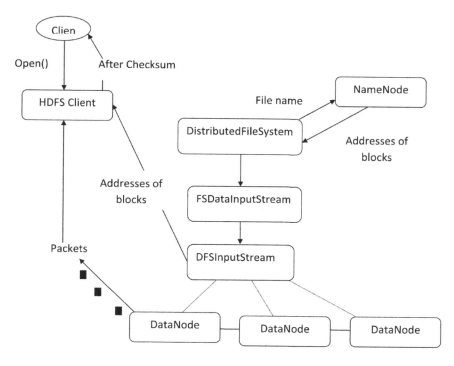

5.   DistributedFileSystem returns FSDataInputStream which is an input stream supporting file read operations. It uses a wrapper DFSInputStream for managing I/O operations.

6.   When the client calls read(), DFSInputStream returns the list of addresses where the first few blocks of the file are stored. The closest DataNode is selected.

7.   On the selected DataNode, the Block reader is initialized with block ID, offset from where data to be read, number of data bytes to be read and the client name.

8.   The data is streamed from DataNode to client in terms of packets (smaller unit of data block to reduce network overload during data transfer).

9.   HDFS client reads packets, performs checksum and then writes data into client's buffer.

10.   The read() operation is called repeatedly till end of block is reached.

11.   If end of block is reached, DFSInputStream takes the next address where next block is available and repeats the entire procedure.

12. If the entire file is read, the client calls close() on FSDataInputStream to close the connection.

HDFS FILE WRITE OPERATION

The various steps in File write operation are indicated in Figure 7.

1. Client creates the required file using create() on FileSystem object. This object is an instance of DistributedFileSystem.
2. DistributedFileSystem makes an RPC call to the NameNode to create a new file in the filesystem's namespace, with no blocks associated with it.
3. The NameNode performs various checks and makes sure that the file does not exist already. It also checks the client's permissions to create the file. If file does not exist and the client has proper permission, then

Figure 7. File write operation

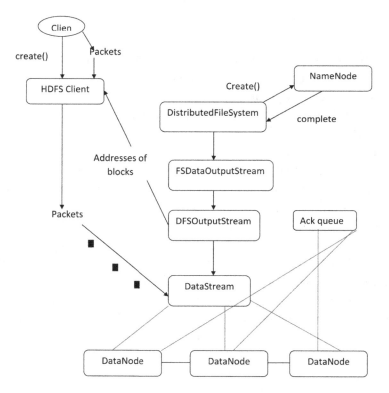

the NameNode makes a record of the new file. Otherwise, it throws an exception.

4. The DistributedFileSystem returns an FSDataOutputStream for writing the data.

5. The FSDataOutputStream wraps DFSOutputStream which handles communication with NameNode and DataNode.

6. The client writes data and the DFSOutputStream splits into packets. These packets are written into an internal queue called "data queue".

7. The "data queue" is consumed by DataStreamer. The DataStreamer asks NameNode to allocate blocks in different DataNodes for storing data including replica also.

8. The list of DataNodes forms the pipeline. By default, the replication factor is three and hence three DataNodes will be in the pipeline.

9. The DataStreamer streams packets into first node in the pipeline. The first node copies the packets and then sends them to second node in the pipeline and so on.

10. Additionally the DFSOutputStream maintains an internal queue for packets that are to be acknowledged by DataNodes. This queue is called "ack queue".

11. The packet is removed from ack queue only after it is acknowledged by all DataNodes in the pipeline.

12. When the client finishes writing data, it calls close().

13. The remaining packets are pushed into the pipeline and acknowledge is awaited.

14. The NameNode now replicates the file in proper locations.

HDFS HIGH AVAILABILITY (HA)

In HDFS cluster, there is only one NameNode. Hence it is Single Point Of Failure (SPOF). If that machine becomes unavailable, then the whole cluster will become unavailable. Then the administrator may start a new NameNode. The new NameNode may take time to start because it has to:

*   Load its NameSpace image into memory
*   Read its EditLog and update information
*   Receive information i.e. Block reports from DataNodes

In very large clusters, this starting time may go upto 30 minutes. This delay is a major issue in a cluster for many applications. Hadoop overcomes this drawback and provides High Availability (HA). The HA can be achieved by providing two NameNodes.

Architecture

One NameNode is called "primary NameNode" and it is in "Active" state. The other NameNode is called "secondary NameNode" and it is in "Standby" state. If the main NameNode fails, the secondary NameNode has to take charge and continue servicing client requests. The major changes needed for implementing this are:

1. Both active NameNode and standby NameNode must have equivalent hardware.
2. Both main NameNode and secondary NameNode must have a shared memory to store and share EditLogs file. When the active NameNode makes any modification, it logs the modification to Edit log file. The standby NameNode must watch this shared memory for any modification and should update its own namespace. If active NameNode fails, then secondary NameNode must read EditLog from shared memory and use it. Then only it can synchronize its operations with the earlier active NameNode and proceed.
3. Block reports are stored in main memory of NameNode . Hence all DataNodes must send their block reports and heartbeat signals to both NameNodes.

The architecture is shown in Figure 8.
The shared storage for High availability can be achieved in two ways:

1. NFS
2. Quorum Journal Manager or Conventional Shared Storage

Network File System (NFS)

NFS mount on Network Attached Storage (NAS) can be used for shared EditLog.

Figure 8. Architecture for HA

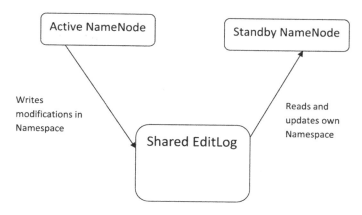

Quorum Journal Manager (QJM)

The architecture is shown in Figure 9. The standby NameNode wants it state to be synchronized with active NameNode.

For this synchronization, both NameNodes communicate via a group of separate daemons called Journal Nodes (JN). If active NameNode modifies its namespace, it is written into majority of Journal nodes. The standby NameNode can read these edits from any of the Journal nodes and can update its namespace. It constantly watches Journal nodes for any change in EditLog. If there is any change, then it immediately updates its namespace.

Figure 9. Architecture of Quorum Journal Managers

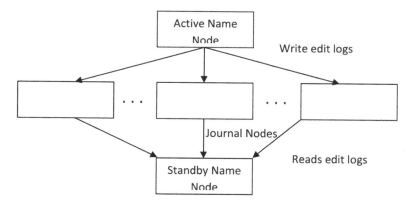

When the active NameNode fails, the standby NameNode ensures that it had read all the edits from Journal Nodes and updates its namespace correctly. Then only it takes the role of active NameNode. Hence synchronization between active NameNode and standby NameNode is correctly achieved.

The Journal Nodes daemon is lightweight process. Hence it can be collocated with other HDFS elements like NameNodes, YARN Resource Manager, etc. EditLog changes are written into majority of JN. Hence there must be at least three JNs. Three JNs will tolerate the failure of single machine. If the system wants to tolerate the failure of more machines, then the number of JNs must be increased. If 'N' JNs are run, then the system can tolerate the failure of (N-1)/2 machines.

FAILOVER CONTROLLER

The transition from active NameNode to standby NameNode is controlled by an entity called "Failover controller". By default, Zookeeper is used as Failover controller. Each NameNode runs a lightweight failover controller process. The main job of this process is to monitor NameNode for failures using Heartbeat mechanism. It triggers a failover if NameNode fails. The failover can be of two types:

1. Graceful failover
2. Ungraceful failover

Graceful Failover

It is the failover initiated by administrator. The transition between two NameNodes is orderly done.

Ungraceful Failover

This failover is not initiated manually. Sometimes even a slow network or network partition can cause failover. There are chances that the previous active NameNode may still run after the standby NameNode takes the control.

FENCING

Due to ungraceful failover, the previous active node may be still active even after the standby NameNode takes control. In this case, the older NameNode should not cause any damage or unwanted modification. Hence a method called "fencing" is used. The older NameNode should be fenced from doing any modification. The QJM allows only one NameNode to do write operation with editLog. But read request from a client could be answered by old NameNode. Hence the older NameNode process must be avoided using Secure Shell (SSH) commands. For Network File System (NFS) still stronger fencing method must be used.

The various fencing methods are:

1. Disabling network port of older NameNode using remote command.
2. Revoking permission of older NameNode to access shared memory.
3. Using specialized power unit to disconnect older NameNode.

CLIENT FAILOVER

The client library handles the client failover transparently. For the implementation, client side configuration is used to control failover. The logical hostname is mapped to both active NameNode and standby NameNode addresses. The client uses the logical hostname and tries to connect with either of the NameNodes.

WORKING WITH COMMAND LINE INTERFACE

Out of the many interfaces, command line interface is one of the simplest ways of doing it and can be used. Initially the HDFS can be implemented in a single machine, for which Hadoop is configured in pseudo distributed mode. After being familiar with the Hadoop in single machine, it can be further expanded to multiple (cluster of) machines. Two properties are to be set up. They are fs.defaultFS and dfs.replication. The first property (fs.defaultFS), which is the default file system is set to hdfs://localhost/. The file system is specified by the URI (hdfs://localhost/). The default port number is 8020. All the HDFS clients use this host name and port to get connected. Since, a single machine is used for the implementation of the Hadoop, the possibilities of replication of data nodes is not there. Hence the second property is dfs. replication, which decides the number of replication factor (default is 3), is set to 1 to suppress the warning message of blocks being under-replicated.

Basic File System Operations

Table 1 shows the list of file system operational commands organized in alphabetic order.

Each command is prefixed by "*hadoop dfs -*".

The following table shows the commands with its description. Almost all commands are self explanatory. Note that each command is prefixed with "*hdfs dfs – *". In the comment line (preceded with //) the return status is indicated (either 0 on success or -1 on error). In the commands, the option–R indicates the operations carried out recursively in the directories. In certain commands to be executed, the user must be the owner(O) of the file or the Super User (SU), which will be indicated by O/SU.

FUTURE RESEARCH DIRECTIONS

Modern applications like IoT generate larger volume of data. Hadoop Distributed File System provides better solution for storing this voluminous data. Hence many users are using HDFS as their data warehouse. But this larger volume may lead to inefficiency. Huang et al. (2011) indicated that HDFS users are mostly concentrating in storing voluminous data only and they assume that the batch processing in Hadoop environment would take care of everything. They do not bother about the time taken for execution and longer time taken by different processes. As the data can be combination of

Table 1.

appendToFile	copyToLocal	get	moveFromLocal	setfacl
cat	count	getfacl	moveToLocal	setrep
chgrp	cp	getmerge	mv	stat
chmod	du	ls	put	tail
chown	dus	lsr	rm	test
copyFromLocal	expunge	mkdir	rmr	Text, touchz

Table 2.

appendToFile	<localsrc> ... <dst> *//return 0 on success and -1 on error*
Append one or more source files from local file system to the destination file system. Also reads input from stdin and appends to destination file system. • hdfs dfs -appendToFile localfile /user/hadoop/hadoopfile • hdfs dfs -appendToFile localfile1 localfile2 /user/hadoop/hadoopfile • hdfs dfs -appendToFile localfile hdfs://nn.example.com/hadoop/hadoopfile • hdfs dfs -appendToFile - hdfs://nn.example.com/hadoop/hadoopfile	
cat	URI [URI ...] *//return 0 on success and -1 on error*
Copies the files specified by the source paths to stdout i.e. display device Example: • hdfs dfs -cat hdfs://nn1.example.com/file1 hdfs://nn2.example.com/file2 • hdfs dfs -cat file://file3 /user/hadoop/file4	
chgrp	[-R] GROUP URI [URI ...]
Change group association of files (O/SU).	
chmod	[-R] <MODE[,MODE]... I OCTALMODE> URI [URI ...]
Change the permissions of files (O/SU) – The format of permission is rwx rwx rwx	
chown	[-R] [OWNER][:[GROUP]] URI [URI]
Change the owner of files. The user must be a super-user.	
copyFromLocal	<localsrc> URI
Similar to put command, except that the source is restricted to a local file reference. Options: The -f option will overwrite the destination if it already exists	
copyToLocal	[-ignorecrc] [-crc] URI <localdst>
Similar to get command, except that the destination is restricted to a local file reference	
Count	[-q] <paths> *//return 0 on success and -1 on error*
Count the number of directories, files and bytes under the paths that match the specified file pattern. The output columns with -count are: • DIR_COUNT • FILE_COUNT • CONTENT_SIZE FILE_NAME The output columns with -count -q are: • QUOTA • REMAINING_QUATA • SPACE_QUOTA • REMAINING_SPACE_QUOTA • DIR_COUNT • FILE_COUNT • CONTENT_SIZE • FILE_NAME Example: • hdfs dfs -count hdfs://nn1.example.com/file1 hdfs://nn2.example.com/file2 • hdfs dfs -count -q hdfs://nn1.example.com/file1	
cp	[-f] URI [URI ...] <dest> *//return 0 on success and -1 on error*
Copy files from source to destination. This command allows multiple sources as well in which case the destination must be a directory. Options: The -f option will overwrite the destination if it already exists. Example: • hdfs dfs -cp /user/hadoop/file1 /user/hadoop/file2 • hdfs dfs -cp /user/hadoop/file1 /user/hadoop/file2 /user/hadoop/dir	

continued on following page

Table 2. Continued

du	[-s] [-h] URI [URI ...] *//return 0 on success and -1 on error*

displays sizes of files and directories contained in the given directory or the length of a file in case its just a file.
Options:
- The -s option will result in an aggregate summary of file lengths being displayed, rather than the individual files.
- The -h option will format file sizes in a "human-readable" fashion (e.g 64.0m instead of 67108864)

Example:
- hdfs dfs -du /user/hadoop/dir1 /user/hadoop/file1 hdfs://nn.example.com/user/hadoop/dir1

dus	<args>

Displays a summary of file lengths. This is an alternate form of hdfs dfs -du -s.

expunge	-expunge

Empty the Trash.

get	[-ignorecrc] [-crc] <src> <localdst> *//return 0 on success and -1 on error*

Copy files to the local file system. Files that fail the CRC check may be copied with the -ignorecrc option. Files and CRCs may be copied using the -crc option.
Example:
- hdfs dfs -get /user/hadoop/file localfile
- hdfs dfs -get hdfs://nn.example.com/user/hadoop/file localfile

getfacl	[-R] <path> *//return 0 on success and -1 on error*

Displays the Access Control Lists (ACLs) of files and directories. If a directory has a default ACL, then getfacl also displays the default ACL.
Options: *path*: File or directory to list.
Examples:
- hdfs dfs -getfacl /file
- hdfs dfs -getfacl -R /dir

getmerge	<src> <localdst> [addnl]

Takes a source directory and a destination file as input and concatenates files in src into the destination local file. Optionally addnl can be set to enable adding a newline character at the end of each file.

ls	<args> *//return 0 on success and -1 on error*

For a file returns stat on the file with the following format:
permissions, number_of_replicas, userid. Groupid, filesize, modification_date, modification_time, filename
For a directory it returns list of its direct children as in Unix. A directory is listed as:
Permissions, userid, groupid, modification_date, modification_time, dirname
Example: hdfs dfs -ls /user/hadoop/file1

lsr	<args>

Recursive version of ls. Similar to Unix ls -R.

mkdir	[-p] <paths> *//return 0 on success and -1 on error*

Takes path uri's as argument and creates directories.
Options: The -p option behavior is much like Unix mkdir -p, creating parent directories along the path.
Example:
- hdfs dfs -mkdir /user/hadoop/dir1 /user/hadoop/dir2
- hdfs dfs -mkdir hdfs://nn1.example.com/user/hadoop/dir hdfs://nn2.example.com/user/hadoop/dir

moveFromLocal	<localsrc> <dst>

Similar to put command, except that the source localsrc is deleted after it's copied

continued on following page

Table 2. Continued

moveToLocal	[-crc] <src> <dst>
Displays a "Not implemented yet" message.	
mv	URI [URI ...] <dest> *//return 0 on success and -1 on error*
Moves files from source to destination. This command allows multiple sources as well in which case the destination needs to be a directory. Moving files across file systems is not permitted. Example: • hdfs dfs -mv /user/hadoop/file1 /user/hadoop/file2 • hdfs dfs -mv hdfs://nn.example.com/file1 hdfs://nn.example.com/file2 hdfs://nn.example.com/file3 hdfs://nn.example.com/dir1	
put	<localsrc> ... <dst> *//return 0 on success and -1 on error*
Copy single src, or multiple srcs from local file system to the destination file system. Also reads input from stdin and writes to destination file system. • hdfs dfs -put localfile /user/hadoop/hadoopfile • hdfs dfs -put localfile1 localfile2 /user/hadoop/hadoopdir • hdfs dfs -put localfile hdfs://nn.example.com/hadoop/hadoopfile • hdfs dfs -put - hdfs://nn.example.com/hadoop/hadoopfile	
rm	[-skipTrash] URI [URI ...] *//return 0 on success and -1 on error*
Delete non empty directory and files. If the -skipTrash option is specified, the trash, if enabled, will be bypassed and the specified file(s) deleted immediately. This can be useful when it is necessary to delete files from an over-quota directory. Example: hdfs dfs -rm hdfs://nn.example.com/file /user/hadoop/emptydir	
rmr	[-skipTrash] URI [URI ...] *//return 0 on success and -1 on error*
Recursive version of delete. If the -skipTrash option is specified, the trash, if enabled, will be bypassed and the specified file(s) deleted immediately. This can be useful when it is necessary to delete files from an over-quota directory. Example: • hdfs dfs -rmr /user/hadoop/dir • hdfs dfs -rmr hdfs://nn.example.com/user/hadoop/dir	
setfacl	[-R] [-b|-k -m|-x <acl_spec> <path>]|[--set <acl_spec> <path>] *//return 0 on success and -1 on error*
Sets Access Control Lists (ACLs) of files and directories. Options: • -b: Remove all but the base ACL entries. The entries for user, group and others are retained for compatibility with permission bits. • -k: Remove the default ACL. • -R: Apply operations to all files and directories recursively. • -m: Modify ACL. New entries are added to the ACL, and existing entries are retained. • -x: Remove specified ACL entries. Other ACL entries are retained. • --set: Fully replace the ACL, discarding all existing entries. The *acl_spec* must include entries for user, group, and others for compatibility with permission bits. • *acl_spec*: Comma separated list of ACL entries. • *path*: File or directory to modify. Examples: • hdfs dfs -setfacl -m user:hadoop:rw- /file • hdfs dfs -setfacl -x user:hadoop /file • hdfs dfs -setfacl -b /file • hdfs dfs -setfacl -k /dir • hdfs dfs -setfacl --set user::rw-,user:hadoop:rw-,group::r--,other::r-- /file • hdfs dfs -setfacl -R -m user:hadoop:r-x /dir • hdfs dfs -setfacl -m default:user:hadoop:r-x /dir	

continued on following page

Table 2. Continued

setrep	[-R] [-w] <numReplicas> <path> *//return 0 on success and -1 on error*
Changes the replication factor of a file. If *path* is a directory then the command recursively changes the replication factor of all files under the directory tree rooted at *path*. Options: • The -w flag requests that the command wait for the replication to complete. This can potentially take a very long time. • The -R flag is accepted for backwards compatibility. It has no effect. Example: hdfs dfs -setrep -w 3 /user/hadoop/dir1	
stat	URI [URI ...] *//return 0 on success and -1 on error*
Returns the stat information on the path. Example: hdfs dfs -stat path	
tail	[-f] URI *//return 0 on success and -1 on error*
Displays last kilobyte of the file to stdout. Options: The -f option will output appended data as the file grows, as in Unix. Example: hdfs dfs -tail pathname	
test	-[ezd] URI
Options: • The -e option will check to see if the file exists, returning 0 if true. • The -z option will check to see if the file is zero length, returning 0 if true. • The -d option will check to see if the path is directory, returning 0 if true. Example: hdfs dfs -test -e filename	
Text	<src>
Takes a source file and outputs the file in text format. The allowed formats are zip and TextRecordInputStream	
touchz	URI [URI ...] *//return 0 on success and -1 on error*
Create a file of zero length. Example: hadoop -touchz pathname	

unstructured, structured and combination of both, the efficiency of HDFS must be increased to handle all type of data.

Mustafa Hajeer et al. (2017) suggested a data driven HDFS model for solving the above problem. They transformed the data and stored it in graph based scalable stores which can store streaming data also. They constructed vertex-to-vertex triples for data points. The data points are clustered using novel distributed encoding method and novel operators in Genetic algorithm. The cluster affiliations are indicated for various data. Thus data are represented using quads. The created network graph database is stored in the distributed environment of HDFS. The proposed algorithm is capable of adapting to dynamic changes coming from different data sources. It improves the ability of HDFS to handle different types of data by building data aware modules. Also the queries for retrieving data are processed in parallel and hence it results in lesser resource usage. The future works suggested are studying the impact of intelligent data placement methods, improving the distributed encoding method and genetic operators, dynamic updates for large velocity of data flow, using lambda architecture and next-generation analytic tools. The Lambda architecture is data processing architecture to handle larger volume of data by using both batch processing and stream processing.

The backup mechanism of Hadoop Distributed File System increases the data reliability but it increases the storage space. In HDFS, triple duplicates are generated when a file is created, an old file is updated or even if few blocks of a file are updated. Even small and medium enterprises will suffer from this storage space problem. Hence utility of storage space in HDFS has to be improved. Ruay-Shiung Chang et al. (2014) suggested dynamic deduplication decision algorithm to improve HDFS. Two-tier deduplication is used here. It runs on two components *prefilter* and *postfilter*. The *prefilter* is responsible for deduplication in file level. The *postfilter* is responsible for eliminating redundant blocks. When the user wants to save data, the file filter in *prefilter* checks whether saving this file will cause overflow. If so, it will deny the user request. Otherwise, the file filter will compare the attributes of file with that of metadata table. If there is a match, the data will be dropped from file filter. Otherwise, the file is divided into several blocks and the attributes of file will be updated in metadata table. After that, the data is stored. The data centre associated with *postfilter* stores the data and metadata that are collected in metadata server. The *postfilter* will wipeout the blocks which are already stored in storage area. The fingerprint of the block will be calculated with hash function. It is compared with the fingerprints available in metadata server. If there is a match, then the duplicate block will not be stored. Two thresholds *threshold$_1$* and *threshold$_2$* are maintained. If the Utility of storage space UM$_T$ is greater than or equal to *threshold$_1$*, then any number of copies of cold data which is greater than 1, then all copies of cold data will be removed. If UM$_T$ is greater than or equal to *threshold$_2$*, one of the copies of hot data will be eliminated gradually. Here offsite backup is also maintained. To have offsite backup, backups in both LAN and WAN are maintained. When only one block is extinct, the target file can be recovered from offsite backup. The evaluation shows that this method can save more data than that of other methods. But the data reliability will get reduced. The suggested future works are increasing data reliability without loss of storage space, overcoming the transmission issue on the networks for offline backup and testing on large scale cluster systems.

Most of the generated data, both structured and unstructured data are in text format only. Compression of data can be done to reduce the data size to save storage space and to reduce the transmission cost over the network. But the compressed data cannot be directly used in MapReduce environment at present. The compressed data must be decompressed first and then only it can be analyzed in HDFS environment. This decompression can create delay which mainly depends upon decompression method used. Moreover more storage space is needed to store the decompressed data. Since the decompression has to be done in parallel in the Hadoop distributed environment, we have to ensure that the compressed data is splittable and each data split is self-contained. The data split is further divided into logical records and then each record will be processed in parallel. To handle all these cases, a new compression method is needed. Dapeng Dong and John Herbert (2017) suggested a context-free compression scheme so that the data can be processed without decompression. They introduced Record- aware Partial Compression (RaPC) algorithm which is more suitable for big textual data. RaPC is an embedded two layer compression scheme. The main goal of the outer layer compression is to reduce the size of data so that the loading time for data can be reduced. The Layer-1 algorithm is a byte-oriented, word based partial compression scheme. The characters in the group a-z, A-Z, 0-9 are taken as informational contents. Other characters are taken as functional contents. RaPC Layer-1 algorithm compresses only informational contents. The Layer-2 compression is used to compress Layer-1 compressed data. The main aim of Layer-2 compression is to compress data and to package logical records into fixed length blocks so that the compressed data is made splittable for HDFS. Also a set of utility functions is provided which includes RaPC *TextWritable data type* equivalent to Hadoop Text data type, *SequnceFileAsBinaryOutputFormat* Record writer for writing RaPC Layer-1 compressed data and binary data to HDFS, *Record Reader* for decoding Layer-2 compressed data. The developed algorithms were tested with standard real world benchmarks like Data Preprocessing, Event Identification, Server Log Analysis, etc. A special indexer program is used to index and record splittable boundaries of the compressed data. The output of this program is a set of indexing file for the input files. As the number of files increases, maintaining the index files becomes more complicated. The suggested future work is to find ways for maintaining index files efficiently.

In the recent social network and the sensor based network the arrival of the data stream and the need for the analysis of the data is inevitable. For such kind of analysis, the sub-dataset is separated from the rest of the data set based on some events or features. Due to the nature of size of the data

Hadoop file system is the mostly used one. However, the storage of sub-datasets over HDFS blocks, suffer from imbalanced or inefficient parallel execution. Consequently, the clustering of sub-datasets results in unbalance work for some computational nodes. Due to this the sampling of the data for data analytics becomes inefficient with large amounts of irrelevant data. Hence a storage distribution aware method is proposed by Jun Wang et.al (2018) to optimize sub-dataset analysis over distributed storage systems referred to as DataNet. The work is implemented by extracting the meta data of the sub-dataset distributions. Following this an elastic storage structure called ElasticMap based on the HashMap and BloomFilter techniques to store the meta-data. Then the distribution aware algorithms designed for sub-dataset applications to achieve balanced and efficient parallel execution.

Many events happen within short duration of the real world data production due to various web traffic, social network, and sensor network activities. All such kind of events are logged, where each log entry is considered to be a record with many fields with information such as user id, log time, destination etc. There is a need for clustering data based on some event and features. The storage of the Hadoop based on block granularity does not guarantee efficient execution in the different nodes leading to unbalanced workload to each node. Also the storage of the data in different nodes leads to the inefficient sampling of the data. This causes the nodes under parallel execution makes asymmetric delay in the completion of the task leading to variable wait time. Hence there is a need for the effective data set management is there. This set of data has to be effectively stored using appropriate data structure. The choices are HashMap and Bloom filter. An efficient method is required to decide to select the data structure, which is called ElasticMap. Also there is a need for the sampling which is aware of the data subset distribution. The effectiveness of work is analysed in terms of time taken for finding the moving average, word count, histogram, top k search with the data taken from DataNet. Also it is analysed the data size in each block. The proposed work achieved the balancing of the work load among the computational node.

The limitations of the Hadoop based distributed system is the delay incurred in the storing and retrieval of the data in multiple machines. However the data size increases in enormous manner also requiring fast response. Hence alternate mechanism is required so that the disk I/O can be minimized, which leads to in-memory architecture. However for very large data, even the distributed is not sufficient, but additional machines with sufficient memory could be deployed in the future. The flink architecture is evolving based on these techniques.

CONCLUSION

This chapter presents the basic architecture of HDFS and explains how the different modes of data replications is done. The effect of the block cache in the performance of the HDFS is outlined. Also the step by step procedure of the file operations is discussed. The means for achieving the high availability in HDFS is presented. Following this, the operations of the fail over controller are discussed. The effect of Fencing for protecting the data is presented. Also the procedure for working with the command line interface is outlined.

REFERENCES

Beal, V. (2017). *Hadoop Distributed File system- HDFS*. Retrieved April 2017, from http://www.webopedia.com/TERM/H/hadoop_distributed_file_system_hdfs.html

Chang, Liao, & Fan, & Wu. (2014). Dynamic Deduplication Decision in a Hadoop Ditributed File System. *International Journal of Distributed Sensor Networks*, *2014*, 1–14.

Cloudera Inc. (2017). *HDFS Key Features*. Retrieved April 2017, from https://www.cloudera.com/products/open-source/apache-hadoop/hdfs-mapreduce-yarn.html

Dong & Herbert. (2017). Content-aware Partial Compression for Textual Big Data Analysis in Hadoop. *IEEE Transactions on Big Data*. doi:10.1109/TBDATA.2017.2721431

Hajeer, M., & Dasgupta, D. (2017). *Handling Big Data Using a Data-Aware HDFS and Evolutionary Clustering Technique*. *IEEE Transactions on Big Data*. doi:10.1109/TBDATA.2017.2782785

HortonWorks. (2017). *Apache Hadoop HDFS*. Retrieved April 2017, from https://hortonworks.com/apache/hdfs/

Huang, J., Ahadi, D. J., & Ren, K. (2011). Scalable SPARQL querying of large RDF graphs. *Proceedings of the VLDB Endowment, 4*(11), 1123–1130.

TechTarget. (2013). *Hadoop Distributed File System (HDFS).* Retrieved April 2017, from http://searchbusinessanalytics.techtarget.com/definition/ Hadoop-Distributed-File-System-HDFS

Wang, J. (2018). Speed Up Big Data Analytics by Unveiling the Storage Distribution of Sub-Datasets. *IEEE Transactions on Big Data, 5*(2).

Chapter 6
YARN

ABSTRACT

Apache Hadoop YARN (Yet Another Resource Negotiator) is the cluster resource management technology in Hadoop version 2. The YARN provides multiple accesses for batch and real-time processing across multiple clusters and has the benefit over utilization of cluster resources during dynamic allocation. The chapter shows the YARN architecture, schedulers, resource manager phases, YARN applications, commands, and timeline server. The architecture of YARN splits the task into resource management and job scheduling. This is managed by Resource Manager and Node Manager. The chapter addresses the Timeline Server, which stores and retrieves the present and past information in a generic way.

INTRODUCTION

YARN as an architectural core of Hadoop is a platform for consistent operations that allows data processing operations like streaming, real time analytics and governance across multiple clusters. Hadoop cluster feature multi-tenancy is enhanced by YARN improving the enterprise's return with multiple accesses for batch, interactive and real time engines working on a same data at a particular time. YARN perk up the cluster utilization with dynamic allocation of cluster resources. Data center expands for processing to thousands of nodes handling zettabytes of data. YARN's resource manager centres wholly on scheduling and highly compatible than mapreduce used in Hadoop 1.

DOI: 10.4018/978-1-5225-3790-8.ch006

BACKGROUND

Hadoop being the foundation of the big data era, there is processing model difference between hadoop 1 and hadoop 2. Hadoop 1 includes the progress with HDFS for storage and the processing by batch oriented MapReduce jobs. The version 1 is potential for distributed processing but not much suitable for interactive analysis along with memory intensive algorithms. Hence hadoop 2 includes new version of HDFS federation and resource manager YARN. HDFS federation combines the measure of scalability and reliability to hadoop, YARN supports and implements a flexible execution engine with high end processing models. It further separates processing and resource management of Mapreduce in Hadoop 1. Additionally, it is responsible for administering workloads with security controls and to maintain multi tenant environment amid high availability features.

YARN ARCHITECTURE

YARN (Yet Another Resource Negotiator) is split up with two major tasks i.e. resource management and job scheduling to act on a global environment and as per application. An application can either refer to a job or a DAG of jobs. In Hadoop 1, inflexible slots are configured on nodes which gets underutilized when more map or reduce tasks are running and also can't share resources with non map reduce applications running on Hadoop cluster like Impala, Giraph etc. A host in Hadoop refers to a node and cluster is the connection of two or more nodes joined by a high speed network. Nodes may be partitioned in racks and blocks as in hardware part of hadoop infrastructure. There can be thousands of hosts in a cluster. In Hadoop, there is one master

Figure 1. Hadoop 1 => Hadoop 2 Comparison

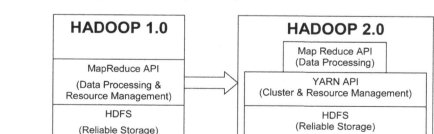

host with multiple worker hosts. Master sends jobs to the worker host. The basic overall structure of Apache Hadoop running environment including YARN is given in Figure 2.

In Figure 2, MapReduce framework is the software layer implementing the map and reduce tasks paradigm. The HDFS Federation provides permanent, reliable and distributed storage for input and output whereas storage can include any alternative storage service from other providers like Amazon.

YARN is responsible for computational processing and memory for application executions. The data computation framework in YARN is formed by resource manager and the node manager. These two form the new generic system for managing applications in a distributed processing network environment. YARN and HDFS are independent since one provides resource and other provides storage.

RESOURCE MANAGER AND NODE MANAGER

The Resource Manager (RM) acts as eventual authority to manage resources among all jobs presently executing in the system. The Node Manager (NM) is per host agent which is responsible for containers to monitor the usage of memory, CPU, network etc. and in turn it states to the Resource Manager Scheduler. There exists an Application Master per host which is a library to execute and monitor tasks in Node Manager and also negotiates the resources from Resource Manager.

Figure 2. Structure of Apache Hadoop v2

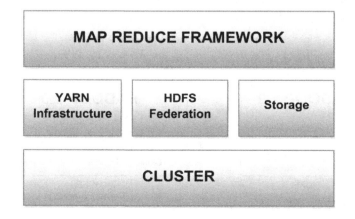

The Resource Manager includes two components: Scheduler and Applications Manager. The scheduler allocates resources to executing real applications with the constraints of capacities, other applications in waiting queues etc. This does not track or monitor the status of jobs and also doesn't bother about job failure having no guarantee to restart it again. This scheduler has association with the container in every host to get records on memory, CPU, network and other related features. The scheduler also has the capability to partition the resources across hosts in the cluster i.e. between applications.

The next component Applications Manager accepts job agreeing the container's request for executing the application and also can restart the job in case of failure. Generally, per Application Master in every host negotiates resources from scheduler, tracks status and monitors the progress.

The YARN application setup is given as a step by step procedure in Figure 3.

The application processing of jobs using YARN setup consists of the following steps:

- A client submits the job or an application to the Resource Manager.
- The Resource Manager allocates a container.
- Resource manager divides the job into different Node Managers as connected.
- Node Manager launches the container.
- Container then executes the Applications Master.
- Application Master requests container for resources from resource scheduler and executes job on the obtained containers. MapReduce framework provides its processing framework on Application Master.

Figure 3. Yarn application setup

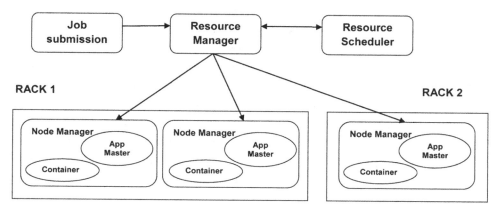

The Resource Manager is a single point of failure for YARN. Using Application Master, YARN spreads across cluster for running applications. Hence it reduces the load of Resource Manager.

SCHEDULERS

A scheduler identifies the job running when and where along with the resources allocated to the job. The YARN computation framework supports the following types of schedulers:

- **Fair Scheduler:** Allocates resources with fair sharing within each weighted pool.
- **Capacity Scheduler:** Allocates resources to pools with FIFO (First In First Out) scheduling within each pool.

Fair Scheduler

It is a pluggable scheduler in Hadoop that allocates YARN applications with resources in large clusters fairly. The resources are assigned to applications either on average or an equal share over time. By default, fair scheduler makes fairness decisions only on memory. The configuration for scheduling both memory and CPU is by resource type policy named as Dominant Resource Fairness. When there is a single application, all the resources can be utilized with entire cluster. When more than application is submitted, resources that are freed are assigned to new application so that each application are allotted same amount of resources.

Unlike default scheduler, which forms queue of applications to allot resources, this allocates resources for short applications over reasonable time than long lived applications. It works with application priorities to calculate the ratio of total resources that each application would utilize.

The scheduler organizes applications into queues and shares the resources fairly between those in queues. It is also allowed to assign a particular application with request through configuration. Within each queue, a scheduling policy is allotted for sharing of resources between executing applications. The default method is memory based fair sharing. Others can be FIFO or multiple resource type Dominant Resource Fairness method. Queues divide the resources given in hierarchy configured with weights to share the clusters.

When an application in queue requests resource, it gets atleast the minimum share allotted for every application. In case of excess, it splits the share and gives to other running applications. This lets the scheduler utilize the resource efficiently.

Fair scheduler also includes the provision to restrict the running applications and those in queue through configuration file. Limiting the applications doesn't mean that some application may fail but it remains as wait in the scheduler's queue until those executing finish.

Configuration

To assign the Fair scheduler, set the configuration in the file yarn-site.xml as follows:

```
<property>
 <name>yarn.resourcemanager.scheduler.class</name>
 <value>org.apache.hadoop.yarn.server.resourcemanager.
scheduler.fair.FairScheduler</value>
</property>
```

Fair scheduler also allows nesting the queues to create a hierarchical structure where every level comes under its parent queue. All queues descend under a queue named "root". Available resources are shared among root's children using fair scheduling method. Additionally, fair scheduler policy of allotting resources can be set by any custom policy seeting the config as,

```
"org.apache.hadoop.yarn.server.resourcemanager.scheduler.fair.
SchedulingPolicy.FifoPolicy, FairSharePolicy (default), and
DominantResourceFairnessPolicy"
```

Some of the other properties which can be set for yarn-site.xml are listed below:

- **Yarn.scheduler.fair.allow-undeclared-pools:** When set to true, uses the username as default pool name. [Default – true]
- **Yarn.scheduler.fair.user-as-default-queue:** When set to true, pools specified in applications are created at run time with default settings. [Default – true]

- **Yarn.scheduler.fair.preemption:** When enabled, fair scheduler preempts the applications in other pools. [Default – false]
- **Yarn.scheduler.fair.preemption.cluster-utilization-threshold:** The preemption is triggered based on cluster ultisation threshold. [Default – 0.8]

Example: yarn-site.xml properties:

```
...
  <property>
    <name>yarn.scheduler.fair.allow-undeclared-pools</name>
    <value>true</value>
  </property>
  <property>
    <name>yarn.scheduler.fair.user-as-default-queue</name>
    <value>true</value>
  </property>
  <property>
    <name>yarn.scheduler.fair.preemption</name>
    <value>true</value>
  </property>
  <property>
    <name>yarn.scheduler.fair.preemption.cluster-utilization-
threshold</name>
    <value>0.8</value>
  </property>
...
```

Some of the properties for fair-scheduler.xml config file are:

- **queuePlacementPolicy:** Policy for assigning jobs to resource pools.
- **userMaxAppsDefault:** Default running application limit for a user whose limit is not otherwise specified.
- **queueMaxAppsDefault:** Default running app limit for pools; overridden by the equivalent element in a pool.
- **queueMaxAMShareDefault:** Default ApplicationMaster resource limit for the pool; overridden by the equivalent element in a pool.
- **defaultFairSharePreemptionThreshold:** Fair share preemption threshold for pools; overridden by the equivalent element in a pool. The threshold value is between 0 and 1.
- **defaultFairSharePreemptionTimeout and defaultMinSharePreemptionTimeout:** Default number of seconds a resource pool is under its fair share or minimum share before it

will preempt containers to take resources from other resource pools.; overridden by the equivalent element in a pool.

- **defaultQueueSchedulingPolicy:** Default scheduling policy for pools.

The sub elements of the property "queue" are stated as follows:

- **Weight:** Weight given to the resource pool when determining how to allocate resources relative to other resource pools.
- **schedulingPolicy:** Policy to determine how resources are allocated to the resource pool: fair, fifo, or drf.
- **aclSubmitApps:** Users and groups that can submit jobs to the pool.
- **aclAdministerApps:** Users and groups that can administer the pool.
- **minResources, maxResources:** Minimum and maximum share of resources that can allocated to the resource pool in the form *X* mb, *Y* vcores.
- **maxAMShare:** Fraction of the resource pool's fair share that can be used to run ApplicationMasters.

Example: fair-scheduler.xml:

```
<allocations>
    <queue name="root">
        <weight>1.0</weight>
        <schedulingPolicy>drf</schedulingPolicy>
        <aclSubmitApps> </aclSubmitApps>
        <aclAdministerApps>*</aclAdministerApps>
        <queue name="example">
            <minResources>1024 mb, 10 vcores</minResources>
            <maxResources>5120 mb, 20 vcores</maxResources>
            <weight>4.0</weight>
            <schedulingPolicy>drf</schedulingPolicy>
            <aclSubmitApps>*</aclSubmitApps>
            <aclAdministerApps>*</aclAdministerApps>
        </queue>
        <queue name="develop">
            <weight>1.0</weight>
            <schedulingPolicy>drf</schedulingPolicy>
            <aclSubmitApps>*</aclSubmitApps>
            <aclAdministerApps>*</aclAdministerApps>
        </queue>
    </queue>
    <defaultQueueSchedulingPolicy>drf</
defaultQueueSchedulingPolicy>
    <queuePlacementPolicy>
```

```
        <rule name="specified" create="true"/>
        <rule name="user" create="true"/>
    </queuePlacementPolicy>
</allocations>
```

Capacity Scheduler

A scheduler of Hadoop, that allocates resources in a timely mode across large cluster for multiple tenants securely with the constraint of allocated capacity. This operation for shared multi tenant clusters maximizes the throughput and cluster utilization is good. In traditional methods, resources are shared to meet the organization's SLA under peak condition but this results in an average utilization and causes overhead when working with multiple clusters. This is done in an efficient way by sharing resources across cluster in large Hadoop applications.

The basic concept behind capacity scheduler is that available resources are shared among clusters based on their computing needs. An additional benefit is that application can use the excess resource not being used by any other. Hence provides flexibility for the execution of application in a cost effective manner. The Capacity Scheduler fixes severe limits on consumption of disproportionate resources for a single application or user or queue and also ensures the stability of the cluster.

Queues are maintained by the administrators to reflect the cost of the shared cluster. Further to control the sharing of resources, hierarchical queues are supported to ensure whether sub-queues of an application are served before other queues can use free resources, thereby provides affinity among the applications sharing free resources.

For example:

- Let's assume that a queue is configured to share 5 users where each one is allotted 20% share. At the beginning, if a single job is active in queue for user1, then the entire resource can be utilized for the completion of user1's job.
- If another user2 creates a job, then resources are shared between the two users as 50% each. In case if user2 doesn't require 50% for its completion, then the excess can be assigned to user1.
- Next if user3 enters with the job, all three are assigned with 33.3% of the queue capacity assuming its sufficient for each job. This continues until 5 users can get 20% each.

- Now, if there come user6 to submit the job, it waits in the queue and resource will not be shared rather Capacity Scheduler allows the 5 users to complete jobs.
- The logic behind is that, it prevent large volume of users to divide resources across too many jobs which may spread the resources to complete tasks.

Other features of Capacity Scheduler are listed as follows:

- **Security:** Each queue includes access control lists of users who can submit the application. In addition, users cannot view or modify the applications of other users' utilizing the resources across a shared cluster.
- **Flexibility:** Free resources can be shared by other users in the queue. When a job has a resource beyond its capacity, this can be assigned to applications on queues with below capacity. This helps in resource utilization.
- **Multi-Tenant Share:** Stringent limits are fixed to prevent a single application to receive more resource in the queue. Hence cluster sharing doesn't get overwhelmed.
- **Capacity Share:** All applications submitted to a queue will have access to utilize the resource based on the total allotted fraction of the capacity of the resource.
- **Priority on Queue Mapping:** Users are allowed to map an job application to any specific queue which can be based on user or group.
- **Operability:** Administrators have the power to modify the runtime configuration of users like viewing the current allocation of resource, adding additional queues at runtime, stopping the execution of an application and allows another to continue etc… But queues can never be deleted.

Configuration

To assign the Capacity scheduler, set the configuration in the file yarn-site.xml

```
<property>
 <name>yarn.resourcemanager.scheduler.class</name>
 <value>org.apache.hadoop.yarn.server.resourcemanager.
```

```
scheduler.capacity. CapacityScheduler</value>
</property>
```

To assign queues, the Capacity Scheduler has a predefined queue as root. All other queues assigned in system are the children of root queue. Further queues can be configured under the property "yarn.scheduler.capacity.root. queues" with comma separated child queues as values. Queue's children can be defined with configuration property as "yarn.scheduler.capacity.<queue-path>.queues" where <queue-path> takes the form root.<child>, root.<child>.<child>, and so on.

An example to set the queues in capacity-scheduler.xml configuration file is stated as follows:

```
<property>
  <name>yarn.scheduler.capacity.root.queues</name>
  <value>A,B</value>
  <description>The queues at the this level (root is the root
queue)  </description>
</property>
<property>
  <name>yarn.scheduler.capacity.root.A.queues</name>
  <value>A1,A2</value>
  <description>The queues at the this level (root is the root
queue).  </description>
</property>
<property>
  <name>yarn.scheduler.capacity.root.B.queues</name>
  <value>B1,B2,B3</value>
  <description>The queues at the this level (root is the root
queue).  </description>
</property>
```

Some of the properties of queue resource allocation, setting application limits, queue administration is listed as follows:

- **yarn.scheduler.capacity.<queue-path>.capacity:** Queue capacity is given in %. The sum of capacity is 100.
- **yarn.scheduler.capacity.<queue-path>.maximum-capacity:** Maximum Queue Capacity.
- **yarn.scheduler.capacity.<queue-path>.minimum-user-limit-percent:** Sets minimum value of resource to be allotted.

- **yarn.scheduler.capacity.<queue-path>.user-limit-factor:** Allows a single user to acquire minimum resource.
- **yarn.scheduler.capacity.resource-calculator:** Compare resources in scheduler. Default is disk based.
- **yarn.scheduler.capacity.maximum-applications:** Maximum number of applications that can be active. Limits the value in every queue since it is proportional to queue capacity. Application submitted when limit is reached gets rejected. The default is 10000.
- **yarn.scheduler.capacity.<queue-path>.maximum-applications:** Fixes maximum application on queue basis.
- **yarn.scheduler.capacity.maximum-am-resource-percent:** Maximum percentage of resources that can be utilized to execute an application in a cluster.
- **yarn.scheduler.capacity.<queue-path>.state:** State of an application can either be RUNNING or STOPPED.
- **yarn.scheduler.capacity.root.<queue-path>.acl_submit_ applications:** Access Control List of users/groups who can submit the applications into queue.
- **yarn.scheduler.capacity.root.<queue-path>.acl_administer_ queue:** Administers the applications in the queue based on given Access Control List.

For changing the queue configuration, the following command is used:

- **yarn rmadmin:** RefreshQueues

RESOURCE MANAGER RESTART

Resource Manager being responsible for managing resources and scheduling the application, it runs on top of YARN. Also, it can be mentioned as single point of failure in Hadoop cluster for YARN processing. Here, the resource manager needs to restart adequately while functioning which should be invisible to end-users.

This feature Resource Manager Restart is broadly done in two phases:

- Phase 1 (Non- work Preserving)
- Phase 2 (Work Preserving)

PHASE 1: NON WORK PRESERVING RESOURCE MANAGER RESTART

The overall idea is that Resource Manager will keep up the metadata in a state-store whenever the client submits a job and saves the status of the job at its completion which may be failed, killed or completed. In addition, resource manager also keeps the credentials of users like security token in a private environment. When there is a failure, Resource Manager Restart is done by retrieving the secure credential and metadata from state store thereby resuming the processing of job without any interruption. This doesn't happen if the job gets completed before Resource Manager Failure.

The cause of Resource Manager Restart may be because of hardware failure, bugs, errors or down-time during a cluster upgrade. This happens in an invisible transparent way. There is no need for users to monitor the events in disruption and to submit the job manually.

Node Managers during down-time just keeps polling till the Resource Manager resumes the action. Once Resource Manager resumes, a heartbeat is sent to all Application Masters in Node Manager and it also passes a resynchronize command to proceed. Node Manager kills the already existing containers and registers newly with the Resource Manager. Hence, after the restart of Resource Manager the details of each job are taken from state-store and populate into memory as a new attempt and proceeds as usual. The work of the applications' submitted already will get lost as it is killed by Resource Manager and resynchronized on restart.

Figure 4. Resource Manager Restart Process

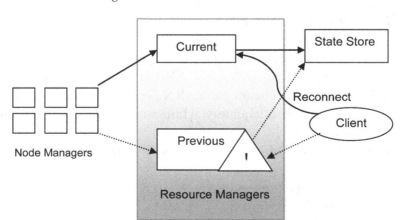

Resource Manager State-Store

When Resource Manager restarts, the data of the job gets loaded back into the memory. The persistant state-store maintained by Resource Manager is called as *RMStateStore*. The available state-store implementation are:

- ZKRMStateStore: ZooKeeper-based state-store implementation
- FileSystemRMStateStore: State-store on FileSystem

When a new job is submitted, it is written into RMStateStore and similarly when the job completes it records the final state into state store. When there is an interruption, job is killed and then on restart begins as new application by taking the user's *ApplicationSubmissionContest* available on state-store and executes as a new instance of ApplicationMaster.

Client

During Resource Manager downtime, the communicating clients i.e. node managers should wait and have to retry until it comes back. This implementation is stated in *RMProxy* – configuration file. The maximum wait time is restricted and also the interval between each retry is mentioned. The java client libraries *YarnClient* and *AMRMClient* can be modified to set the proxy. Node Managers are intimated by a resynchronize command by Resource Manager once it restarts. Application Master in Node Manager does the process of retrying the Resource Manager to invoke the application again.

Configuration

To facilitate Phase 1 Resource Manager Restart, the following config changes are made:

- **yarn.resourcemanager.recovery.enabled**: The configuration property is set to true, Resource Manager will enable the restart functionality.
- **yarn.resourcemanager.store.class**: This specifies the state-store implementation to store the application and credential information in a secure environment. The two options available are:
  - org.apache.hadoop.yarn.server.resourcemanager.recovery. ZKRMStateStore – zookeeper based state-store implementation

○   org.apache.hadoop.yarn.server.resourcemanager.recovery. FileSystemRMStateStore – filesystem based state-store implementation

- **yarn.resourcemanager.am.max-attempts**: Specifies the maximum number of attempts an application can have.

Configuration for Zookeeper State-Store

- **yarn.resourcemanager.zk.state-store.address**: Has the address of server in Zookeeper address in the format as Host:Port (127.0.0.1:2089).
- **yarn.resourcemanager.zk.state-store.parent-path**: Specify the path where Resource Manager State is stored.
- **yarn.resourcemanager.zk.state-store.timeout.ms:** To identify when a client session expires in milliseconds. Default is 10 milliseconds.
- **yarn.resourcemanager.zk.state-store.num-retries:** Number of times a client can try for reconnection.Default is 2.
- **yarn.resourcemanager.zk.state-store.acl:** List of nodes allowed to read and write in a zookeeper state-store.

Configuration for Filesystem State-Store

- **yarn.resourcemanager.fs.state-store.ur**i: Specifies the URI where the Resource Manager State should be stored. This URI is configured to the FileSystemRMStateStore. An example can be hdfs://localhost:9000/ rmstore which allows read and write operations only by Resource Manager.
- **yarn.resourcemanager.fs.state-store.retry-policy-spec:** Specification for retrying the Resource Manager given as sleep time and number of entries pair. Default is (2000,500) milliseconds.

PHASE 2: WORK PRESERVING RESOURCE MANAGER RESTART

The phase 2 work preserving completely focuses on renovating the running state of the Resource Manager by merging the status information available in Container and Application Masters of Node Managers upon restart. The major difference is that in phase 1, the application gets killed when interrupted and starts as new application when Resource Manager restarts but in phase 2 applications won't lose the already completed task due to Resource Manager Outage.

Phase 1 centers on persistency of application state and reload on recovery yet Phase 2 centers on renovating the entire YARN cluster, including scheduler which keeps track of resource request, resource utilization of jobs in queue, etc. Hence, applications can resynchronize back with Resource Manager and resume where it left off and there is no need to re-run from scratch as in phase 1.

Resource Manager can continue the progress of running state by taking the status information from container in Node Manager since the container does not get killed completely on failure. Resource Manager reconstructs with container instance and job's scheduling status and also Application Master resends the resource request. Resource Manager loses the entire data on failure, so the data in AMRM client library is utilized by the Application Master to resend to resource request and to resynchronize automatically.

The options remembered on state-store are, all applications submitted to YARN cluster with the metadata information i.e. credentials, attempt level information, state of jobs and container allocations.

Resource Manager

Resource Manager retains the queue state in state-store at runtime and resumes backs the state into memory when restarts. The queue state includes the metadata of applications but no information is present about its running state i.e. tracking of dynamically changing queue's resource usage. All this information gets erased on Resource Manager shut down. And retaining all the information including scheduler's state is difficult as it requires space and time. In phase 2, to manage all these in an efficient manner the container statuses are reported by Node Managers which contains data to recover the job and the process reloads by gathering other information from state-store.

Node Manager

During the downtime of Resource Manager, containers in Node Manager have details and it keeps trying until it gets the resource. If an application gets completed, the status will be reported to Resource Manager by Node Manager.

After Resource Manager restarts, it sends a resynchronize command to Node Manager as heartbeat comes in. This Node Manager resumes by using the containers that has preserved the work-in-progress of every application. After that, Resource Manager continues the process across clusters and reports if it is finished.

Application Master

After Resource Manager restarts, it stacks the data from state-store. In phase 1, once Resource Manager notifies, the Node Manager kills the containers including Application Master and creates a new container. The case in phase 2 varies in such a way that Application Master is not killed and continues running by retrying the communication with Resource Manager. Once restarts, it reregisters with the Resource Manager else it will throw an "ApplicationMasterNotRegistered" Exception. Application Master also resends the uncompleted resource request to the newly started Resource Manager.

WRITING YARN APPLICATIONS

The general idea is to implement a new YARN application is to submit an application to YARN Resource Manager. This is done by setting a YARN object and once the YARN client starts, it prepares the container and

Figure 5. Comparison of RM restart Phase 1 and Phase 2

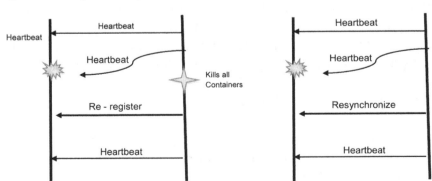

Application Master for processing. The YARN resource should identify the jars required with the Operating System environment settings. Once done, YARN Resource Manager launches the Application Master on allocated container. This handles the process execution and its operation in an asynchronous way. The main task behind Application Master is to allocate and negotiate resource for container, after allocation communicates with Node Managers to launch the application. It's made using an event handler given as "AMRMClientAsync.CallbackHandler". The event handler must launch a runnable object when containers are allocated. The Application Master must specify the "ContainerLaunchContext" that includes the launch information like command line specification, environment etc…

While executing, Application Master communicates with Node Managers using "NMClientAsync" object. All callback handler events like client start,stop,update or error is handled by "NMClientAsync.CallbackHandler". The report on execution progress is given by Application Master to Resource Manger using getProgress() method of "AMRMClientAsync. CallBackHandler".

In brief, the interfaces needed are given as follows:

- Client -> Resource Manager using YarnClient objects
- ApplicationMaster -> Resource Manager using AMRMClientAsync objects handled asynchronously by AMRMClientAsync. CallbackHandler
- ApplicationMaster -> Node Manager using NMClientAsync objects handling events by NMClientAsync.CallbackHandler

WRITING AND SUBMITTING A CLIENT APPLICATION

- The initial step to start a client is to initilaise a YarnClient and begin by start()

```
YarnClient yarnClient = YarnClient.createYarnClient();
yarnClient.init(conf);
yarnClient.start();
```

- Once the client is initialized, need to create a new application with id and name. The response from this contains the information about cluster like maximum/minimum resource capabilities of the cluster.

```
YarnClientApplication app = yarnClient.createApplication();
GetNewApplicationResponse appResponse = app.
getNewApplicationResponse();
```

- Next step of the client is to setup the ApplicationSubmissionContext that includes all the information needed by Resource Manager to launch Application Master:

```
ApplicationSubmissionContext appContext = app.
getApplicationSubmissionContext();
ApplicationId appId = appContext.getApplicationId();
appContext.setKeepContainersAcrossApplicationAttempts(keepCont
ainers);
appContext.setApplicationName(appName);
```

- Set the local resources for the Application Master including jar files:

```
Map<String, LocalResource> localResources = new HashMap<String,
LocalResource>();
LOG.info("Copy App Master jar from local filesystem and add to
local environment");
```

- Copy the application master jar to the filesystem and Create a local resource to point to the destination jar path:

```
FileSystem fs = FileSystem.get(conf);
addToLocalResources(fs, appMasterJar, appMasterJarPath, appId.
toString(),
    localResources, null);
if (!log4jPropFile.isEmpty()) {
  addToLocalResources(fs, log4jPropFile, log4jPath, appId.
toString(),
      localResources, null);
}
```

- Set the environment variables and classpath as required for execution:

```
LOG.info("Set the environment for the application master");
Map<String, String> env = new HashMap<String, String>();
env.put(DSConstants.DISTRIBUTEDSHELLSCRIPTLOCATION,hdfsShellScr
iptLocation);
env.put(DSConstants.DISTRIBUTEDSHELLSCRIPTTIMESTAMP,Long.toStri
ng(hdfsShellScriptTimestamp));
env.put(DSConstants.DISTRIBUTEDSHELLSCRIPTLEN,Long.
toString(hdfsShellScriptLen));
```

```
// Add AppMaster.jar location to classpath:
StringBuilder classPathEnv = new StringBuilder(Environment.
CLASSPATH.$$()) .append(ApplicationConstants.CLASS_PATH_
SEPARATOR).append("./*");
for (String c: conf.getStrings(YarnConfiguration.YARN_
APPLICATION_CLASSPATH,
YarnConfiguration.DEFAULT_YARN_CROSS_PLATFORM_APPLICATION_
CLASSPATH)) {
classPathEnv.append(ApplicationConstants.CLASS_PATH_SEPARATOR);
classPathEnv.append(c.trim());
}
classPathEnv.append(ApplicationConstants.CLASS_PATH_SEPARATOR).
append(
"./log4j.properties");
```

- Set java execution commands including the memory usage, virtual cores, containers, priority etc…

```
LOG.info("Setting up app master command");
vargs.add(Environment.JAVA_HOME.$$() + "/bin/java");
```

- Set Xmx based on am memory size:

```
vargs.add("-Xmx" + amMemory + "m");
```

- Set class name:

```
vargs.add(appMasterMainClass);
```

- Set params for Application Master:

```
vargs.add("--container_memory " + String.
valueOf(containerMemory));
vargs.add("--container_vcores " + String.valueOf(containerVirtu
alCores));
vargs.add("--num_containers " + String.valueOf(numContainers));
vargs.add("--priority " + String.valueOf(shellCmdPriority));
for (Map.Entry<String, String> entry: shellEnv.entrySet()) {
vargs.add("--shell_env " + entry.getKey() + "=" + entry.
getValue());
}
vargs.add("1>" + ApplicationConstants.LOG_DIR_EXPANSION_VAR +"/
AppMaster.stdout");
vargs.add("2>" + ApplicationConstants.LOG_DIR_EXPANSION_VAR +
"/AppMaster.stderr");
```

```
StringBuilder command = new StringBuilder();
for (CharSequence str: vargs) {
command.append(str).append(" ");
}
LOG.info("Completed setting up app master command " + command.
toString());
List<String> commands = new ArrayList<String>();
commands.add(command.toString());
```

- ContainerLaunchContext defines all required information to run the application like libraries, classpath, security tokens etc…

```
ContainerLaunchContext amContainer = ContainerLaunchContext.
newInstance(
  localResources, env, commands, null, null, null);
Resource capability = Resource.newInstance(amMemory, amVCores);
appContext.setResource(capability);
```

- To setup the security tokens,

```
if (UserGroupInformation.isSecurityEnabled()) {
Credentials credentials = new Credentials();
String tokenRenewer = conf.get(YarnConfiguration.RM_PRINCIPAL);
if (tokenRenewer == null | | tokenRenewer.length() == 0) {
throw new IOException(
"Can't get Master Kerberos principal for the RM to use as
renewer");
}
final Token<?> tokens[] =
fs.addDelegationTokens(tokenRenewer, credentials);
if (tokens != null) {
for (Token<?> token: tokens) {
LOG.info("Got dt for " + fs.getUri() + "; " + token);
}
    }
DataOutputBuffer dob = new DataOutputBuffer();
credentials.writeTokenStorageToStream(dob);
ByteBuffer fsTokens = ByteBuffer.wrap(dob.getData(), 0, dob.
getLength());
amContainer.setTokens(fsTokens);
}
appContext.setAMContainerSpec(amContainer);
```

- Once the setup is complete, queue and priority information can be specified for the application:

```
Priority pri = Priority.newInstance(amPriority);
appContext.setPriority(pri);
appContext.setQueue(amQueue);
yarnClient.submitApplication(appContext);
```

- At this state, Resource Manager accepts and allocates container as specified in configuration for the application and launches the Application Master on the allotted container.
- The progress of the client can be tracked by communicating with the Resource Manager using getApplicationReport() method on YarnClient object:

```
ApplicationReport report = yarnClient.
getApplicationReport(appId);
```

- The report consists of general information like application id, queue, user details along with application status,tracking information and application master details.
- If a client needs to kill an application or abort it because of time or other factor then the method used is:

```
yarnClient.killApplication(appId);
```

WRITING AN APPLICATION MASTER (AM)

- Once the Resource Manager launches and client provides necessary resources about the job it can be tasked by the Application Master to complete. As soon as the Application Master starts, parameters like container ID, submission time, node manager host in which it runs etc… are noted. Resource Manager requires an ApplicationAttemptId from Application Masters container.

```
Map<String, String> envs = System.getenv();
String containerIdString =    envs.get(ApplicationConstants.
AM_CONTAINER_ID_ENV);
if (containerIdString == null) {
  throw new IllegalArgumentException("ContainerId not set in
the environment");
}
```

```
ContainerId containerId = ConverterUtils.toContainerId(containe
rIdString);
ApplicationAttemptId appAttemptID = containerId.
getApplicationAttemptId();
```

- As the Application Master has been initialized, the Node Manager and Resource Manager are setup with customized event handlers.

```
AMRMClientAsync.CallbackHandler allocListener = new
RMCallbackHandler();
amRMClient = AMRMClientAsync.createAMRMClientAsync(1000,
allocListener);
amRMClient.init(conf);
amRMClient.start();
containerListener = createNMCallbackHandler();
nmClientAsync = new NMClientAsyncImpl(containerListener);
nmClientAsync.init(conf);
nmClientAsync.start();
```

- Application Master releases heartbeat to Resource Manager for showing that it is alive and running. The timeout for expiry can be set using the following configuration:

```
appMasterHostname = NetUtils.getHostname();
RegisterApplicationMasterResponse response = amRMClient
.registerApplicationMaster(appMasterHostname, appMasterRpcPort,
appMasterTrackingUrl);
```

- The maximum resource capability for registration of an application is given by the configuration:

```
int maxMem = response.getMaximumResourceCapability().
getMemory();
LOG.info("Max mem capability of resources in this cluster " +
maxMem);
int maxVCores = response.getMaximumResourceCapability().
getVirtualCores();
LOG.info("Max vcores capability of resources in this cluster "
+ maxVCores);
if (containerMemory > maxMem) {
LOG.info("Container memory specified above max threshold of
cluster."
+ " Using max value." + ", specified=" + containerMemory + ",
max="
```

```
+ maxMem);
containerMemory = maxMem;
}
if (containerVirtualCores > maxVCores) {
LOG.info("Container virtual cores specified above max threshold
of cluster."
+ " Using max value." + ", specified=" + containerVirtualCores
+ ", max="
+ maxVCores);
containerVirtualCores = maxVCores;
}
List<Container> previousAMRunningContainers =
response.getContainersFromPreviousAttempts();
LOG.info("Received " + previousAMRunningContainers.size()
+ " previous AM's running containers on AM registration.");\
```

- Based on the given task for execution, containers requirement are calculated and allotted by the Resource Manager:

```
List<Container> previousAMRunningContainers =
    response.getContainersFromPreviousAttempts();
LOG.info("Received " + previousAMRunningContainers.size()
    + " previous AM's running containers on AM registration.");
int numTotalContainersToRequest =
    numTotalContainers - previousAMRunningContainers.size();
for (int i = 0; i < numTotalContainersToRequest; ++i) {
  ContainerRequest containerAsk = setupContainerAskForRM();
  amRMClient.addContainerRequest(containerAsk);
}
```

- While setting up the container, the two concepts to be concentrated are resource capability and priority:

```
private ContainerRequest setupContainerAskForRM() {
  Resource capability = Resource.newInstance(containerMemory,
    containerVirtualCores);
  ContainerRequest request = new ContainerRequest(capability,
null, null, pri);
  LOG.info("Requested container ask: " + request.toString());
  return request;
}
```

- On retrieval of heartbeat, the event handler should report the progress by getProgress() method for the application:

```
public float getProgress() {
  // set progress to deliver to RM on next heartbeat
  float progress = (float) numCompletedContainers.get()
     / numTotalContainers;
  return progress;
}
```

- Similar process to YARN client is assigned for setting up ContainerLaunchContext for the ultimate task running on the allotted container.
- The NMClientAsyn object handles the events like container stop, start, update etc....
- Once the Application Master identifies that work is done, the application needs to unregister releasing all resources and stops the client. The config used for unregister is,

```
try {
  amRMClient.unregisterApplicationMaster(appStatus, appMessage,
null);
} catch (YarnException ex) {
  LOG.error("Failed to unregister application", ex);
} catch (IOException e) {
  LOG.error("Failed to unregister application", e);
}
amRMClient.stop();
```

YARN COMMANDS

Yarn commands are called upon using bin/yarn script. The command "yarn" without any arguments prints the description of all YARN commands.

```
Usage: yarn [--config] COMMAND
--config refers to the default configuration directory
```

Command refers to any user given command.

The commands can be classified as User commands and Administration commands for a Hadoop cluster. They are listed in detail below.

USER COMMANDS

- **Jar:** The code can be bundled as a jar file and executed using the command,

```
yarn jar <jar> [mainclass] arguments
```

- **Application:** Used to descript the application report as running or killed application given as,

```
yarn application <options>
```

The options can be any one of the following:

- ○ List => lists all applications from resource manager
- ○ AppStates States => filter applications based on input state specified. Can be ALL, NEW, ACCEPTED, KILLED, SUBMITTED, FINISHED, FAILED, RUNNING
- ○ AppTypes Types => filter applications based on input application type specified
- ○ Status ApplicationId => prints the status of the application
- ○ Kill ApplicationId => kills the application

- **Node:** Prints the report of every node:

```
yarn node <options>
```

The options can be any one of the following:

- ○ List => lists all the applications from the resource manager
- ○ States States => filter nodes based on input node states specified
- ○ All => works with list of all nodes
- ○ Status NodeId => prints status report of every node

- **Logs:**

```
yarn logs -applicationId < application Id>  <options>
```

- applicationId => specifies an application Id
- appOwner AppOwner => Owner can be current user
- containerId ContainerId => address of current node specified
- nodeAddress NodeAddress => specified in format nodename:port
- **Classpath:**
  - yarn classpath
  - Prints the class path including the Hadoop jar libraries
- **Version:**
  - yarn version
  - Prints the version

ADMINISTRATION COMMANDS

- Resource Manager
  - Start the Resource Manager
  - yarn resourcemanager
- Node Manager
  - Start the Node Manager
  - yarn nodemanager
- Proxy Server
  - Start the web proxy server
  - Yarn proxyserver
- Rmadmin
  - Executes the Resource Manager admin client
  - yarn   rmadmin   [-refreshQueues]   [-refreshNodes]
    [-refreshUserToGroupsMapping]

- *[-refreshSuperUserGroupsConfiguration] [-refreshAdminAcls]*

  - [-refreshServiceAcl] [-getGroups [username]] [-help [cmd]]
  - [-transitionToActive <serviceId>]
  - [-transitionToStandby <serviceId>]
  - [-getServiceState <serviceId>]
  - [-checkHealth <serviceId>]
  - refreshQueues => Reload the Access Control List of queue states configuration file
  - refreshNodes => Refer the host information at resource manager
  - refreshUserToGroupsMapping

- ◦ refreshSuperUserGroupsConfiguration
- ◦ refreshAdminAcls
- ◦ refreshServiceAcl
- ◦ getGroups [username]
- ◦ help [cmd]
- ◦ transitionToActive <serviceId> => Transitions the service provided into an active state
- ◦ transitionToStandby <serviceId>
- ◦ getServiceState <serviceId>
- ◦ checkHealth <serviceId> => Resource Manager admin check for service if failure it exits the code
- Daemonlog
  - ◦ Get/set the log level for each daemon
  - ◦ yarn daemonlog -getlevel <host:port> <name>
  - ◦ yarn daemonlog -setlevel <host:port> <name> <level>

Prints or sets the log level of the daemon running at the given host and port address.

YARN TIMELINE SERVER

Timeline server in YARN addresses the process of storing retrieving the past and present information in a generic way. The timeline server can be proceeded either as specific information for an application or generic for all applications.

- **Application Specific**: This restricts the storage and retrieval to a single application on framework. In case of Hadoop, the information may include number of map task, reduce task, counters etc… This information is published through "TimelineClient" in Application Master or container to the Timeline Server. This can be retrieved using REST APIs for the particular application specific UI.
- **Generic for All Applications:** The timeline server will be provided with generic information of application level data that includes, user information, queue name, application attempts, containers used and information about each container. This is published by YARN Resource Manager to the timeline storage and uses web UI to display about any completed application.

CURRENT STATUS

Timeline server is given generic history service stored in a database preserving the status in memory. Application specific is available via RESTful APIs using JSON type. The single server implementation places a limit on the scalability and prevents the service being highly available component of the YARN infrastructure.

TIMELINE STRUCTURE

The timeline structure includes timeline domain with multiple host timeline entities containing user information with applications. Each domain has a unique ID and comprises owner information, Access Control List and Timestamp data. The entities contain metadata of events. The events can be specific to an application, container or any user-defined object that defines starting of an application, allocation in container, failure or any other related information. Each entity is represented by a unique EntityId and EntityType. Primary Filters are used for indexing the entities in Timeline store.

CONFIGURATION

The timeline server is to be configured in the file yarn-site.xml using hadoop/etc folder to set the host name of the Timeline server:

```
<property>
  <description>The hostname of the Timeline service web
application.</description>
  <name>yarn.timeline-service.hostname</name>
  <value>0.0.0.0</value>
</property>
```

For enabling the timeline service the additional configurations that can be included in the Timeline. Server are given by:

```
<property>
  <description>Defines the clients whether Timeline service is
enabled or not.  If enabled, the TimelineClient library used
by end-users will post entities and events to the Timeline
Server.</description>:
```

```
    <name>yarn.timeline-service.enabled</name>
    <value>true</value>
</property>
<property>
    <description>Setting to manage whether yarn system metrics is
published on the timeline server or not by Resource Manager.</
description>
    <name>yarn.resourcemanager.system-metrics-publisher.enabled</
name>
    <value>true</value>
</property>
<property>
    <description> Defines the clients whether to query generic
application data from timeline history-service or not. If not
enabled then application data can be queried only from Resource
Manager.</description>
    <name>yarn.timeline-service.generic-application-history.
enabled</name>
    <value>true</value>
</property>
```

TIMELINE SERVER EXECUTION

After all configurations are set, admin can begin the Timeline server history service with the command:

```
Yarn timelineserver
```

To begin the same service as a daemon,

```
$HADOOP_YARN_HOME/sbin/yarn-daemon.sh start timelineserver
```

FUTURE RESEARCH DIRECTIONS

Nowadays data are generated from different geographical locations. Some applications that process geo-distributed data are sensor networks, data generated by different branches of a company in different countries, and stock exchanges. Frameworks like Hadoop and Spark (stream processing for big data) force all the data to be moved to one location and all processing is done locally. It cannot support geo-distributed data processing. The main advantages of having geo-distributed data processing are data processing across nodes of multiple clusters, resource sharing, load balancing, fault-tolerance, dynamic scaling during execution, optimization of computation cost, etc. Shlomi Dolev et al., (2017) discussed this issue in detail and they suggested geo-distributed data processing framework for Hadoop and Spark. They classified geo-distributed data into two categories – prelocated (data is already geographically distributed before computation begins) and user located (user distributes the data to *n* locations explicitly). In prelocated geo-distributed data, jobs (not data) are distributed to different locations and outputs of all sites are aggregated at one specified site. For prelocated geo-distributed batch processing, the frameworks recommended by the authors are G-Hadoop (Wang, Tao, Ranjan, Martan, Streit, Chen & Chen, 2013), G-MR (Jayalath, Stephen, & Eugster, 2014), Nebula (Ryden Oh, Chandra, & Weissman, 2014), and Medusa (Costa, Bai, & Correia, 2016). G-Hadoop processes data across multiple clusters without changing the cluster architecture. It uses Gfarm file system which is based on Master-Slave architecture. G-MR is a Hadoop based framework which executes Map-Reduce jobs in the geo-distributed environment. It uses Data Transformation Graph (DTG) algorithm that finds an optimized path for execution based on characteristics of data set, MapReduce jobs, etc. Nebula is also a master-slave system that selects the best node in the cluster for minimizing overall execution time. Medusa is also MapReduce based system but it handles three types of faults efficiently – processing corruption that leads to wrong output, malicious attacks, and unavailability of MapReduce instances. The frameworks for prelocated geo-distributed stream processing are Iridium (Pu, Ananthanarayanan, Bodik, Kandula, Akella, Bahl, & Stocia, 2015) which is designed on top of Apache Spark, JetStream (Rabkin, Arye, Sen, Pai, & Freedman, 2014) which minimizes the amount of inter-cluster traffic, SAGE (Tudoran, Antoniu & Bouge, 2013) which is cloud based architecture and G-cut (Zhou, Ibrahim & He, 2017) which does graph partitioning over multiple clusters.

In user located geo-distributed data, both data and jobs are distributed to different sites and aggregation of outputs is optional depending upon the application. For user located geo-distributed batch processing, the frameworks recommended by the authors are Hierarchical MapReduce-HMR (Luo & Plale, 2012) which is a trivial framework for MapReduce map intensive jobs, Resilin (Iordache, Morin, Parlavantzas, Feller, Riteau, Rennes & Rennes, 2013) which provides hybrid cloud based MapReduce computation framework for exploiting the best available public resources, SEMROD (Oktay, Mehrotra, Khadikar & Kantarcioglu, 2015) which differentiates sensitive and non-sensitive data and then sends non-sensitive data to the cloud, Hadoop on Grid – HOG (He, Weitzel, Swanson & Lu, 2012) which accesses the grid resources in an opportunistic manner, and HybridMR (Tang, He & Gilles, 2015) which allows a MapReduce job on both desktop grid and cloud infrastructures simultaneously.

For user located geo-distributed stream processing, the frameworks recommended by the authors are Google's Photon (Ananthanarayanan, Basker, Das, Gupta, Jiang, Qiu… Venkataraman, 2013) which is a highly scalable, very low latency system helping Google Advertising System, Google's Mesa, (Gupta, Yang, Govig, Krisch, Chan, Lai, Wu…Agrawal, 2014) which is a highly scalable analytic data warehousing system, etc. The open issues suggested by the authors are:

- Security and privacy of data
- Fine-grain solutions to different types of compatibilities
- Global reducer at a predefined location
- Dynamic selection of global reducer
- Wide variety of operations on geographically distributed framework
- Job completion time
- Consistency Vs performance
- Geo-distributed IoT data processing
- Geo-distributed machine learning

All data centres are consuming more electricity and hence the cost is increased. Hence green-aware systems are most wanted. MapRedue framework also has more and more workloads and hence the cost for energy is more. To overcome this issue, (Niu, He & Liu, 2018) suggested a green-aware data processing framework. The main idea by the authors is to delay the workload according to job's deadline so as to match the low-price electricity. The authors proposed JouleMR, a cost-effective and green-aware MapReduce framework. The users can specify slack for each MapReduce job. The slack of each job is decided based on its deadline. The system consists of Hadoop cluster, a charge controller, an inverter, batteries and switch. It has both green source (solar energy) and brown energy(public grid). If the power demand is higher than that of green source, it immediately draws power from brown resources. The energy efficient execution plan is implemented using multiple queues for incoming jobs. The future works suggested by the authors are:

- Predicting the workload
- Predicting the amount of green energy for very long epoch size
- Time-series algorithms to support long term prediction
- Dynamic and fine-grained resource allocation model

CONCLUSION

The chapter deals with the detailed description of the working of YARN infrastructure in Hadoop environment. Dealing with Hadoop version 1 and 2, the issues and configuration setup incase of Mapreduce was compared with YARN and its usage. YARN (Yet Another Resource Negotiator) is comprised of two main tasks resource management and job scheduling to act on a global environment for any application. Scheduling of resources as fair and capacity scheduler was defined. In case of a Resource Manager failure, restart process works with the renewal of Application Master and containers in Node Manager. Further YARN application configurations can be setup in yarn-site.xml. The user commands and administration can be utilized for checking the execution of nodes, Resource Manager, jar included etc... Finally the Timeline Server is used to monitor the historical service of YARN using RESTful API's for any particular UI application.

REFERENCES

Ananthanarayanan, R., Basker, V., Das, S., Gupta, A., Jiang, H., Qiu, T., ... Venkataraman, S. (2013). Photon: Fault-tolerant and Scalable Joining of Continuous Data Streams. *2013 ACM SIMOD/PODS Conference*, 577-588. 10.1145/2463676.2465272

Costa, P., Bai, X., & Correia, M. (2016). Medusa: An Efficient Cloud Fault-Tolerant MapReduce. *16th IEEE/ACM International Symposium on Cluster, Cloud, and Grid Computing (CCGrid)*, 443-452.

Dolev, S., Florissi, P., Gudes, E., Sharma, S., & Singer, I. (2017). *A Survey on Geographically Distributed Geoprocessing using MapReduce. IEEE Transactions on Big Data*. doi:10.1109/TBDATA.2017.2723473

Eadline. (2016). Hadoop 2 Quick-Start Guide: Learn the Essentials of Big Data Computing in the Apache Hadoop 2 Ecosystem. Addison Wesley.

Gupta, Yang, Govig, Krisch, Chan, Lai, … Agrawal. (2014). Mesa: Geo-Replicated, Near Real-Time, Scalable Data Warehousing. *Proceedings of the Very Large DataBase Endowment,* 1259-1270.

He, C., Weitzel, D. J., Swanson, D., & Lu, Y. (2012). HOG: Distributed Hadoop MapReduce on the Grid. *CSE Conference and Workshop,* 1276-1283. 10.1109/SC.Companion.2012.154

Iordache, A., Morin, C., Parlavantzas, N., Feller, E., & Riteau, P. (2013). Resilin: Elastic MapReduce over Mulyiple Clouds. *Proceedings of the 13ʰ IEEE/ACM International Symposium on Cluster, Cloud and Grid Computing,* 261-268.

Jayalath, C., Stephen, J., & Eugster, P. (2014). From the cloud to the atmosphere: Running MapReduce across Data Centres. *IEEE Transactions on Computers,* *63*(1), 74–87. doi:10.1109/TC.2013.121

Lizhe, Wang, Ranjan, Martan, Streit, Chen, & Chen. (2013). G-Hadoop: Mapreduce across distributed data centres for data-intensive computing. *Future Generation Computer Systems,* *29*(3), 739–750. doi:10.1016/j.future.2012.09.001

Luo, Y., & Plale, B. (2012). Hierarchical MapReduce Programming Model and Scheduling Algorithms. *Proceedings of the 12th IEEE/ACM International Symposium on Cluster, Cloud and Grid Computing,* 769-774. 10.1109/CCGrid.2012.132

Murthy, Vavilapalli, Eadline, Niemiec, & Markham. (2014). *Apache Hadoop YARN: Moving beyond MapReduce and Batch Processing with Apache Hadoop 2.* Addison Wesley.

Niu, Z., He, B., & Liu, F. (2018). *JouleMR: Towards Cost-Effective and Green-Aware Data Processing Frameworks. IEEE Transactions on Big Data.*

Oktay, K. Y., Mehrotra, S., Khadilkar, V., & Kantarcioglu, M. (2015). SEMROD: Secure and Efficient MapReduce over HybriD Clouds. *Proceedings of the ACM SIGMOD International Conference on Management of Data,* 153-166.

Pu, Q., Ananthanarayanan, G., Bodik, P., Kandula, S., Akella, A., Bahl, P., & Stocia, I. (2015). *Low Latency Geo-distributed Data Analytics. ACM SIGCOMM.* doi:10.1145/2785956.2787505

Rabkin, A., Arye, M., Sen, S., Pai, V. S., & Freedman, M. J. (2014). Aggregation and Degradation in JetStream: Streaming Analytics in the Wide Area. *11th USENIX Symposium on Networked Systems Design and Implementation*, 275-288.

Ryden, M., Oh, K., Chandra, A., & Weissman, J. (2014). Nebula: Distributed Edge Cloud for Data Intensive Computing. *IEEE International Conference on Cloud Engineering*, 57-66.

Tang, B., He, H., & Fedak, G. (2015). HybridMR: a New Approach for Hybrid MapReduce combining desktop Grid and Cloud Infrastructures. In Concurrency and Computation: Practice and Experience (pp. 4140–4155). Wiley.

Tudoran, R., Antoniu, G., & Bouge, L. (2013). SAGE: Geo-Distributed Streaming Data Analysis in Clouds. *IEEE International Parallel and Distributed Processing Symposium Workshops*, 2278-2281.

White, T. (2015). *Hadoop the definitive guide*. O'Reilly.

Zhou, A., Ibrahim, S., & He, B. (2017). On Achieving Efficient Data Transfer for Graph Processing in Geo-Distributed Datacentres. *ICDCS'17-The 37th IEEE International Conference on Distributed Computing Systems*.

Chapter 7
Hadoop MapReduce Programming

ABSTRACT

The second major component of Hadoop is MapReduce. It is the software framework for Hadoop environment. It consists of a single resource manager, one node manager per node, and one application manager per application. These managers are responsible for allocating necessary resources and executing the jobs submitted by clients. The entire process of executing a job is narrated in this chapter. The architecture of MapReduce framework is explained. The execution is implemented through two major operations: map and reduce. The map and reduce operations are demonstrated with an example. The syntax of different user interfaces available is shown. The coding to be done for MapReduce programming is shown using Java. The entire cycle of job execution is shown. After reading this chapter, the reader will be able to write MapReduce programs and execute them. At the end of the chapter, some research issues in the MapReduce programming is outlined.

INTRODUCTION

The major components of Hadoop systems are Hadoop Distributed File System (HDFS) and MapReduce. The MapReduce is a software framework for easily writing applications. It is mainly used for processing larger amounts of data in-parallel on large clusters (thousands of nodes) in a reliable and fault-tolerant manner. This chapter gives an overview of MapReduce programming.

DOI: 10.4018/978-1-5225-3790-8.ch007

Also it explains clearly the different APIs available for programming. The programming can be done in different languages like C, C++, C#, Java, Perl, PHP, Python and Ruby. But this chapter focuses on programming with Java only.

BACKGROUND

The growth of data in the recent applications in the Internet is highly alarming. Analyzing such kind of large data (data analytics) is the demand in the business process requirements. Though many algorithms and techniques have been developed to mine such kind of large data and have been invested in the analytics, the turnaround time is not satisfactory. The huge storage requirements and computing requirements have dictated the distributed computing environment. The Hadoop based Distributed File System has enabled this. The principle involves dividing the jobs into small independent pieces (in many cases split manually) and mapping to various computing system and combining the solution back in a synchronized manner.

WORKING OF MAPREDUCE

The MapReduce framework consists of a single master ResourceManager, one slave NodeManager per cluster-node, and AppMaster per application. The user/application can submit the work to be executed as a job. The input and output of the job are stored in file system. The framework takes care of splitting the job into number of smaller tasks, scheduling the tasks across different nodes and monitoring them. If the task fails, the framework re-executes the job automatically without user intervention. The tasks are normally scheduled in the nodes where data is already present and hence the network bandwidth is properly utilized.

The applications can specify the input/output locations and other job parameters in "job configuration". Then the client submits the jar/executable file of the job along with its configuration to the ResourceManager. The ResourceManager then:

- Distributes software/configuration to the slaves
- Schedules the tasks

- Monitors the tasks
- Provides status and diagnostic information to the client

Execution of Job

The various steps in execution of MapReduce job is shown in Figure 1. The job is executed as follows:

1. The application process submits the job and initiates "Job" object with the help of Java Virtual Machine (JVM).
2. The ResourceManager in the Master node checks if any new application comes in.

Figure 1. Execution of job in MapReduce

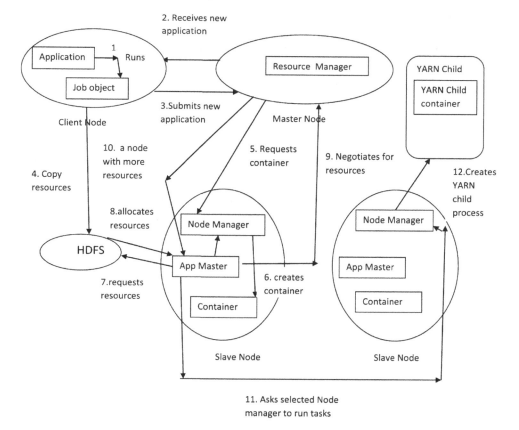

3. The details of new application such as application id are submitted to the ResourceManager.
4. The client application copies all needed resources ie. files into HDFS.
5. Then the ResourceManager requests Slave nodes for containers.
6. The NodeManager in the Slave node creates container.
7. The AppMaster in the Slave node requests the needed files from HDFS.
8. The requested files are given by HDFS.
9. The AppMaster requests the ResourceManager for resources.
10. The ResourceManager indicates the slave node with more resources.
11. The AppMaster requests the NodeManager in the selected slave node to run the task.
12. Then the NodeManager creates a YARN child process to execute the task.
13. The YARN child container executes the task.

Inputs and Outputs

The MapReduce framework views the input to the job as a set of <key, value> pairs and produces a set of <key, value> pairs as the output of the job, possibly of different types.

MapReduce Operations

A MapReduce *job* usually splits the input data-set into independent chunks which are processed by the *map tasks* in a completely parallel manner. The framework sorts the outputs of the maps, which are then input to the *reduce tasks.* Each map operation processes one input key/value pair and produces a set of key/value pairs.

Each reduce operation:

*   Merges all intermediate values (produced by map tasks) for a particular key.
*   Produce final key/value pairs.

Hence the Input and Output types of a MapReduce job are:

```
(input) <k1, v1> -> map -> <k2, v2> ->  reduce -> <k3, v3>
(output)
```

Architecture of MapReduce Framework

The architecture of MapReduce is shown in Figure 2.

The input file is split into smaller portions and it is given to the mapper in the proper format. The mapper maps the input key, value pairs into appropriate intermediate key/ value pairs. Those intermediate key, value pairs are grouped based on the key value. The reducer reduces the intermediate key, value pairs into smaller set and produces the output.

Example for MapReduce

Let us consider the task of counting the votes for different contestants in an election. The votes are indicated as contestant names and it is available as a file for each region. The files for different regions have to be processed and

Figure 2. Architecture of MapReduce

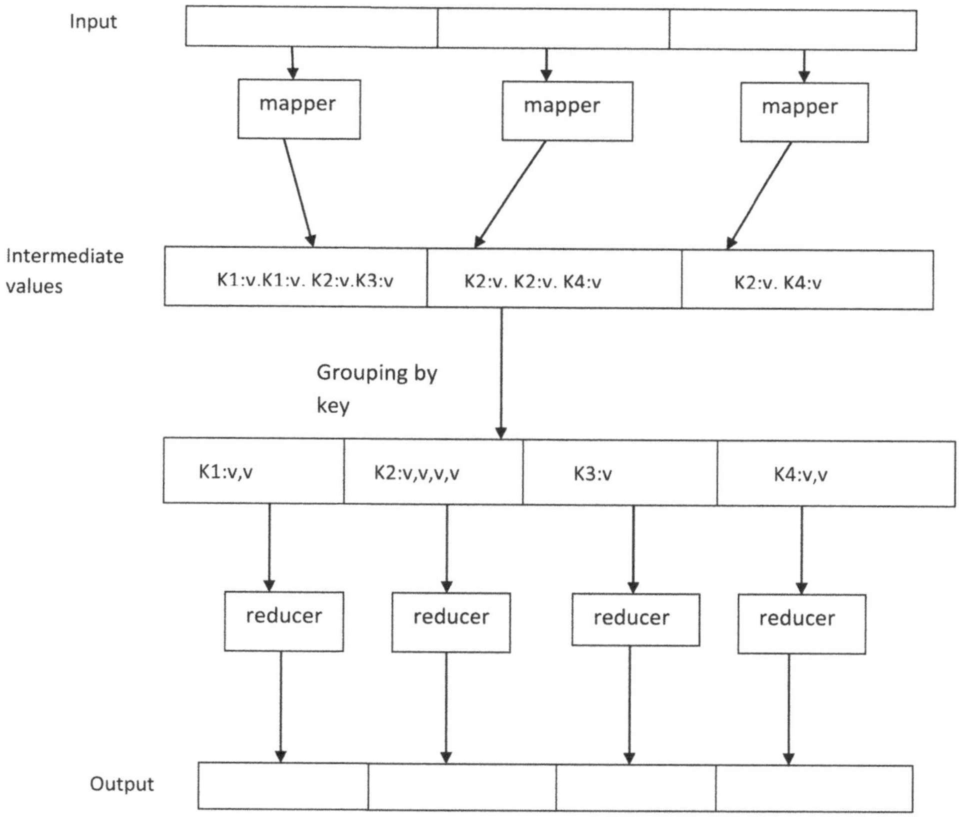

the total count for each contestant has to be calculated. If we implement the task using MapReduce, the working is shown in Figure 3.

The input is the different files for different regions. The files are having the contestant names who gained the vote. It is given to the mappers. The mapper reads each name in the file and take it as a key. The corresponding value is the count ie.1. Then it can be shuffled, if needed and sorted in the alphabetical order. These key, value pairs are given to the reducers. The reducers combine them based on the key. Also the values of combinations are added and it gives the total count of votes for that particular contestant.

Input and Output Formats

The formats of the input and output for MapReduce are shown in detail in Figure 4.

Figure 3. Working of MapReduce

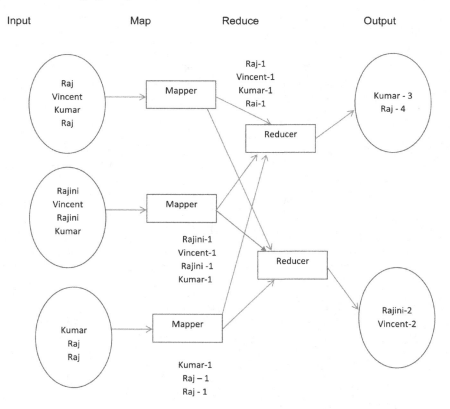

Figure 4. Input and Output

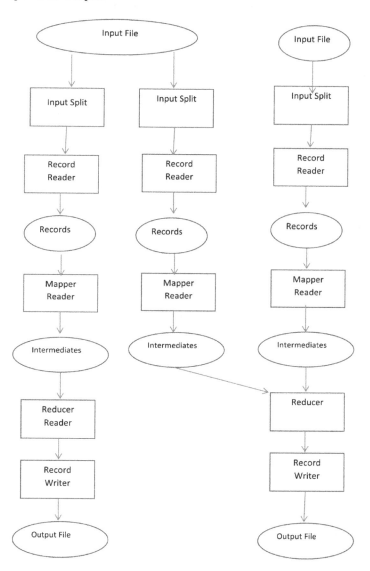

Each input file is splitted into number of logical "InputSplit" instances. Each InputSplit instance is assigned to a mapper. "RecordReader" implementation is used to collect input records from the logical InputSplit. It maintains record boundaries and shows a record oriented view of logical InputSplit to the tasks. The input records are processed by the mappers. The mappers produce intermediates. The intermediates are further processed by the reducers. "RecordWriter" implementation is used to write the output files of the job. The output files are stored in a file system.

MapReduce User Interfaces

The following user interfaces are provided in the MapReduce:

- Mapper
- Reducer
- InputFormat
- OutputFormat
- OutputCommitter
- Partitioner
- Job
- Counter
- Shuffle
- Sort
- Secondary Sort

InputFormat

The InputFormat describes the input specification for a MapReduce job. The InputFormat is used to:

1. Validate the input specification of the job
2. Split the input file into logical InputSplit instances
3. Provide the RecordReader implementation

The InputFormat is the interface for the implementation classes such as FileInputFormat. It is used to split the input file into logical InputSplit instances based on the total size of the input file in bytes. The FileSystem blocksize is treated as an upper bound for input splits.

A lower bound on the split size can be set via *mapreduce.input. fileinputformat.split.minsize*. The logical splits based on input-size are insufficient for many applications since record boundaries must be processed. In such cases, the application should implement a RecordReader.

TextInputFormat is the default InputFormat. With TextInputFormat, the framework detects input-files with the *.gz* extensions and automatically decompresses them using the appropriate CompressionCodec.

FileInputFormat specifies the set of input files. The various methods supported by the implementation class are as follows:

- **FileInputFormat.setInputPaths(JobConf, Path...):** Input paths
- **FileInputFormat.addInputPath(JobConf, Path):** Add to the existing paths
- **FileInputFormat.setInputPaths(Job, String..):** Comma separated input paths
- **FileInputFormat.addInputPaths(Job, String):** Add to the existing paths

InputSplit

InputSplit represents the data to be processed by an individual Mapper. It presents a byte-oriented view of the input. It is the responsibility of the RecordReader to process and present a record-oriented view. FileSplit is the default InputSplit. It sets mapreduce.map.input.file to the path of the input file for the logical split.

RecordReader

The RecordReader reads <key, value> pairs from an InputSplit. It converts the byte-oriented view of the input, provided by the InputSplit, and presents a record-oriented view to the Mapper implementations for processing. It assumes the responsibility of processing record boundaries and presents the tasks with keys and values.

OutputFormat

The OutputFormat describes the output-specification for a MapReduce job. It is used to:

- Validate the output-specification of the job; for example, check that the output directory doesn't already exist.

- Provide the RecordWriter implementation used to write the output files of the job.

TextOutputFormat is the default OutputFormat.

The class FileOutputFormat has the methods related to file based output format. It has the methods to:

- To check for validity of the output-specification for the job.
- To decide whether the job is output compressed
- To get the default path and filename for the output format.
- To get the output committer for this output format.
- To get the CompressionCodec for compressing the job outputs. Get the base output name for the output file.
- To get the Path to the output directory for the map-reduce job.
- To get the RecordWriter for the given task.
- To generate a unique filename, based on the task id, name, and extension.
- To get the Path to the task's temporary output directory for the map-reduce job.
- To set whether the output of the job is compressed.
- To set the CompressionCodec to be used to compress job outputs.
- To set the base output name for output file to be created.
- To set the Path of the output directory for the map-reduce job

SequenceFileOutputFormat

This writes binary files suitable for reading into subsequent MapReduce jobs.

NullOutputFormat

It disregards its inputs.

OutputCommitter

The OutputCommitter describes the commiting of task output for a MapReduce job.

It is used to:

- Setup the job during initialization. For example, create the temporary output directory for the job during the initialization of the job. Job setup is done by a separate task when the job is in PREP state and after initializing tasks. Once the setup task completes, the job will be moved to RUNNING state.
- Cleanup the job after the job completion. For example, remove the temporary output directory after the job completion. Job cleanup is done by separate task at the end of the job. Job is declared SUCCEDED/ FAILED/KILLED after the cleanup task completes.
- Setup the task temporary output. Task setup is done as part of the same task, during task initialization.
- Check whether a task needs a commit. This is to avoid the commit procedure if a task does not need commit.
- Commit of the task output. Once task is done, the task will commit its output if required.
- Discard the task commit. If the task has been failed/killed, the output will be cleaned-up. If task could not cleanup (in exception block), a separate task will be launched with same attempt-id to do the cleanup.

FileOutputCommitter is the default OutputCommitter. Job setup/cleanup tasks occupy map or reduce containers, whichever is available on the NodeManager. And JobCleanup task, TaskCleanup tasks and JobSetup task have the highest priority, and in that order.

Mapper

The Mapper maps input key-value pairs to a set of intermediate key/value pairs. The instance of Mapper must be provided by user and it should extend Mapper class. The framework creates one map task for each InputSplit generated by InputFormat for the job. The output pairs do not need to be of the same types as input pairs. The Mapper calls map(WritableComparable, Writable, Context) for each key/value pair in the InputSplit for that task. The output pairs are collected with calls to context.write(WritableComparable, Writable).

Writable

Writable is an interface in Hadoop and value types in Hadoop must implement this interface. Hadoop provides these writable wrappers for almost all Java primitive types. MapReduce uses implementations of Writables for interacting with user-provided Mappers and Reducers. The data needs to be transmitted between different nodes in a distributed computing environment. This requires serialization and deserialization of data to convert the data that is in structured format to byte stream and vice-versa. Hadoop therefore uses simple and efficient serialization protocol to serialize data between map and reduce phase and these are called Writable. All values are instances of *Writable*. All keys are instances of *WritableComparable*.

The Writable wrapper classes for Java primitives are indicated in Table 1.

WritableComparable

WritableComparable interface is just a subinterface of the Writable and java. lang.Comparable interfaces. Any type which is to be used as a key in the Hadoop Map-Reduce framework should implement this interface. WritableComparable objects can be compared to each other using Comparators.

Table 1. Writable Wrapper classes

Java Primitive	Writable Implementation	Serialized Size (bytes)
boolean	BooleanWritable	1
byte	ByteWritable	1
short	ShortWritable	2
int	IntWritable	4
	VIntWritable (VariableLength)	1-5
float	FloatWritable	4
long	LongWritable	8
	VLongWritable	1-9
double	DoubleWritable	8
String	Text	Variable length

Number of Maps

The number of Maps depends on the total size of the inputs that is, the total number of blocks of the input files. The right level of parallelism for maps seems to be around 10-100 maps per-node, although it has been set up to 300 maps for very cpu-light map task. It is best if the maps take at least a minute to execute.

Eg:

If input data size is 10TB and have a block size of 128MB, then the number of maps would be 82,000 maps.

Partitioner

Mapper outputs are sorted and then partitioned per Reduce. The total number of partitions is same as the number of reduce tasks for the job. The users can control which keys (and hence records) go to which Reducer by implementing a custom Partitioner. The Partitioner partitions the key space. The key (or a subset of the key) is used to derive the partition, typically by a *hash function*. It controls which of the m reduce tasks the intermediate key (and hence the record) is sent to for reduction.

HashPartitioner is the default Partitioner.

Eg 1:

```
 Partitioner = new HashPartitioner<WritableComparable,Writab
le>();
```

Eg 2:

```
public interface Partitioner<K, V> extends Configuration
{
  int getPartition(K key, V value, int numPartitions);
 }
```

Reducer

Reducer reduces a set of intermediate values which share a key to a smaller set of values.

The number of reduces for the job is set by the user via Job. setNumReduceTasks(int).

Overall, Reducer implementations are passed for the job via the Job. setReducer Class(Class) method and can override it to initialize themselves. The framework then calls reduce(WritableComparable, Iterable<Writable>, Context) method for each <key, (list of values)> pair in the grouped inputs. Iterable<T> returns an iterator (for each) over a set of elements of type T. The Context represents a naming context, which consists of a set of name-to-object bindings. It contains methods for examining and updating these bindings. The output of the reduce task is typically written to the FileSystem via Context.write(WritableComparable, Writable). The applications can use the Counter to report its statistics. The output of the Reducer is *not sorted*.

Applications can then override the cleanup(Context) method to perform any required cleanup.

Reducer has 3 primary phases: shuffle, sort and reduce.

Shuffle

Input to the Reducer is the sorted output of the mappers. In this phase the framework fetches the relevant partition of the output of all the mappers, via HTTP.

Sort

The framework groups Reducer inputs by keys (since different mappers may have output the same key) in this stage. The shuffle and sort phases occur simultaneously; When map-outputs are being fetched they are merged.

Secondary Sort

If equivalence rules for grouping the intermediate keys are required to be different from those for grouping keys before reduction, then one may specify a Comparator via Job.setSortComparatorClass(Class). Since Job.setGroupin gComparatorClass(Class) can be used to control how intermediate keys are grouped, these can be used in conjunction to simulate *secondary sort on values*.

Number of Reduces

The right number of reduces seems to be 0.95 or 1.75 multiplied by (*<no. of nodes>* * *<no. of maximum containers per node>*). With 0.95, all of the reduces can launch immediately and start transferring map outputs as the maps finish. With 1.75 the faster nodes will finish their first round of reduces and launch a second wave of reduces doing a much better job of load balancing.

Increasing the number of reduces increases the framework overhead, but increases load balancing and lowers the cost of failures. The scaling factors above are slightly less than whole numbers to reserve a few reduce slots in the framework for speculative-tasks and failed tasks.

It is possible to set the number of reduce-tasks to *zero* if no reduction is desired. In this case the outputs of the map-tasks go directly to the FileSystem, into the output path set by FileOutputFormat.setOutputPath(Job, Path) . The framework does not sort the map-outputs before writing them out to the FileSystem.

Counter

Counter is used for MapReduce applications to report its statistics. Mapper and Reducer can use it to report statistics. Each Counter can be of any Enum type. The Counters of particular Enum are grouped in Counters.Group. The applications can update the Counter via. Counters.incrCounter(Enum, long) or Counters.incrCounter(String, String, long) in the map and reduce methods. These counters are then globally aggregated by the framework.

Task Execution

The MRAppMaster executes the Mapper/Reducer *task* as a child process in a separate jvm.

The child-task inherits the environment of the parent MRAppMaster. The user can specify additional options to the child-jvm via mapreduce. {maplreduce}.java.opts and configuration parameter in the Job such as non-standard paths for the run-time linker to search shared libraries via -Djava. library.path=<> etc. If the mapreduce.{maplreduce}.java.opts parameters contains the symbol *@taskid@*, it is interpolated with value of taskid of the MapReduce task.

Anatomy of Job

MapReduce program in Hadoop is called Hadoop job. The jobs are divided into map and reduce tasks. An instance of running a task is called a task attempt.

If a task fails, another task attempt will be done automatically. Multiple jobs can be composed into a workflow. The client (i.e., driver program) creates a job, configures it, and submits it to Job. The input and output specifications of the job are checked. The InputSplit values for the job are computed. The requisite accounting information for the DistributedCache of the job, if necessary is setup.

The job's jar files and configuration files are copied into the MapReduce system directory on the FileSystem. Then the job is submitted to the ResourceManager. Optionally the status of the job can be monitored.

Job Configuration

The Job represents a MapReduce job configuration. It is the primary interface for a user to describe a MapReduce job to the Hadoop framework for execution, which tries to faithfully execute the job as described by Job. However, some of the configuration parameters could not be altered since they are marked as final by administrators. Some of the parameters could be directly set and others could be set with little extra efforts. The Job is typically used to specify the Mapper, combiner, Partitioner, Reducer, InputFormat, OutputFormat implementations. The input and output are specified with FileInputFormat and FileOutputFormat.setOutputPath(Path) respectively.

Apart from these, the specification such as Speculative execution and Maximum number of attempts per task can be set. Speculative execution is done to optimize the time delay by doing some operations in advance (which sometimes to be undone). The methods setMapSpeculativeExecution(), and setReduceSpeculativeExecution() passing the Boolean parameter turns ON/OFF. The maximum number of attempts per task can be specified by the methods: setMaxMapAttempts(int) and setMaxReduceAttempts(int).

Configuration.set(String,String), Configuration.get(String) methods are used to set/get arbitrary parameters needed by applications. It is preferable to use the DistributedCache for large amounts of (read-only) data.

The typical configuration file looks as follows:

```
<?xml version="1.0"?>
<?xml-stylesheet type="text/xsl" href="configuration.xsl?>
<property>
<name>mapred.reduce.tasks</name>
<value> some numbers </value>
<description>the default number of  reduce tasks per job </
description>
```

```
</property>
<property> …. </property>
. . . . . . .
<property> …. </property>
```

The parameters could be manually set or the defaults values could be used. Around 190 parameters are involved in working with the map reduce based work.

Job History

The history of the job transactions could be logged into the user specified directory: mapreduce.jobhistory.intermediate-done-dir and mapreduce. jobhistory.done-dir, which defaults to job output directory. The commands "$ mapred job –history output.jhist" can be used to see the history of all the tasks.

Job Control

The methods job.submit() and job.waitForCompletion (Boolean) are used to submit the jobs. The difference between these two methods is that the first one submits the job and return immediately and the second method submits and waits till completion.

Example Program

So far, all the classes and their methods for the map-reduce concept has been discussed. As a concrete example, a problem to count the number of similar names (a typical contestant in an election scenarios is considered). Figure 3 shows the working principle of an example problem. The following is the code for solving the above problem. If the number of text with the contestant name is huge, and if the real time solution is required, Hadoop based distribute computing promises the solution.

Code

```
import java.io.IOException;
import java.util.StringTokenizer;
import org.apache.hadoop.conf.Configuration;
import org.apache.hadoop.fs.Path;
import org.apache.hadoop.io.IntWritable;
import org.apache.hadoop.io.Text;
```

```
import org.apache.hadoop.mapreduce.Job;
import org.apache.hadoop.mapreduce.Mapper;
import org.apache.hadoop.mapreduce.Reducer;
import org.apache.hadoop.mapreduce.lib.input.FileInputFormat;
import org.apache.hadoop.mapreduce.lib.output.FileOutputFormat;
public class NameCount
{
  public static class ContestantMapper
      extends Mapper<Object, Text, Text, IntWritable>
  {
    private final static IntWritable one = new IntWritable(1);
    private Text name = new Text();
    public void map(Object key, Text value, Context context
                  ) throws IOException, InterruptedException
      {
      StringTokenizer itr = new StringTokenizer(value.
toString());
      while (itr.hasMoreTokens())
          {
        name.set(itr.nextToken());
        context.write(name, one);
      }
    }
  }
  public static class Adder
      extends Reducer<Text,IntWritable,Text,IntWritable>
  {
    private IntWritable result = new IntWritable();
    public void reduce(Text key, Iterable<IntWritable> values,
                    Context context
                  ) throws IOException, InterruptedException
      {
      int sm = 0;
      for (IntWritable val: values)
          {
        sm += val.get();
      }
      result.set(sm);
      context.write(key, result);
    }
  }
  public static void main(String[] args) throws Exception
  {
    Configuration conf = new Configuration();
    Job job = Job.getInstance(conf, "name count");
    job.setJarByClass(NameCount.class);
    job.setMapperClass(ContestantMapper.class);
    job.setCombinerClass(Adder.class);
    job.setReducerClass(Adder.class);
```

```
    job.setOutputKeyClass(Text.class);
    job.setOutputValueClass(IntWritable.class);
    FileInputFormat.addInputPath(job, new Path(args[0]));
    FileOutputFormat.setOutputPath(job, new Path(args[1]));
    System.exit(job.waitForCompletion(true) ? 0: 1);
  }
}
```

RESEARCH ISSUES WITH MAPREDUCE

MapReduce programming is part of the Hadoop System. However programming with MapReduce for the real world scenarios for large application and in turn analyzing is challenging and hence Guozhang Wang et.al (2010) attempted to do the behavior simulations. In many scientific domains, researchers are turning to large-scale behavioral simulations to better understand real-world phenomena. The authors presented Big Red Agent-based Computation Engine (BRACE), extending the MapReduce framework to process these simulations efficiently across a cluster and leveraged spatial locality to treat behavioral simulations as iterated spatial joins and achieved the reduced communication overhead between nodes. They emphasized the importance of the optimization in the single node for addressing the complexity of computation and communication across the nodes. Though processing behavioral simulations in parallel as iterated spatial joins can be very efficient, it can be much simpler for the domain scientists to program the behavior of a single agent. Furthermore, many simulations include a considerable amount of complex computation and message passing between agents, which makes it important to optimize the performance of a single node and the communication across nodes. To address both of these challenges, BRACE includes a high-level language called Big Red Agent SImulation Language (BRASIL), which has object-oriented features for programming simulations, compiled to a dataflow representation for automatic parallelization and optimization. By means of working with various algebraic optimization techniques, they claimed to achieve both linear scalability and single-node performance similar to that of a hand-coded simulation.

MapReduce programming finds it applications in numerous domains. One such application is proposed by Emad et.al (2014), since the massive dataset in a clinical side is faced with the challenges of storage and analytics. For such kind of the data access approaches, it must be precisely tailored to large volumes of semi-structured/unstructured data. MapReduce offers some advantages over the existing parallel processing methods and Graphical Processing Unit (GPU) methods in terms of redundant storage which makes the fault-tolerant storage system and replicating the computing tasks across the nodes in the cluster to give high-throughput data processing. Using these features of MapReduce programming, high tech clinical big data analytics was achieved.

In the two phases of Map and Reduce, there are lot of sub tasks present. The number of Map tasks that is equal to the number of data blocks is decided in the input. However the number of reduce tasks could not be determined based on the number of intermediate data that is produced by the Map tasks. Since the reduce tasks have to bring the data into main memory, the memory management for such kind of reduce tasks could not be planned leading to the inefficient execution of application and even application failure. Seyed Morteza Nabavinejad et.al (2016) introduced Mnemonic approaches which makes uses of the profile of the application behavior to predict the memory requirements for the reduce task from the intermediate data generated. By means of the profiling mechanism, they have reduced the likelihood of the application failure and the execution time.

Machine learning techniques have an impact on the industries due to its own inherent features and find its applications in many domains. It is meant for imitation of the human behavior in the machine. Basically Artificial Intelligence (AI) and Artificial Neural Network (ANN) are being used in varieties of data mining applications. The basic idea behind the machine learning techniques is to imitate the human brain activities. The brain is made of huge number of neurons (approximately 10^{14} neurons) and each neuron is associated with nearly 10000 neurons. Hence the complexity of connections is very high. Hence human computing infrastructure that is needed to imitate the brain is very high. AI is not new in the research. Due to limitations of the memory and processing power, it was limited only to the researchers. However due to the huge infrastructure for computing and storage (like in Hadoop) is nowadays available, the realization of ANN is feasible. The objective of ANN is to make the machine to be intelligent which has lot of research potential. Knowledge extraction or data mining from the massive data is a part of business analytics, which always deals in terms of prediction, description and association rule mining. Xuan Liu et.al (2015) used MapReduce programming to provide a feasible framework for programming mining algorithms with Map and Reduce functions, which is scalable with a weakness of not supporting the iterations. Hence they proposed to apply Meta-learning programmed with MapReduce to avoid parallelizing machine learning algorithms but at the same time improved their scalability to big datasets. They conducted experiments on Hadoop's fully distributed mode on Amazon EC2, and reduced training computational complexity as the number of computing nodes increases while obtaining smaller error rates than those on a single node.

CONCLUSION

In this chapter, the entire specification and setting up of the Hadoop system is elaborated. The working principle has been outlined with appropriate diagram and example. The HDFS has been already deployed in many industrial applications. Deployment of the HDFS in various applications such as clustering of large data has not been explored since there are limitations in terms of the dependencies of the job subsequence, lack of automatic identification of the job independences, lack of compiler support for the distributed computing environment.

REFERENCES

Eadline, D. (2016). *Hadoop 2 Quick-Start Guide: Learn the Essentials of Big Data Computing in the Apache Hadoop 2 Ecosystem*. Addison Wesley.

Liu, Wang, Matwin, & Japkowicz. (2015). Meta-MapReduce for scalable data mining. *Journal of Big Data*, 1-23.

Mohammed, Far, & Naugler. (2014). Applications of the MapReduce programming framework to clinical big data analysis: current landscape and future trends. *Big Data Mining*. Retrieved from http://www.biodatamining.org/content/7/1/22

Murthy, A., Vavilapalli, V., Eadline, D., Niemiec, J., & Markham, J. (2014). *Apache Hadoop YARN: Moving beyond MapReduce and Batch Processing with Apache Hadoop 2*. Addison Wesley.

Nabavinejad, S. M., Goudarzi, M., & Mozaffari, S. (2016). The Memory Challenge in Reduce Phase of MapReduce Applications, IEEE Transactions On. *Big Data*, 2(4), 380–386.

Wang, G., Salles, M. V., Sowell, B., Wang, X., Cao, T., Demers, A., ... White, W. (2010). Behavioral Simulations in MapReduce. *Proceedings of the VLDB Endowment International Conference on Very Large Data Bases*, *3*(1), 952–963. doi:10.14778/1920841.1920962

White, T. (2015). *Hadoop the definitive guide*. O'Reilly.

Chapter 8
MapReduce and YARN API

ABSTRACT

Apache Hadoop includes Java APIs for different functions on a HDFS file system like creation of a file, renaming, deletion, and to set read-write permissions for directories. This can be done on a single and cluster of systems. In addition, REST (REpresentational State Transfer) APIs is a collection of web services to provide interoperability between a single system and an interconnected distributed network. REST is chosen for its speedy performance, scalability, simplicity, and reliability. YARN REST and MapReduce REST APIs are briefly discussed in this chapter. YARN web service REST API includes URI resources through which the cluster information, nodes, and application information can be accessed. YARN is comprised of Resource manager, node manager, and timeline REST APIs. The application has HTTP request as resource and the response can be in the form XML or JSON. The request URI, response status, header, and body are defined in actual format. Similarly, the REST API is used for MapReduce that comprises the details about the jobs running with the information such as number of tasks, counters, and attempts. Hence, the REST APIs on YARN and resource manager create small modules as a response when a resource is requested. An outline of the research and growth of REST APIs is included in this chapter.

INTRODUCTION

Hadoop provides many Java native APIs that support file system operations like creation of a file or renaming or deletion and operations with directories

DOI: 10.4018/978-1-5225-3790-8.ch008

to set read, write permissions etc… Hadoop cluster requires these operations to manipulate the data in files across HDFS. This is supported by an additional API based on REST functionalities to map these requirements. The Hadoop YARN and Mapreduce REST API's support various services across applications working in the environment.

BACKGROUND

REpresentational State Transfer (REST) is web service to provide interoperability between a single system and an interconnected distributed network. It allows the requesting system to access and manipulate data of web resources using uniform set of stateless operations. In a REST API, requests will be in the form of resource URI which may elicit a response in XML, JSON, and HTML etc… REST is chosen for its fast performance, scalability, visibility, simplicity, reliability, reusing components and gets the system updated without affecting it. The services which adhere to the architectural constraints and properties of REST APIs utilize it. One such case is that Hadoop services that combine the architecture of YARN and Mapreduce based RESTful APIs.

REST uses HTTP protocol for communication in the web world. URI is used for communication among the resources of RESTful services. The HTTP methods supported are:

1. **GET:** Read a resource (Read only).
2. **PUT:** Create new resource.
3. **POST:** Update an existing resource or create a new resource.
4. **DELETE:** Remove a resource.
5. **OPTIONS:** Get the supported operations on the resource.

YARN REST APIs

Hadoop YARN web service REST APIs includes set of URI resources through which the cluster information, nodes and application information can be accessed. The resources can be grouped based on type of information. Some can be together while others using URI resource

The URI of REST based web service is:

```
                          http://{http address of service}/ws/
{version}/ {resourcepath}
```

where,

- {http address of service}: The http address of the service to get information. It can be ResourceManager, NodeManager, MapReduce application master, and history server.
- {version}: The version of the APIs.
- {resourcepath}: A path that defines a resource or as collection

To cite REST API, the application begins with a HTTP operation on the URI linked with the resource. GET is used to retrieve the information about resource specified. The headers in HTTP can be Accept or Accept-Encoding. Accept supports XML and JSON in response whereas Accept-Encoding supports gzip compressed format.

The format of JSON request and response with a single resource can be, HTTP Request:

```
GET  http://rmhost.domain:8088/ws/v1/cluster/app/application\
_1324325439346\_0001
```

Response Status Line:

```
HTTP/1.1 200 OK
```

Response Header:

```
HTTP/1.1 200 OK
Content-Type: application/json
Transfer-Encoding: chunked
Server: Jetty(6.1.26)
```

Response Body:

```
{
  app": {
    "id":"application_1324057493980_0001",
    "user":"user1",
    "name":"",
    "queue":"default",
    "state":"ACCEPTED",
```

```
    "finalStatus":"UNDEFINED",
    "progress":0,
    "trackingUI":"UNASSIGNED",
    "diagnostics":"",
    "clusterId":1324325439346,
    "startedTime":1324057495921,
    "finishedTime":0,
    "elapsedTime":2063, "amContainerLogs":"http:\/\/amNM:2\/
node\/containerlogs\/container_ 1324057493980_0001_01_000001",
    "amHostHttpAddress":"amNM:2"
  }   }
```

RESOURCE MANAGER REST API

Resource Manager REST APIs permit the user to get cluster information in Hadoop environment i.e. the status of cluster, scheduler information, node information and about application in cluster. The cross-origin support can be enabled for the resource manager using the two configurations:

1.   Setting org.apache.hadoop.security.HttpCrossOriginFilterInitializer to hadoop.http.filter.initializers in core-site.xml file
2.   Set yarn.resourcemanager.webapp.cross-origin.enabled to true in yarn-site.xml file

The cluster information can be retrieved using the URI,

```
                http://<rm http address:port>/ws/v1/cluster/
info
```

The HTTP GET operation as a request retrieves a response in JSON or XML type format. The JSON response is given by:
HTTP Request:

```
GET http://<rm http address:port>/ws/v1/cluster/info
```

Response Header:

```
HTTP/1.1 200 OK
Content-Type: application/json
```

```
Transfer-Encoding: chunked
Server: Jetty(6.1.26)
```

Response Body:

```
{
  "clusterInfo":
  {
    "id":1324053971963,
    "startedOn":1324053971963,
    "state":"STARTED",
    "resourceManagerVersion":"0.23.1-SNAPSHOT",
    "resourceManagerBuildVersion":"0.23.1-SNAPSHOT from 1214049
by user1 source checksum 050cd664439d931c8743a6428fd6a693",
    "resourceManagerVersionBuiltOn":"Tue Dec 13 22:12:48 CST
2011",
    "hadoopVersion":"0.23.1-SNAPSHOT",
    "hadoopBuildVersion":"0.23.1-SNAPSHOT from 1214049 by user1
source checksum 11458df3bb77342dca5f917198fad328",
    "hadoopVersionBuiltOn":"Tue Dec 13 22:12:26 CST 2011"
  }
}
```

The XML response with request is given by:

HTTP Request: GET http://<rm http address:port>/ws/v1/cluster/
info

Response Header:

```
HTTP/1.1 200 OK
Content-Type: application/xml
Content-Length: 712
Server: Jetty(6.1.26)
```

Response Body:

```
<?xml version="1.0" encoding="UTF-8" standalone="yes"?>
<clusterInfo>
  <id>1324053971963</id>
  <startedOn>1324053971963</startedOn>
  <state>STARTED</state>
  <resourceManagerVersion>0.23.1-SNAPSHOT</
resourceManagerVersion>
  <resourceManagerBuildVersion>0.23.1-SNAPSHOT from 1214049
by user1 source checksum 050cd664439d931c8743a6428fd6a693</
```

```
resourceManagerBuildVersion>
  <resourceManagerVersionBuiltOn>Tue Dec 13 22:12:48 CST 2011</
resourceManagerVersionBuiltOn>
  <hadoopVersion>0.23.1-SNAPSHOT</hadoopVersion>
  <hadoopBuildVersion>0.23.1-SNAPSHOT from 1214049 by
user1 source checksum 11458df3bb77342dca5f917198fad328</
hadoopBuildVersion>
  <hadoopVersionBuiltOn>Tue Dec 13 22:12:48 CST 2011</
hadoopVersionBuiltOn>
</clusterInfo>
```

The Various Elements of the CLUSTERINFO Object are:

- Id => cluster id
- startedOn => The time the cluster started in milliseconds
- state => The ResourceManager state - valid values are: NOTINITED, INITED, STARTED, STOPPED
- resourceManagerVersion => Version of the ResourceManager
- resourceManagerBuildVersion => ResourceManager build string with build version, user, and checksum
- resourceManagerVersionBuiltOn => Timestamp when ResourceManager was built in milliseconds

CLUSTER APPLICATIONS API

The API collects the resources where each represents an application. The HTTP request is by GET and the response as JSON type.
    URI:

```
http://<rm http address:port>/ws/v1/cluster/apps
```

The different operations under GET are:

- **State:** State of the application
- **States:** Applications matching the given application states given as list
- **FinalStatus:** The final status of the application user - user name
- **Queue:** Queue name
- **Limit:** Total number of application objects to be returned
- **StartedTimeBegin:** Applications with start time beginning in milliseconds

- **StartedTimeEnd:** Applications with start time ending
- **finishedTimeBegin:** Applications with finish time beginning
- **finishedTimeEnd:** Applications with finish time ending
- **applicationTypes:** Applications matching the given application type given as list
- **ApplicationTags:** Applications matching any of the given application tags

HTTP Request:

```
GET http://<rm http address:port>/ws/v1/cluster/apps
```

Response Header:

```
HTTP/1.1 200 OK
Content-Type: application/json
Transfer-Encoding: chunked
Server: Jetty(6.1.26)
```

Response Body:

```
{   "apps":
    {      "app":
        [         {
            "finishedTime": 1326815598530,
            "amContainerLogs": "http://host.domain.com:8042/
node/containerlogs/container_1326815542473 _0001_01_000001",
"trackingUI": "History",
            "state": "FINISHED",
            "user": "user1",
            "id": "application_1326815542473_0001",
            "clusterId": 1326815542473,
            "finalStatus": "SUCCEEDED",
            "amHostHttpAddress": "host.domain.com:8042",
            "progress": 100,
            "name": "word count",
            "startedTime": 1326815573334,
            "elapsedTime": 25196,
            "diagnostics": "",
            "trackingUrl": "http://host.domain.com:8088/
proxy/application_1326815542473_0001/jobhistory/job/
job_1326815542473_1_1",
            "queue": "default",
            "allocatedMB": 0,
            "allocatedVCores": 0,
```

```
      "runningContainers": 0,
      "memorySeconds": 151730,
      "vcoreSeconds": 103
    }
]  }  }
```

CLUSTER NODES API

This includes the collection of resources which represents a node. The HTTP Request is by GET and response as JSON type.

HTTP Request:

```
GET http://<rm http address:port>/ws/v1/cluster/nodes
```

Response Header:

```
  HTTP/1.1 200 OK
Content-Type: application/json
Transfer-Encoding: chunked
Server: Jetty(6.1.26)
```

Response Body:

```
{
  "nodes":  {
    "node":     [
      {
        "rack":"\/default-rack",
        "state":"NEW",
        "id":"h2:1235",
        "nodeHostName":"h2",
        "nodeHTTPAddress":"h2:2",
        "healthStatus":"Healthy",
        "lastHealthUpdate":1324056895432,
        "healthReport":"Healthy",
        "numContainers":0,
        "usedMemoryMB":0,
        "availMemoryMB":8192,
        "usedVirtualCores":0,
        "availableVirtualCores":8
      },
      {
        "rack":"\/default-rack",
```

```
"state":"NEW",
"id":"h1:1234",
"nodeHostName":"h1",
"nodeHTTPAddress":"h1:2",
"healthStatus":"Healthy",
"lastHealthUpdate":1324056895092,
"healthReport":"Healthy",
"numContainers":0,
"usedMemoryMB":0,
"availMemoryMB":8192,
"usedVirtualCores":0,
"availableVirtualCores":8
}     ]   }     }
```

CLUSTER DELEGATION TOKENS API

The Delegation Token APIs are used to create, renew and cancel YARN ResourceManager delegation tokens. All delegation token requests must be carried out on a Kerberos authenticated connection (discussed in details in Chapter 10). HTTP operations supported are POST and DELETE for request where the HTTP response is by JSON:

The URI to create and cancel delegation token are,

```
http://<rm http address:port>/ws/v1/cluster/delegation-token
```

and to renew delegation token

```
http://<rm http address:port>/ws/v1/cluster/delegation-token/
expiration
```

HTTP Request:

```
POST http://<rm http address:port>/ws/v1/cluster/delegation-
token
Accept: application/json
Content-Type: application/json
{
  "renewer": "test-renewer"
}
```

Response Header:

```
HTTP/1.1 200 OK
WWW-Authenticate: Negotiate...
Date: Sat, 28 Jun 2014 18:08:11 GMT
Server: Jetty(6.1.26)
Set-Cookie: ...
Content-Type: application/json
```

Response Body:

```
{   token":"MgASY2xpZW50QEVYQU1QTEUuQ09
NDHRlc 3QtcmVuZXdlcgCKAUcki EZpigFHSJTKa
QECFN9EMM9BzfPoDxu572EVUpzqhnSGE1JNX0RF TEVHQVRJT05fVE9LRU4A",
    "renewer":"test-renewer",
    "owner":"client@EXAMPLE.COM",
    "kind":"RM_DELEGATION_TOKEN",
    "expiration-time":1405153616489,
    "max-validity":1405672016489
}
```

NODE MANAGER REST APIs

The NodeManager REST APIs retrieves the information about applications and containers running on the node in cluster. The cross-origin support can be enabled for the node manager using the two configurations,

1. Setting org.apache.hadoop.security.HttpCrossOriginFilterInitializer to hadoop.http.filter.initializers in core-site.xml file
2. Set yarn.nodemanager.webapp.cross-origin.enabled to true in yarn-site. xml file

NodeManager Information API

The overall information about the node resource is available. HTTP request is by GET and response through JSON type.

HTTP Request:

```
GET http://<nm http address:port>/ws/v1/node/info
```

HTTP Response:

```
HTTP/1.1 200 OK
Content-Type: application/json
Transfer-Encoding: chunked
Server: Jetty(6.1.26)
```

Response Body:

```
{
    "nodeInfo": {
        "hadoopVersionBuiltOn": "Mon Jan  9 14:58:42 UTC 2012",
        "nodeManagerBuildVersion": "0.23.1-SNAPSHOT from 1228355
by user1 source checksum 20647f76c36430e888cc7204826a445c",
        "lastNodeUpdateTime": 1326222266126,
        "totalVmemAllocatedContainersMB": 17203,
        "totalVCoresAllocatedContainers": 8,
        "nodeHealthy": true,
        "healthReport": "",
        "totalPmemAllocatedContainersMB": 8192,
        "nodeManagerVersionBuiltOn": "Mon Jan  9 15:01:59 UTC
2012",
        "nodeManagerVersion": "0.23.1-SNAPSHOT",
        "id": "host.domain.com:8041",
        "hadoopBuildVersion": "0.23.1-SNAPSHOT from 1228292 by
user1 source checksum 3eba233f2248a089e9b28841a784dd00",
        "nodeHostName": "host.domain.com",
        "hadoopVersion": "0.23.1-SNAPSHOT"
    }
}
```

APPLICATION APIs

One or more application resource includes information that was run or running on the Node Manager. Request is by GET operation on the resource and JSON as response. Response header remains similar to node information. Response body of a particular application may have one container with status. More applications can be referred with multiple container resource information.

HTTP Request URI:

```
GET http://<nm http address:port>/ws/v1/node/apps
```

Response Body:

```
{
   "app": {
      "containerids": [
         "container_1326121700862_0005_01_000003",
         "container_1326121700862_0005_01_000001"
      ],
      "user": "user1",
      "id": "application_1326121700862_0005",
      "state": "RUNNING"
   }
}
```

CONTAINERS API

Container API includes one or more containers resource information that was run or running on the Node Manager. Request is by GET operation on the resource and JSON as response. Response header remains similar to node information.

HTTP Request URI:

```
GET http://<nm http address:port>/ws/v1/node /containers
```

Response Body:

```
{
   "containers": {
      "container": [
         {
            "nodeId": "host.domain.com:8041",
            "totalMemoryNeededMB": 2048,
            "totalVCoresNeeded": 1,
            "state": "RUNNING",
            "diagnostics": "",
            "containerLogsLink": "http://host.domain.com:8042/
node/containerlogs/container_1326121700862_0006_01_000001/
user1",
            "user": "user1",
            "id": "container_1326121700862_0006_ 01_000001",
            "exitCode": -1000
         },
         {
            "nodeId": "host.domain.com:8041",
            "totalMemoryNeededMB": 2048,
```

```
            "totalVCoresNeeded": 2,
            "state": "RUNNING",
            "diagnostics": "",
            "containerLogsLink": "http://host.domain.com:8042/
node/containerlogs/container_1326121700862_0006_01_000003/
user1",
            "user": "user1",
            "id": "container_1326121700862_0006 _01_000003",
            "exitCode": -1000
        }
    ]
  }
}
```

TIMELINE SERVER REST API

The timeline server can be queried using the REST API calls. There is no specific library in YARN but the Jersey client in JAVA queries and retrieves the data in a secured manner. The REST API is implemented in the root path:

```
                                GET /ws/v1/Timeline as a
Timeline web service.
```

This returns a JSON object describing server instance as,

```
                            {"About":"Timeline API"}
```

If the HTTP request is made using GET to retrieve the list of all domains of user then the request and response is given as follows:

```
GET http://localhost:8188/ws/v1/timeline/ domain?owner=alice
{
"domains":
  [
    {
    "id":"DS_DOMAIN_2",
    "owner":"alice",
    "readers":"peter",
    "writers":"john",
    "createdtime":1430425000337,
    "modifiedtime":1430425000337
    },….. ]
}
```

With the Timeline entity API, it gives the entity information for each entity based on entityType and entityId with GET request and JSON response as follows:

```
GET http://<timeline server http address:port>/ws/v1/timeline/
{entity-type}/{entity-id}
{
   "events":[
     {
     "timestamp":1430424959169,
     "eventtype":"DS_APP_ATTEMPT_START",
     "eventinfo":  {}}],
     "entitytype":"DS_APP_ATTEMPT",
     "entity":"appattempt_1430424020775_0003_000001",
     "starttime":1430424959169,
     "domain":"DS_DOMAIN_1",
     "relatedentities":  {},
     "primaryfilters":  {
         "user":["zshen"]
         },
     "otherinfo":  {}
     }  ]    }
```

With the Timeline Event API, we can obtain the event objects list for all the entities under same type. The events under every entity can be sorted based on their timestamp. The HTTP GET request and JSON response as follows:

```
GET http://<timeline server http address:port>/ws/v1/timeline/
entity%20type%200/events
{
"events": [
  {
  "entity":"appattempt_1430424020775_0003_000001",
  "entitytype":"DS_APP_ATTEMPT"}
  "events":[
     {
     "timestamp":1430424963836,
     "eventtype":"DS_APP_ATTEMPT_END",
     "eventinfo":{}},
     {
     "timestamp":1430424959169,
     "eventtype":"DS_APP_ATTEMPT_START",
     "eventinfo":{}}
     ],    }  ]    }
```

MAPREDUCE REST APIs

The mapreduce REST API allows user to view the status of a running Application Master. The information retrieved includes the details about the job that's running like number of tasks, counters, attempts. The proxy is used to access Application Master by configuring on the resource manager or any other host. The URL proxy is http://<proxy http address:port>/proxy/appid.

Mapreduce Application Master API

The Application Master information resources comprises application id, timestamp, user etc... The HTTP GET request, response as JSON type with the header and body are stated as follows:
HTTP Request URI:

```
GET http://<proxy http address:port>/proxy/application_
1326232085508_0003/ ws/v1/mapreduce/info
```

Response Header:

```
HTTP/1.1 200 OK
Content-Type: application/json
Transfer-Encoding: chunked
Server: Jetty(6.1.26)
```

Response Body:

```
{
  "info": {
      "appId": "application_1326232085508_0003",
      "startedOn": 1326238244047,
      "user": "user1",
      "name": "Sleep job",
      "elapsedTime": 32374
   }
}
```

The same request with XML response with user defined tags is by,

```
<?xml version="1.0" encoding="UTF-8" standalone="yes"?>
<info>
  <appId>application_1326232085508_0003</appId>
  <name>Sleep job</name>
```

```
    <user>user1</user>
    <startedOn>1326238244047</startedOn>
    <elapsedTime>32407</elapsedTime>
</info>
```

JOB API

This includes information resource of a particular job or jobs. Some fields define the user permission based on access control list settings. The HTTP GET request and response as JSON type are stated below. The Response header remains the same as mapreduce REST API. The response body is similar for multiple jobs API with the additional tag as jobs.

HTTP Request URI:

```
GET http://<proxy http address:port>/proxy/application_
1326232085508_0004/ws/v1/ mapreduce/jobs/job_1326232085508_4_4
```

Response Body:

```
{
    "job": {
        "runningReduceAttempts": 1,
        "reduceProgress": 100,
        "failedReduceAttempts": 0,
        "newMapAttempts": 0,
        "mapsRunning": 0,
        "state": "RUNNING",
        "successfulReduceAttempts": 0,
        "reducesRunning": 1,
        "acls": [
            {
                "value": " ",
                "name": "mapreduce.job.acl-modify-job"
            },              {
                "value": " ",
                "name": "mapreduce.job.acl-view-job"
            }          ],
        "reducesPending": 0,
        "user": "user1",
        "reducesTotal": 1,
        "mapsCompleted": 1,
        "startTime": 1326238769379,
        "id": "job_1326232085508_4_4",
```

```
      "successfulMapAttempts": 1,
      "runningMapAttempts": 0,
      "newReduceAttempts": 0,
      "name": "Sleep job",
      "mapsPending": 0,
      "elapsedTime": 59437,
      "reducesCompleted": 0,
      "mapProgress": 100,
      "diagnostics": "",
      "failedMapAttempts": 0,
      "killedReduceAttempts": 0,
      "mapsTotal": 1,
      "uberized": false,
      "killedMapAttempts": 0,
      "finishTime": 0
  }     }
```

Job Attempts API

Collection of resources that includes the job attempts. The HTTP GET request and response as JSON type are stated below. The Response header remains the same as mapreduce REST API.

HTTP Request URI:

```
GET http://<proxy http address:port>/proxy/
application _1326232085508_0004/ ws/v1/mapreduce/jobs/
job_1326232085508_4_4/jobattempts
```

Response Body:

```
{
   "jobAttempts": {
      "jobAttempt": [
          {
              "nodeId": "host.domain.com:8041",
              "nodeHttpAddress": "host.domain.com:8042",
              "startTime": 1326238773493,
              "id": 1,
              "logsLink": "http://host.domain.com:8042/node/
containerlogs/ container_1326232085508_0004_01_000001",
              "containerId":
"container_1326232085508_0004_01_000001"
          }     ]   }   }
```

Job Configuration API

It contains information resource about the job configuration. The HTTP GET request and response as JSON type are stated below. The Response header remains the same as mapreduce REST API.

HTTP Request URI:

```
GET http://<proxy http address:port>/proxy/application_
1326232085508_0004/ ws/v1/mapreduce/jobs/job_1326232085508_4_4/
conf
```

Response Body:

```
{
   "conf": {
      "path": "hdfs://host.domain.com:9000/user/user1/.staging/
job_ 1326232085508_0004/job.xml",
      "property": [
         {
            "value": "/home/hadoop/hdfs/data",
            "name": "dfs.datanode.data.dir",
            "source": ["hdfs-site.xml", "job.xml"]
         },
         {
            "value": "/home/hadoop/tmp",
            "name": "mapreduce.cluster.temp.dir"
            "source": ["mapred-site.xml"]
         },
         ...          ]    }    }
```

Job Counters API

It contains group of resources that signifies all counters for the job. The HTTP GET request and response as JSON type are stated below. The Response header remains the same as mapreduce REST API.

HTTP Request URI:

```
GET http://<proxy http address:port>/proxy/
application_1326232085508 _0004/ws/v1/ mapreduce/jobs/job
_1326232085508_4_4/counters
```

Response Body:

```
{
    "jobCounters": {
        "id": "job_1326232085508_4_4",
        "counterGroup": [
            {
                "counterGroupName": "Shuffle Errors",
                "counter": [
                    {
                        "reduceCounterValue": 0,
                        "mapCounterValue": 0,
                        "totalCounterValue": 0,
                        "name": "BAD_ID"
                    },    {
                        "reduceCounterValue": 0,
                        "mapCounterValue": 0,
                        "totalCounterValue": 0,
                        "name": "CONNECTION"
                    }, ...............
}
```

Tasks API

It contains group of resources that signifies all tasks for the job. The HTTP GET request and response as JSON type are stated below. The Response header remains the same as mapreduce REST API.

HTTP Request URI:

```
GET http://<proxy http address:port>/proxy/application
_1326232085508_0004/ws/v1/ mapreduce/jobs/job
_1326232085508_4_4/tasks
```

Response Body:

```
{
    "tasks": {
        "task": [
            {
                "progress": 100,
                "elapsedTime": 2768,
                "state": "SUCCEEDED",
                "startTime": 1326238773493,
                "id": "task_1326232085508_4_4_m_0",
                "type": "MAP",
                "successfulAttempt": "attempt_1326232085508_4_4
_m_0_0",
```

```
      "finishTime": 1326238776261
},           {
       "progress": 100,
       "elapsedTime": 0,
       "state": "RUNNING",
       "startTime": 1326238777460,
       "id": "task_1326232085508_4_4_r_0",
       "type": "REDUCE",
       "successfulAttempt": "",
       "finishTime": 0
}        ]    }      }
```

Similar to the Jobs API is the Tasks API for counters and attempts.

RESEARCH ISSUES WITH REST

REST being one of the web architecture standard, it finds its applications in various domain recently. In this chapter, the study of YARN and Hadoop APIs is done, where there is a need for the accessing the resources distributed in the internet world. To justify the need for the REST based architecture in the Hadoop and YARN, the remaining part of this section outlines some of the uses of the REST API in other related domains.

Li Li, Wu Chou et.al (2016) in their research used REST architectural as one of the prevalent choices for working with distributed resources such as northbound API of Software-Defined Networking (SDN). To meet out the changing services, the REST API also needs to be changed. They suggested a method to make hypertext-driven navigation easy and made provision to deal the changes in the API. The hypertext-driven navigation in REST APIs are addressed in three aspects: (1) First, they presented REST Chart, a Petri-Net-based REST service description framework and language to extend REST APIs, which the enable the rapid evolution of SDN northbound APIs; (2) They outlined the design patterns, within the REST Chart framework to navigate through large scale APIs; and (3) They presented differential cache mechanism in the client side to reduce the overhead of hypertext-driven navigation that affects the application of REST API. REST again find its role in northbound API of Software-Defined Networking (SDN), defining the process of accessing the network resources truly with RESTful services as proposed by Wei Zhou et.al (2014T). They made the HTTP content negotiation mechanism to allow the clients to select different representation formats to access the same resource URI. Also they exhibited the design of RESTful northbound API of SDN in the context of OpenStack.

With the evolving APIs, REST documentation became time consuming and expensive process to capture usage examples as proposed by S M Sohan el.al (2017). They addressed the cost of capturing the usage examples and benefits and insisted to need for prioritizing them. Obviously capturing the usage examples, the productivity from clients will suffer by using correct data types, formats, required HTTP headers and request body when the documentation lacks usage examples. In the applications involving with the Big Data, the primary focus will be the storage of data and applications in the distributed environment and completing the tasks earlier. Over the time the question of using data at multiple locations and platform will arise question like: what to do? Ultimately the inference from the data will be demanded. Kesinee Boonchuay et.al (2017), addressed the association rule mining to manage the jobs in an organization which are also based on several types of platforms with the challenges of interoperability issues with solution of addressing them with RESTful API.

CONCLUSION

Hence the RESTful web service approach is used along with YARN and Mapreduce as an API to retrieve the information about various resources. The HTTP request used is GET and POST, while response is by either JSON or XML type. REST API creates a series of small modules as a part of response while requesting each resource. Hence this provides the users with lot of reliability, flexibility and scalability.

REFERENCES

Boonchuay, K., Intasorn, Y., & Rattanaopas, K. (2017). Design and implementation a REST API for association rule mining. *14th International Conference on Electrical Engineering/Electronics, Computer, Telecommunications and Information Technology.* 10.1109/ECTICon.2017.8096326

Li, Chou, Zhou, & Luo. (2016). Design Patterns and Extensibility of REST API for Networking Applications. *IEEE Transactions on Network and Service Management, 13*(1), 154 – 167.

Murthy, A., Vavilapalli, V., Eadline, D., Niemiec, J., & Markham, J. (2014). *Apache Hadoop YARN: Moving beyond MapReduce and Batch Processing with Apache Hadoop 2.* Addison Wesley.

Sohan, Maurer, Anslow, & Robillard. (2017). A study of the effectiveness of usage examples in REST API documentation. *IEEE Symposium on Visual Languages and Human-Centric Computing.* 10.1109/VLHCC.2017.8103450

White, T. (2015). *Hadoop the definitive guide, O'reilly Subbu Allamaraju,(2010), RESTful Web Services Cookbook.* O'Reilly.

Zhou, W., Li, L., Luo, M., & Chou, W. (2014). EST API Design Patterns for SDN Northbound API. *2014 28th International Conference on Advanced Information Networking and Applications Workshops.* Retrieved from http://hadoop.apache.org/docs/current/hadoop-yarn

Chapter 9
Hadoop Tools

ABSTRACT

As the name indicates, this chapter explains the various additional tools provided by Hadoop. The additional tools provided by Hadoop distribution are Hadoop Streaming, Hadoop Archives, DistCp, Rumen, GridMix, and Scheduler Load Simulator. Hadoop Streaming is a utility that allows the user to have any executable or script for both mapper and reducer. Hadoop Archives is used for archiving old files and directories. DistCp is used for copying files within the cluster and also across different clusters. Rumen is the tool for extracting meaningful data from JobHistory files and analyzes it. It is used for statistical analysis. GridMix is benchmark for Hadoop. It takes a trace of job and creates a synthetic job with the same pattern as that of trace. The trace can be generated by Rumen tool. Scheduler Load Simulator is a tool for simulating different loads and scheduling methods like FIFO, Fair Scheduler, etc. This chapter explains all the tools and gives the syntax of various commands for each tool. After reading this chapter, the reader will be able to use all these tools effectively.

INTRODUCTION

The core part of the Hadoop is MapReduce which supports distributed processing of huge amount of data in a cluster of commodity machines. Another major part is Hadoop Distributed File System (HDFS) which maintains the needed file system. Although the HDFS and MapReduce support the major operations, additional tools are provided to support the users. This chapter describes all the additional tools available and how each one can be used.

DOI: 10.4018/978-1-5225-3790-8.ch009

BACKGROUND

Even though Hadoop framework supports all necessary functions for distributed processing, some more tools are needed. The archiving of data, running executable files and more data analysis are needed for efficient processing. Also benchmarking has to be done. These additional functionalities are provided with the help of some tools. Those tools are described in this chapter.

TOOLS

The additional tools provided by the Hadoop distribution are:

- Hadoop Streaming
- Hadoop Archives
- DistCp
- Rumen
- Gridmix
- Scheduler Load Simulator
- Benchmarking

Let us see all these tools one by one in detail.

HADOOP STREAMING

Hadoop streaming is a utility that is used to create and run Map/Reduce jobs with any executable or script as the mapper and/or the reducer.

Working of Hadoop Streaming

Both mapper and reducer can be executables. These executables read the input line by line from stdin and gives the output to stdout. When the mapper is initialized, each mapper task will launch the executable as a separate process. The mapper tasks covert its input into lines and feed them to stdin. The mapper collects lines from stdout of the process and coverts each line to key, value pair. This key, value pair is output of the mapper.

The reducer tasks convert its input key,value pairs into lines and feed them to stdin. The reducer collects line oriented output from stdout of the process and converts each line to key, value pair. This key, value pair is output of the reducer. This is the basis for the communication protocol between the Map/ Reduce framework and the streaming mapper/reducer.

The streaming tasks exiting with non-zero status are considered to be failed tasks. The user can indicate this by setting stream.non.zero.exit.is.failure to be true or false. By default, it is true.

Streaming Commands

The streaming commands are of the following form:

```
hadoop command [genericOptions] [streamingOptions]
```

The generic options must be placed before streaming options.

Required Streaming Parameters

The required streaming options are described in the Table 1.

Optional Streaming Parameters

The optional streaming parameters are described in the Table 2.

Example for Hadoop Streaming

```
hadoop jar hadoop-streaming-2.8.0.jar \
-input InputDirs \
-output  OutputDir \
-inputformat org.apache.hadoop.mapred.KeyValueTextInputFormat \
-mapper  /usr/bin/CountMap \
-reducer  /usr/bin/CountReduce
```

Table 1. Required Streaming parameters

Sl. No.	Required Parameters	Description
1.	-input directoryname or filename	Input location for mapper
2.	-output directoryname	Output location for mapper

Table 2. Optional Streaming parameters

Sl. No.	Optional Parameters	Description
1.	-mapper Executable or JavaClassName	Mapper executable; If not indicated, IdentityMapper is used by default.
2.	-reducer Executable or JavaClassName	Reducer executable; If not indicated, IdentityReducer is used by default.
3.	-file FileName	Mapper or Reducer or Combiner available locally in a file
4.	-inputformat JavaClassName	Class for format of returning key,value pairs. If not specified, TextInputFormat is used by default.
5.	-outputformat JavaClassName	Class for format of storing key,value pairs. If not specified, TextOutputFormat is used by default.
6.	-partitioner JavaClassName	Partitioner executable for reduce input
7.	-combiner streamingCommand or JavaClassName	Combiner executable for map output
8.	-cmdenv name = value	Passing environment variables to streaming commands
9.	-inputreader	RecordReader class (for backward compatibility)
10.	-verbose	Wording output
11.	-numReduceTasks	Specify the number of reducers
12.	-mapdebug	Script to be called if map task fails
13.	-reducedebug	Script to be called if reduce task fails
14.	-lazyOutput	Creating output at a later time. Eg: If FileOutputFormat is used, output is created only after Context.write is called.

Here "InputDirs" is the directory names where input is available. "OutputDir" is the directory where output must be stored. The mapper executable is available in /usr/bin/CountMap and the reducer executable is available in /usr/bin/CountReduce. The input format is specified as KeyValueTextInputFormat.

Example 2

The executables need not pre-exist on the machines. The "-file" option can be used to tell the framework to pack executable files. The example for the command with "-file" option is:

```
hadoop jar hadoop-streaming-2.8.0.jar \
-input InputDirs \
-output  OutputDir \
-inputformat org.apache.hadoop.mapred.KeyValueTextInputFormat \
-mapper  /usr/bin/CountMap \
```

```
-reducer  /usr/bin/CountReduce \
-file  myScript
```

In addition to executable files, the other auxiliary files such as dictionaries, configuration files, etc which may be used by the mapper /the reducer can also be indicated.

Example 3

The example for Hadoop streaming with more options is:

```
hadoop jar hadoop-streaming-2.8.0.jar \
-input InputDirs \
-output  OutputDir \
-inputformat org.apache.hadoop.mapred.KeyValueTextInputFormat \
-mapper  /usr/bin/CountMap \
-reducer  /usr/bin/CountReduce \
-file  myScript\
-outputFormat \   org.apache.hadoop.mapreduce.lib.output.
TextOutputFormat\
-partitioner PartitionerClass \
-combiner  CombinerClass\
-cmdenv EXAMPLE_DIR = /home/example/dictionaries/
```

Generic Command Options

The generic command options supported by Hadoop streaming are indicated in Table 3.

Table 3. Generic Streaming parameters

Sl. No.	Generic Optional Parameters	Description
1.	-conf configurationFile	Specifying application configuration file
2.	-fs host:port or local	Specifying NameNode
3.	-files	Comma separated files to be copied into the cluster
4.	-libjars	Comma separated jar files to be included in the classpath
5.	-D property = value	Indicating directory and assigning value for any property
6.	-archives	Comma separated archives to be unarchived

Specifying Directories

To change the local temporary directory to "tmp"

```
-D dfs.data.dir = /tmp
```

To specify additional local temporary directories:

```
-D mapred.local.dir=/tmp/localDir
-D mapred.system.dir=/tmp/systemDir
-D mapred.temp.dir=/tmp/tempDir
```

To specify the number of reducers:

```
-D mapreduce.job.reduces = 2
-D mapreduce.job.reduces = 0 (or) -reducer NONE
```

Customizing Splitting of Lines

The stdout of the mapper is read as line to be split as key/value pair by the Map/Reduce framework. The string from the first column to the first tab character is treated as key and rest of the line is taken as its value. Instead of the tab character, some other field separator is also possible. In addition, the extraction of the key can be specified by a position of the separator into the line other than the first separator character.

Example:

```
hadoop jar hadoop-streaming-2.8.0.jar \
  -D stream.map.output.field.separator=, \
  -D stream.num.map.output.key.fields=3 \
```

In this case the separator is comma (,) and the key will be extracted up to the third comma in a line. Similar principle is used for the input also as follows:

```
-D stream.map.input.field.separator=, \
  -D stream.num.map.input.key.fields=3 \
```

The options -files and –archives enables the files and archives to be available to the tasks. The URI of the files or archives that are already loaded is used to specify them. These files and archives will be cached so that another job can make use of it. The NameNode and the service is specified by the hostname:portnumber, which can be retrieved the fs.default.name config variable.

As we have already seen, the option –files informs the list of file(s) to be copied into the cluster.

```
-files hdfs://host:fs_port/user/firstfile.txt
-files hdfs://host:fs_port/user/firstfile.txt#onefile
-files hdfs://host:fs_port/user/firstfile.txt, hdfs://host:fs_
port/user/secondfile.txt
-files hdfs://host:fs_port/user/ firstfile.txt, hdfs://host:fs_
port/user/ secondfile.txt#twofiles
```

The terms *onefile* and *twofiles* are the symbolic names for the above mentioned files:

```
hadoop jar hadoop-streaming-2.8.0.jar \
                -archives 'hdfs://hadoop-nn1.example.com/user/
me/samples/cachefile/cachedir.jar' \
                -D mapreduce.job.maps=1 \
                -D mapreduce.job.reduces=1 \
                -D mapreduce.job.name="Experiment" \
                -input "/user/me/samples/cachefile/input.txt" \
                -output "/user/me/samples/cachefile/out" \
                -mapper "xargs cat" \
                -reducer "cat"
```

Example to Demonstrate the Working With Hadoop Streaming Concept

There are two text files (Rama.txt and Sita.txt are placed into a directory Input) to be concatenated into a single file.

The command to view these files is:

```
$ ls Input/
Rama.txt   Sita.txt
```

These two files are archived as JAR file as follows:

```
$ jar cvf RamaSita.jar -C Input/ .
added manifest
adding: Rama.txt(in = 30) (out= 29)(deflated 3%)
adding: Sita.txt(in = 37) (out= 35)(deflated 5%)
```

The archived Jar file is copied into a new directory called *Work* using the command:

```
$ hdfs dfs -put RamaSita.jar samples/Work
```

The list of the files to be concatenated is stored in a file called In.txt, which can be listed as follows:

```
$ hdfs dfs -cat /user/me/samples/Work/In.txt
RamaSita.jar/Rama.txt
RamaSita.jar/Sita.txt
```

To view and visualize the contents of the files, the commands are executed as follows:

```
$ cat Input/Rama.txt
I am Rama, Hero of Ramayana
$ cat Input/Sita.txt
I am Sita, Heroine of Ramayana
```

After storing the necessary files in the folders, the following Hadoop streaming command is executed as follows:

```
hadoop jar hadoop-streaming-2.8.0.jar \
 -archives 'hdfs://hadoop-n1.example.com/user/me/samples/Work/
RamaSita.jar' \
                -D mapreduce.job.maps=1 \
                -D mapreduce.job.reduces=1 \
                -D mapreduce.job.name="StreamingExperiment" \
                -input "/user/me/samples/Work/In.txt" \
                -output "/user/me/samples/Work/out" \
                -mapper "xargs cat" \
                -reducer "cat"
```

After executing the command, the result can be viewed using the command as follows:

```
$ hdfs dfs -ls /user/me/samples/Work/out
Found 2 items
-rw-r--r--* 1 me supergroup 0 2013-11-14 17:00
                                /user/me/samples/cachefile/
Out/_SUCCESS
-rw-r--r--* 1 me supergroup 69 2013-11-14 17:00
                                /user/me/samples/Work/Out/
```

```
part-00000
$ hdfs dfs -cat /user/me/samples/Work/Out/part-00000
I am Rama, Hero of Ramayana
I am Sita, Heroine of Ramayana
```

Additional Streaming Classes

Hadoop has some library classes which are useful for certain purposes. Some of them are:

- Hadoop Partitioner Class
- Hadoop Comparator Class
- Hadoop Aggregate
- Hadoop Field Selection Class

The details about these classes are as follows:

Hadoop Partitioner Class

This class is based on a class KeyFieldBasedPartitioner. It is useful to partition map outputs based on certain key fields. An example is given below:

```
hadoop jar hadoop-streaming-2.8.0.jar \
   -D stream.map.output.field.separator=. \
   -D stream.num.map.output.key.fields=4 \
   -D map.output.key.field.separator=. \
   -D mapreduce.partition.keypartitioner.options=-k1,2 \
   -D mapreduce.job.reduces=12 \
   -input myInputDirs \
   -output myOutputDir \
   -mapper /bin/cat \
   -reducer /bin/cat \
   -partitioner org.apache.hadoop.mapred.lib.
KeyFieldBasedPartitioner
```

The option "-D stream.map.output.field.separator=." indicates that the separator is ".".

The option "-D stream.num.map.output.key.fields=4" indicates that the map output keys of the Map/Reduce job have four fields separated by "."

The option "-D mapreduce.partition.keypartitioner.options=-k1,2" indicates that the framework will partition the map outputs by the first two fields of the keys.

Table 4 shows a set of six data with four keys as shown in the first column. The second shows the partitioning of the keys with respect to the first two keys. The third column sort the keys within each partitioning.

Hadoop Comparator Class

This class provides facilities for sorting with appropriate specification. The command to be executed is:

```
hadoop jar hadoop-streaming-2.8.0.jar \
-D mapreduce.job.output.key.comparator.class=org.apache.hadoop.
mapreduce. \ lib.partition.KeyFieldBasedComparator \
   -D stream.map.output.field.separator=. \
   -D stream.num.map.output.key.fields=4 \
   -D mapreduce.map.output.key.field.separator=. \
   -D mapreduce.partition.keycomparator.options=-k2,2nr \
   -D mapreduce.job.reduces=1 \
   -input myInputDirs \
   -output myOutputDir \
   -mapper /bin/cat \
   -reducer /bin/cat
.option=-k2,2nr indicates the sorting to be done based on the
second key for the numerical values and the sorted values must
be in reverse order.
```

An example is as shown in Table 5.

Hadoop Aggregate Package

This package provides the facilities for the aggregation of the collection of values. Some of the aggregate operations are: sum, min, max etc.

Table 4. Example for the portioning and Sorting

Keys Without Partitioning	Partitioning With First Two Keys	Sorting Within the Partitioning
23.12.45.23	22.45.34.56	22.45.22.10
45.65.23.11	22.45.22. 10	22.45.34.56
23.12.55.33	23.12.45.23	23.12.45.23
45.65.20.70	23.12.55.33	23.12.55.33
22.45.34.56	45.65.20.70	45.65.20.70
22.45.22.10	45.65.23.11	45.65.23.11

Table 5. Sorting of keys using Comparator class

Keys Without Sorting	Keys After Sorting
23.12.45.23 23.65.23.11 23.12.55.33 23.65.20.70 23.45.34.56 23.45.22.10	23.12.55.33 23.12.45.23 23.45.34.56 23.45.22.10 23.65.20.70 23.65.23.11

The Hadoop example is as shown below:

```
hadoop jar hadoop-streaming-2.8.0.jar \
  -input myInputDirs \
  -output myOutputDir \
  -mapper myAggregatorForKeyCount.py \
  -reducer aggregate \
  -file myAggregatorForKeyCount.py \
```

For working with the aggregator operations a python code is used as the specification and *"-reducer aggregate"* does the job.

Hadoop Field Selection Class

This is similar to one of the Linux Command like "cut". By using this class, the field and its associated key value pair could be selected. By appropriately configuring, any arbitrary keys and values of the keys can be selected. The command for doing the field selection is as follows:

```
hadoop jar hadoop-streaming-2.8.0.jar \
  -D mapreduce.map.output.key.field.separator=. \
  -D mapreduce.partition.keypartitioner.options=-k1,2 \
  -D mapreduce.fieldsel.data.field.separator=. \
  -D mapreduce.fieldsel.map.output.key.value.fields.spec=6,5,1-
3:0- \
  -D mapreduce.fieldsel.reduce.output.key.value.fields.spec=0-
2:5- \
  -D mapreduce.map.output.key.class=org.apache.hadoop.io.Text \
  -D mapreduce.job.reduces=12 \
  -input myInputDirs \
  -output myOutputDir \
  -mapper org.apache.hadoop.mapred.lib.FieldSelectionMapReduce
\
  -reducer org.apache.hadoop.mapred.lib.FieldSelectionMapReduce
\
```

```
-partitioner org.apache.hadoop.mapred.lib.
KeyFieldBasedPartitioner
```

Hadoop Archives

A Hadoop archive maps to a file system directory. A Hadoop archive has a *.har extension. The archive directory contains the following two parts:

- Metadata
- Data

The metadata consists of _index and _masterindex files. The _index file contains the name of files and its index i.e. location within the data file. The data consists of part_* files.

Since the archives are immutable, the operations such as create, delete, renames return error.

Creating an Archive

An archive can be created with the following command:

```
hadoop archive -archiveName name -p <parent> [-r <replication
factor>] <src>* <dest>
```

- Where 'name' is the name of the archive to be created
- '-p' is used to indicate the parent path and relative paths to the parent
- '-r' indicates the replication factor; By default, it is 3
- 'SRC' indicates the source of the files to be archived
- 'Dest' indicates the destination where archive is to be stored

Example: For creating an archive of the directories 'myFiles1' and 'myFiles2' in /usr/myFiles with the name 'archiFiles', the command is:

```
hadoop archive -archiveName archiFiles.har -p /usr/myFiles
myFiles1 myFiles2  -r 3 /destDir
```

The archive is stored in 'destDir' directory. Depending on whether the file is in secure zone or not, the file will be encrypted or decrypted matching to the area under storage.

Looking Up Files in Archives

All the file system commands work in the archives also except with the different URI, whose format is given as:

```
har://scheme-hostname:port/archivepath/fileinarchive
If scheme is not provided it assumes the underlying file
system, where the URI is as follows:
har:///archivepath/fileinarchive
```

For looking up files, the command *ls* and *lsr* are used as that in the conventional commands.

Unarchiving an Archive

Unarchive is like the copy commands. The command cp and distcp indicates copying the files in a sequence and in parallel respectively. The syntax for cp and distcp is as follows:

```
hdfs dfs -cp har:///user/zoo/foo.har/dir1 hdfs:/user/zoo/newdir
hadoop distcp har:///user/zoo/foo.har/dir1 hdfs:/user/zoo/
newdir
```

Archive Logs

Large number of YARN aggregate logs from multiple clusters could be aggregated to reduce the burden of maintaining many small files. Job History server can read the aggregated logs in Hadoop archives and using "yarn logs" command.

The syntax to archive the log is:

```
mapred archive-logs options
```

Options

- **Force:** Force recreating the folder if it already exists
- **Help:** Displays the help message
- **MaxEligibleApps <n>:** Maximum number of eligible applications to process
  - ◦ (default: -1 all applications)

- maxTotalLogsSize
- **<Megabytes>:** Max log size (Default: 1024)
- **Memory <megabytes>:** Amount of memory for each container (default: 1024)
- **MinNumberLogFiles <n>:** Minimum of log files (default: 20)
- **NoProxy:** Decides to delegate the application or to do it by itself
- **Verbose:** Print more details

Distributed Copy (DistCp)

The DistCp is a tool used for intra/inter cluster copying. It uses MapReduce for its copying, error handling and reporting. The list of directories/files is given to map tasks. Each map will copy a portion of file in parallel. Each Node Manager can have communication with both source and destination file system. Both source and destination must run the same version /compatible version of protocols.

Failure of Distributed Copying

The DistCp uses both Map/Reduce and FileSystem API. Hence any issues in any one of them would affect distributed copying. It is the responsibility of the user to check if the copying is done properly or not. The distributed copying will fail in the following cases:

1. If another client is still writing to source file
2. If another client is still writing to destination file
3. If source file is moved/removed before copying (FileNotFoundException is thrown)

Architecture of DistCp

The three major components of DistCp are:

1. Copy-listing Generator
2. DistCp driver
3. InputFormats and Map-Reduce components

Copy-Listing Generator

The list of directories/files to be copied is created by copy-listing-generator classes. They create a SequenceFile which contains all the source-paths including wildcards after testing its content.

This SequenceFile is used by Hadoop Job for parallel copying. The main classes used are:

- **CopyListing:** It is an interface. Any copy listing generator class must implement this interface.
- It provides the factory method which is used to choose the CopyListing implementation.
- **SimpleCopyListing:** It is an implementation of *CopyListing*. It accepts different source paths containing directories and files. It recursively lists all directories and files for copying.
- **GlobbedCopyListing:** It is also an implementation of *CopyListing*. It expands wild-cards in the source paths. The expansions are forwarded to *SimpleCopyListing*. Then the *SimpleCopyListing* onstructs the entire listing. It is used when there is no listing of source files.
- **FileBasedCopyListing:** It is also an implementation of *CopyListing*. But it reads the source path list from a specified file. After reading the source path list, it is forwarded to *GlobbedCopyListing*. Then it is implemented by *GlobbedCopyListing*.

It is also possible for the user to customize the method for copy-listing by extending the *CopyListing* interface. The file size and checksum check are done by MapReduce jobs only and hence time is saved.

DistCp Driver

The major works done by DistCp driver are:

- **Parsing the Arguments:** The arguments passed to DistCp through command line are parsed using OptionsParser and DistCpOptionsSwitch
- **Initializing *DistCp*:** The following command arguments are taken:
  - Source paths
  - Target location
  - Copy Options: Update or overwrite or append, which file attributes to preserve, etc.

These arguments are assembled into a *DistCpOptions* object. The DistCp is initialized with *DistCpOptions* object.

- **Orchestrating Copy Operation:** The appropriate copy-listing-generator is initiated to generate the list of files to be copied. The Map-Reduce job is launched to carry out the copying operation in parallel. Based on the option indicated by the user, a handle is returned to Hadoop MapReduce immediately or the waiting is done till the job completes.

InputFormats and Map-Reduce Components

The InputFormats and MapReduce components are responsible for implementing the actual copying operation. The following classes are used as indicated:

- **UniformSizeInputFormat:** The listing file is split into groups of paths such that the sum of file sizes in each InputSplit is almost equal to that of other maps. The splitting is not 100% correct but tries to do better. The uniform splitting reduces the setup time.
- **DynamicInputFormat and DynamicRecordReader:** The *DynamicInputFormat* splits the listing file into several chunk-files using rg.apache.hadoop.mapreduce.InputFormat. The number of chunk-files is a multiple of the number of maps. Each map is assigned one of the chunk-files. The paths from chunk are read by *DynamicRecordReader* and processed in CopyMapper. After processing all paths in a chunk, the chunk is deleted. Then tha map acquires a new chunk and processes it. This procedure is repeated until all chunks are processed. This method allows faster maps to process more number of chunks than that of slower ones. Hence the overall speed is increased.
- **CopyMapper:** This class implements the actual file copy. The input paths are checked against the input options to decide whether copying is needed. The file will be copied if at least one of the following is true:
  - A file with same name does not exist in the target
  - A file with same name exists in the target but with different size
  - A file with same name exists in the target but overwrite is indicated
  - A file with same name exists in the target but with different block size

- A file with same name exists in the target but with different checksum and -skipcrccheck is not mentioned
- **CopyCommitter:** The *CopyCommitter* implements the commit phase and does:
  - Preserving directory permissions (if mentioned in options)
  - Cleaning temporary files, working directories, etc.

Inter-Cluster Copying

The example for inter-cluster copying is shown as follows:

```
bash$ Hadoop distcp hdfs://nn1:8020/CopyDir/AllFiles \
        hdfs://nn10:8020/DestiFiles/myFiles
```

For executing this command, the NameSpace under /CopyDir/AllFiles in nn1 is expanded into a temporary file. Then it partitions its content into a set of map tasks. These map tasks copy the files from nn1 to nn10 using NodeManagers.

Copying From Multiple Source Directories

Multiple directories can be indicated on the source side. If the files already exist at the destination, it is not replaced but just skipped. If two sources collide, DistCp will abort the copy with an error message. The collisions at the destination will be processed according to the options indicated.

Eg:

```
bash$ Hadoop distcp hdfs://nn1:8020/CopyDir/AllFiles \
                hdfs://nn1:8020/CopyDir/DitinctFiles\
        hdfs://nn10:8020/DestiFiles/myFiles
```

Copying From File

For copying from file, -f option is used.

Eg:

```
'copyList' contains the following three files:
nn1:8020/CopyDir/AllFiles\File1
nn1:8020/CopyDir/AllFiles\File2
nn1:8020/CopyDir/AllFiles\File3
```

Then it can be copied as:

```
bash$ Hadoop distcp -f hdfs://nn1:8020/copyList \
        hdfs://nn10:8020/DestiFiles/myFiles
```

Copying With Update

The –update option is used to copy files that do not exist at the target or different from target version. It overwrites if source and destination differ in size, block size or checksum.

Example:

Consider a source from nn1 with the following files:

```
hdfs://nn1:8020/sourceFiles/eg1/1
hdfs://nn1:8020/sourceFiles/eg1/2
hdfs://nn1:8020/sourceFiles/eg2/11
hdfs://nn1:8020/sourceFiles/eg2/22
```

If DistCp is invoked without –update option as follows,

```
bash$ Hadoop distcp hdfs://nn1:8020/sourceFiles/eg1 \
                hdfs://nn1:8020/sourceFiles/eg2 \
                hdfs://nn10:8020/target
then
```

DistCp will create directories 'eg1' and 'eg2' under 'target' in destination machine. After copying, the 'target' directory will contain the following:

```
hdfs://nn10:8020/target/eg1/1
hdfs://nn10:8020/target/eg1/2
hdfs://nn10:8020/target/eg2/11
hdfs://nn10:8020/target/eg2/22
If -update option is used as follows:
bash$ Hadoop distcp -update hdfs://nn1:8020/sourceFiles/eg1 \
                hdfs://nn1:8020/sourceFiles/eg2 \
                hdfs://nn10:8020/target
```

then the contents of the directories are copied into the destination. But directories from source are not copied. After copying, the 'target' directory will contain the following:

```
hdfs://nn10:8020/target/1
hdfs://nn10:8020/target/2
```

```
hdfs://nn10:8020/target/11
hdfs://nn10:8020/target/22
```

If the source folders 'eg1' and 'eg2' contain the files with same number (Eg:2), then both sources would map to the same entry at the destination. Hence DistCp will abort.

Copying With Different Sizes

Consider the above example again with sizes as follows:
Sizes in Source:

```
hdfs://nn1:8020/sourceFiles/eg1/1    32
hdfs://nn1:8020/sourceFiles/eg1/2    32
hdfs://nn1:8020/sourceFiles/eg2/11   64
hdfs://nn1:8020/sourceFiles/eg2/22   32
```

Sizes in Target:

```
hdfs://nn10:8020/target/1    32 (contents  same as that of
                                hdfs://nn1:8020/sourceFiles/
eg1/1)
hdfs://nn10:8020/target/11   32
hdfs://nn10:8020/target/22   64
```

If distcp command is used:

- 1 is skipped because file length and content both are same
- 2 is copied because it does not exist in destination
- 11 and 22 are overwritten because contents are not same as that of source

If distcp command with –update option is used:
The results will be same as that for distcp command alone.
If distcp command with –append option is used, then:

- 1 is skipped because file length and content both are same
- 2 is copied because it does not exist in destination
- 11 is overwritten because source length is less than that of destination
- 22 is appended with changes in file (if files match up to destination's original length)

Copying With Overwrite

The –overwrite option overwrites the files in the target, if they already exist. If –overwrite option is used as follows:

```
bash$ Hadoop distcp -overwrite hdfs://nn1:8020/sourceFiles/eg1
\
                    hdfs://nn1:8020/sourceFiles/eg2 \
                    hdfs://nn10:8020/target
```

then the contents of the directories are copied into the destination. But directories from source are not copied. After copying, the 'target' directory will contain the following:

```
hdfs://nn10:8020/target/1
hdfs://nn10:8020/target/2
hdfs://nn10:8020/target/11
hdfs://nn10:8020/target/22
```

Considering the size of the files as similar to that of previous example: If distcp command with –overwrite option is used, then:

- 1 is also overwritten even though file length and content both are same.
- 2 is copied because it does not exist in destination.
- 11 is overwritten because source length is less than that of destination.
- 22 is appended with changes in file (if files match up to destination's original length).

Raw Namespace Extended Attributes Preservation

The system internal functions such as encryption of meta data use 'raw' Namespace extended attributes. These extended attributes (Xattr) are visible to users only when accessed through the /.reserved/raw hierarchy. The raw extended attributes are preserved based solely on whether /.reserved/raw prefixes are supplied. To prevent raw extended attributes from being preserved, the /.reserved/raw prefix is not used on any of the source and target paths. If the /.reserved/rawprefix is specified on only a subset of the source and target paths, an error will be displayed and a non-0 exit code returned.

Copying Between Versions of HDFS

WebHdfsFileSystem is used for copying between two different major versions of Hadoop (e.g. between 1.X and 2.X). It is available for both read and write operations. The remote cluster is specified as webhdfs://<namenode_hostname>:<http_port>. Similarly the "swebhdfs://" is used when webhdfs has to be secured with SSL. When copying between same major versions of Hadoop cluster (e.g. between 2.X and 2.X), hdfs protocol can be used.

MapReduce and Side- Effects

If a map fails to copy one of its inputs, then the following side-effects will be there:

- If a map fails more than the maximum number of attempts (indicated by mapreduce.map,maxattempts), the remaining map tasks will be killed.
- The files already copied by previous maps are marked as "skipped" unless –overwrite option is indicated.
- If speculative operation is set (using mapreduce.map.speculative), the result is undefined.

SSL Configurations for HSFTP Sources

If Hybrid SSH FTP (HSFTP) source is to be used using hsftp protocol, the SSL configuration file has to be specified using –mapredSslConf option. The SSL configuration file must be in the class-path of DistCp. The following three parameters are to be configured in SSL configuration file:

- The local-filesystem location of the trust-store file, containing the certificate for the NameNode using ssl.client.truststore.location
- The format of the trust-store file (optional) using ssl.client.truststore. type
- Password for the trust-store file (optional) using ssl.client.truststore. password

DistCp and ObjectStores

The DistCp can work with object stores such as Amazon S3, Azure WSAB and Openstack Swift. The prerequisites for working with the above mentioned object stores are as follows:

- On the class path, the JAR containing the object store implementation and its dependencies must be present.
- The object store clients must be self registering ie. The jar must automatically register its bundled filesystem. Otherwise, the configuration file needs to be modified accordingly.
- The relevant object store access credentials must be available in the cluster configuration, or in all cluster hosts.

For uploading the data, the command is:

```
hadoop distcp hdfs://nn1:8020/fileSets/eg1 s3a://bucket/
datasets/set1
```

For downloading the data:

```
hadoop distcp s3a://bucket/coded/results hdfs://nn1:8020/
outputs
```

For copying data between object stores:

```
hadoop distcp s3a://bucket/coded/results\
             wasb://copyUpdates@eg1.blob.core.windows.net
```

For Copying data within an object store:

```
hadoop distcp wasb://copyUpdates@eg1.blob.core.windows.net/new
             wasb://copyUpdates@eg1.blob.core.windows.net/older
```

For updating (copying only changed files):

```
hadoop distcp -update -numListstatusThreads 16  \
   swift://history.cluster1/2016 \
   hdfs://nn1:8020/dataFolder/2017
```

Command Line Options

The various command line options for distcp are described in the Table 6.

Table 6. Command Line options for DistCp

Sl.No.	Flag	Description
1.	-p [rbugpcaxt]	• Preserving r – replication factor ; b – block size ▪ u – user ; g – group ; p –permission; ▪ c – checksum type; a – ACL; x – Xattr; ▪ t – timestamp; • When –update is specified, the status updates will not be synchronized, if files are not re-created. • If –pa is specified, DistCp preserves permission Also because ACLs are supersets of permission
2.	-i	Ignore failures; But it maintains logs of failures. It provides more accurate statistics for copying.
3.	-log <LogDir>	Writes logs to LogDir. If map fails, the log will not be maintained for re-execution.
4.	-m <num_maps>	Maximum number of maps to copy data
5.	-f <urilist_uri>	The list at <urilist_uri> will be used as source list. The urilist_uri must be a fully qualified URI.
6.	-filters	Filters certain paths from copying. A file containing list of patterns (one pattern per line) is indicated. The paths matching these patterns will be excluded from copying.
7.	-delete	Delete the files existing in destination but not in source. The deletion is done by FS shell.
8.	-strategy {dynamic | uniformsize}	Uniformsize – copying of the total files is uniformally divided among all maps. Dynamic – All maps use DynamicInputFormat for copying . Default is uniformsize.
9.	-bandwidth	Specifying the maximum bandwidth (MB/sec) to be used by each map. The map throttles its bandwidth so that the net bandwidth will be within the limit.
10.	-atomic {-tmp <tmp_dir> }	Making DistCp to copy the source data to a temporary target location and then move from temporary location to final target location atomically. Optionally the temporary directory can be mentioned with –tmp option. This temporary directory must be on the final target cluster.
11.	-async	Running DistCp asynchronously. As soon as Hadoop Job is launched, it is quit. Job-id is logged for tracking.
12.	-diff <fromSnapShot> <toSnapShot>	Use snapshot differences to identify the differences between source and target. Two snapshots s1 and s2 are created on the source FS. The difference between s1 and s2 will be copied to target FS.
13.	-numListstatusThreads	Number of threads to be used for file listing. Maximum number of threads is 40.
14.	-skipcrccheck	Whether CRC check can be skipped between source and target
15.	-mapredSslconf <ssl_conf_file>	When using HSFTP protocol with source, the security related properties are specified in the configuration file ssl_conf_file.

RUMEN

Rumen is a data extraction and analysis tool for Hadoop. Extracting meaningful data from JobHistory logs is more essential for Hadoop environment. It is hard to write a tool which can tightly couple with Hadoop. Hence it is better to have a built-in tool for performing log parsing and analysis. Also the benchmarking and simulation tools may need statistical analysis of various attributes of MapReduce jobs such as task runtimes, task failures, etc. Rumen generates Cumulative Distribution Functions (CDF) for the Map/Reduce task runtimes. The CDF is also used for extrapolating the runtime of incomplete, missing and synthetic tasks.

Rumen mines JobHistory logs to extract meaningful data and stores it in an easily parsed,condensed format called "digest". It performs a statistical analysis of the digest to estimate the variables that are not supplied by traces. Rumen traces drive both GridMix (a benchmark of Hadoop MapReduce clusters) and Mumak (a simulator for JobTracker).

Components of Rumen

There are two components of Rumen. They are Trace builder and Folder.

Trace Builder

It converts JobHistory logs into an easily-parsed format. It outputs the trace in JSON (JavaScript Object Notation) format. The JSON data is written as name/value pairs. It consists of a field name in double quotes followed by a colon followed by value.

Example 1

```
{ "name": "John"}
```

Example 2

```
{"id": 1001, "name": "Ram"}
```

Example 3: Array Called faculty

```
{"faculty": [
{ "name": "Raj", "Dept": "EEE"},
{ "name": "Kamal", "Dept": "ECE"},
{ "name": "Nirma", "Dept": "CSE"}
] }
```

Folder

The trace obtained from *TraceBulder* simply summarizes the jobs in input folders and files. The Folder is a utility to scale the input trace. The time span within which all jobs in a given trace finish is called the runtime of trace. The Folder can be used to scale the run time of trace. If the trace runtime is decreased, some jobs may drop and the runtime of remaining jobs will be scaled down. If the trace runtime is increased, some dummy jobs may be added and the runtime of jobs will be scaled up.

Using Rumen

The JobHistory logs can be converted into the desired job-trace. It consists of two steps:

1. Extracting the information from JobHistory logs into an intermediate format – It is one time job. It is called "Gold Trace". The extracted information can be reused multiple times.
2. Adjusting the job trace obtained from intermediate trace to have desired properties – The "Gold Trace" can be reused to generate traces with desired values of properties.

The two basic commands provided by Rumen are:

1. TraceBuilder
2. Folder

TraceBuilder

The TraceBuilder converts JobHistory files into a series of JSON objects . It then writes JSON objects into <jobtrace-output> file. It also extracts the cluster layout (topology) and writes it in <topology-output> file. The

<inputs> represents a space separated list of JobHistory folders and files. The input and output of TraceBuilder must be fully qualified FileSystem path. Hence file:// is used to indicate files on local file system and hdfs:// is used to indicate files on HDFS. The input files or folders are FileSystem paths and hence they can be globbed. It is useful for specifying multiple paths using regular expression.

Only the files that are placed under the input folder will be considered for generating the trace. To add all the files under input directory by recursively scanning, the option ' –recursive' must be used.

The cluster topology is used:

1. To reconstruct the splits and make sure that the distances/latencies seen in the actual run are modeled correctly.
2. To extrapolate splits information for tasks with missing splits or synthetically generated tasks.

The syntax of TraceBuilder command is:

```
java org.apache.hadoop.tools.rumen.TraceBuilder [options]
<jobtrace-output> <topology-output> <inputs>
```

The options for TraceBuilder command are explained in Table 7.

Example for TraceBuilder

```
java org.apache.hadoop.tools.rumen.TraceBuilder \
  file:///tmp/job1-trace.json \
  file:///tmp/job1-topology.json \
  hdfs:///tmp/hadoop-yarn/staging/history/done_intermediate/
user1
```

Table 7. Options for TraceBuilder command

Sl. No.	Parameter	Description
1.	Demuxer	It is used to read the JobHistory files. The default is DefaultInputDemuxer. The JobHistory logs and job configuration files are smaller in size. They can be easily embedded in some container file format like SequenceFile or TFile. To store like that, one can write customized demuxer class.
2.	Recursive	It is used to inform TraceBuilder to recursively traverse input paths for JobHistory logs and process all files. By default, only the files under input folder are used for generating the trace.

This command will analyse all the jobs in *tmp/hadoop-yarn/staging/history/ done_intermediate/user1* stored in HDFS file system. It outputs the job traces in /tmp/job1-trace.json along with topology information in /tmp/job1-topology. json stored on local filesystem.

Folder

The Folding means that the output duration of the resulting trace is fixed and job timelines are adjusted to respect the final output duration. The command for invoking Folder utility is:

```
java org.apache.hadoop.tools.rumen.Folder [options] [input]
[output]
```

The options for Folder command are explained in Table 8.

Table 8. Options for Folder command

Sl. No.	Parameter	Description
1.	Input-cycle	It defines the basic unit of time for Folding operation. This value must be provided. Eg: -input-cycle 10 m implies that the whole trace run will be sliced at 10 min interval. The possible time units are m-minutes, h-hours, d – days.
2.	Output-duration	It defines the final runtime of the trace. The default value is 1 hour. Eg: -output-duration 30m implies that the resulting trace will have maximum run time of 30min. All jobs in the input file will be folded and scaled to fit this window.
3.	Concentration	It sets the concentration of the resulting trace. If the total run time of the resulting traces is less than the runtime of input trace, then the resulting trace will contain less number of jobs than that of input trace. To avoid this, the concentration parameter should be set to higher value. The default value is 1.
4.	Debug	It runs the Folder in debug mode. In the debug mode, the Folder will print additional statements for debugging. The intermediate files generated in the scratch directory are not cleaned. By default, it is False.
5.	Seed	It is the initial seed to the Random Number Generator. The same sequence of Random numbers can be generated if the same seed is used again. The Folder uses Random Number Generator to decide whether or not to emit the job.
6.	Temp-directory	It is used to indicate the temporary directory for Folder. All temporary files are cleaned except for debug option. By default, the parent directory of the output folder is the temporary directory.
7.	Skew-buffer-length	It enables the Folder to tolerate skewed jobs. By default, this buffer length is 0. Eg: '-skew-buffer-length 100' implies that the jobs appear out of order within a window of 100. If it is within this window limit, then the Folder will emit the job in order. If it is out of this window, the Folder will bail out provided allow-missorting is not set. The Folder reports the maximum skew size seen in the input trace for future use.
8.	Allow-missorting	It enables Folder to tolerate out of order jobs. If missorting is allowed, the Folder will ignore out of order jobs that cannot be skewed using –skew-buffer-length. By default, it is not enabled.

Examples

1. Folding an Input trace with 10 hours of total run time to generate an output trace with 2 hours of runtime

```
java org.apache.hadoop.tools.rumen.Folder \
  -output-duration 2h \
  -input-cycle 20m \
  file:///tmp/ trace1.json \
  file:///tmp/trace-2hr.json
```

2. Folding an Input trace with 10 hours of total run time to generate an output trace with 2 hours of runtime with toleration of skewness

```
java org.apache.hadoop.tools.rumen.Folder \
  -output-duration 2h \
  -input-cycle 20m \
  -allow-missorting \
  -skew-buffer-length 100 \
  file:///tmp/trace1.json \
  file:///tmp/ trace-2hr.json
```

If the folded jobs are out of order, then atmost 100 jobs will be de-skewed. If the 101st job is *out-of-order*, then the command will bail out.

3. Folding an input trace with 10 hours of total runtime to generate an output trace with 1 hour of total runtime in debug mode and with concentration

```
java org.apache.hadoop.tools.rumen.Folder \
  -output-duration 1h \
  -input-cycle 20m \
  -concentration 2
  -debug -temp-directory file:///tmp/debug \
  file:///tmp/trace1.json \
  file:///tmp/trace-2hr.json
```

GRIDMIX

GridMix is a benckmark for Hadoop clusters. The client submits a group of jobs. The jobs are described using JSON. For each job description, GridMix generates a synthetic job with the same byte and record patterns as recorded in the trace. It emulates the load of production jobs and tries to model the resource profiles to identify bottlenecks and to guide the development. To use GridMix, a MapReduce job trace must describe the job mix. The job trace can be generated by using the Hadoop tool "Rumen". For emulating the load of production jobs, the following steps have to be followed:

- First locate the job history files on the production cluster using mapreduce.jobhistory.done-dir (or) mapreduce.jobhistory.intermediate.done-dir configuration property.
- Rumen tool is run to build a job trace in JSON format for all jobs or selected set of jobs.
- GridMix is used with the job trace on the benchmark cluster.

The jobs submitted by the GridMix have names of the form "GRIDMIXnnnnnn" where nnnnnn is a sequence number padded with leading zeros.

Command for using GridMix without configuration parameters is as follows:

```
java org.apache.hadoop.mapred.gridmix.Gridmix [-generate
<size>] [-users <users-list>] <iopath> <trace>
```

Command for using GridMix with configuration parameters is as follows:

```
java org.apache.hadoop.mapred.gridmix.Gridmix \
  -Dgridmix.client.submit.threads=10 -Dgridmix.output.
directory=dd1 \
  [-generate <size>] [-users <users-list>] <iopath> <trace>
```

The configuration parameters "threads" and "output directory" must be indicated before other parameters.

- **<iopath>:** Working directory for GridMix
  - ◦ Can be on local file system or on HDFS
  - ◦ Should be same as that for original job mix
- **Generate:** Option to generate input data and Distributed Cache files for synthetic job
- **<size>:** Size of input data to be generated and can be indicated in TB, GB, etc,
  - ◦ Minimum size is indicated in gridmix.min.file.size
  - ◦ Default value is 128MB
- **<iopath>/input:** Destination directory for generated input data

- **<iopath>/distributedCache:** Directory where HDFS based distributed cache files are generated
  - Only non-existing distributed cache files are generated
- **Users:** Points to users list
- **<trace>:** Path to job trace generated by Rumen
  - If '-' is indicated as a value, then the trace will be in uncompressed format
  - Otherwise, it is in compressed format

Adding JAR of Rumen

The JAR of Rumen must be added to the classpath of both client and jobs. Then GridMix can be run using Hadoop JAR command as follows:

```
HADOOP_CLASSPATH=$HADOOP_HOME/share/hadoop/tools/lib/hadoop-
rumen-2.5.1.jar \
  $HADOOP_HOME/bin/hadoop jar $HADOOP_HOME/share/hadoop/tools/
lib/hadoop-gridmix-2.5.1.jar \
    -libjars $HADOOP_HOME/share/hadoop/tools/lib/hadoop-rumen-
2.5.1.jar \
    [-generate <size>] [-users <users-list>] <iopath> <trace>
```

GridMix Configuration Parameters

The various configuration parameters of GridMix are explained in Table 9.

Job Types

The job trace is a stream of JSON descriptions. For each job description, the submission client:

- Maintains the job submission time
- Reads the records and bytes count for all tasks of that job
- Writes the details of each task

Then the GridMix constructs synthetic jobs of two types:

1. LOADJOB
2. SLEEPJOB

Table 9. GridMix Configuration Parameters

Sl. No.	Configuration Parameter	Description
	gridmix.output.directory	The directory where output will be written. The iopath will be related to this parameter. The submitting user must have read & write permission to the directory. The default value is "gridmix".
2.	gridmix.gen.blocksize	It is the block size of generated data. The default value is 256MB.
3.	gridmix.gen.bytes.per.file	It is the maximum byte written per file. The default value is 1 GB.
4.	gridmix.min.file.size	It is the minimum size of input files. The default value is 128 MB. This parameter has to be changed if the error message "Found no satisfactory file" is got during execution.
5.	gridmix.max.total.scan	It is the maximum size of input files. The default value is 100 TB.
6.	gridmix.client.submit.threads	It indicates the number of threads submitting jobs to the cluster. It also controls how many splits are loaded into memory at a given time. The dense traces may need more submitting threads. The storing splits in memory is expensive and hence it should be cautiously used. The default value is1 for SERIAL job submission policy and number of processors on client machine +1 for other policies.
7.	gridmix.submit.multiplier	It is the multiplier to accelerate or decelerate the submission of jobs. The time separating the two jobs is multiplied by this factor. The default value is 1.0.
8.	gridmix.client.pending.queue.depth	It is the depth of queues in which jobs are waiting for split generation. Normally it is not configured, The default value is 5.
9.	gridmix.task.jvm-options.enable	The simulated task's maximum heap options can be configured using the values obtained from the original task via trace.

LOADJOB

LOADJOB is a synthetic job that emulates the I/O work load indicated by Rumen. It embeds the detailed I/O information of every map and reduce task. The information contains the number of records and bytes read and written into each job's input splits. Also the map tasks relay the I/O patterns of reduce tasks through intermediate output data.

SLEEPJOB

SLEEPJOB is a synthetic job where each tasks does nothing but sleeps for certain time as observed in the production task. The scalability of ResourceManager is limited by the number of heartbeats it can handle. The bench mark cluster is a fraction of production cluster. The heartbeats generated by the clusters is less than that of the production cluster. So multiple NodeManagers can be run on each slave node. Hence the I/O workload generated by synthetic jobs would beat the slave nodes, Hence such a job is used.

The type of job can be set with *gridmix.job.type*. By default, it is LOADJOB. For LOADJOB, the fraction of a record which is used for data for the key can be set using *gridmix.key.fraction*.

By default, its value is 0.1.

The configuration parameters that affect SLEEPJOB are explained in Table 10.

Job Submission Policies

The GridMix controls the rate of job submission based on the trace information or from the statistics it gathers from ResourceManager. There are three different policies for job submission. The GridMix applies the corresponding algorithm based on the policy indicated by the user.

The various policies are explained in Table 11.

The configuration parameters that affect the job submission policy are explained in the Table 12.

Emulating Users and Queues

The GridMix has to emulate the contention of jobs from different users and/ or submitted to different queues. Emulating the multiple queues is easier. The benchmark cluster can be setup with the same queue configuration as that of the production cluster. Hence the synthetic jobs can be configured such

Table 10. Configuration parameters for SLEEPJOB

Sl.No.	Parameter	Description
1.	gridmix.sleep.maptask-only	It indicates whether there is no reduce tasks. By default, it is FALSE.
2.	gridmix.sleep.fake-locations	It indicates the number of fake locations for map tasks for the job. By default, it is zero.
3.	gridmix.sleep.max-map-time	It indicates the maximum runtime for map tasks for the job in millisec. The default value is unlimited.
4.	gridmix.sleep.max-reduce-time	It indicates the maximum runtime for reduce tasks for the job in millisec. The default value is unlimited.

Table 11. Policies for Job Submission

Sl. No.	Policy	Description of Policy
1.	STRESS	The real time load of the cluster is monitored continuously. Based on that, the jobs are submitted so that the cluster remains under stress. The statistics are collected to decide whether the cluster is "underloaded" or "overloaded". The cluster is said to be "underloaded" if • The number of pending and running jobs are under the threshold TJ • The number of pending and running maps are under the threshold TM • The number of pending and running reduces are under the threshold TR The threshold TJ is proportional to the size of the cluster and the threshold TM is proportional to the map slots capacity. The threshold TR is proportional to the reduce slots capacity. If the cluster is overloaded, the job submission is regulated. Each running task is weighed based on its remaining work. For example, if 90% of the task is over, its load is taken as 0.1. To avoid very larger job blocking other jobs, the number of pending/waiting tasks for each job is limited.
2.	REPLAY	The actual job trace is replayed 100% faithfully. Even the time intervals in the job trace are followed exactly.
3.	SERIAL	The next job will be submitted only after completion of previous job.

Table 12. Configuration Parameters for Job Submission

Sl. No.	Configuration Parameter	Description
1.	gridmix.job-submission.policy	This indicates the type of job policy. It can be STRESS or REPLAY or SERIAL. The default value is STRESS.
2.	gridmix.throttle.jobs-to-tracker-ratio	It is the threshold TJ. The default value is 1.0.
3.	gridmix.throttle.maps.task-to-slot-ratio	It is the threshold TM. The default value is 2.0.
4.	gridmix.throttle.reduces.task-to-slot-ratio	It is the threshold TR. The default value is 2.5.
5.	gridmix.throttle.maps.max-slot-share-per-job	In STRESS mode, it is the maximum share of a cluster's map slots capacity that can be counted towards a job's incomplete map tasks in overload calculation. The default value is 0.1.
6.	gridmix.throttle.reduces.max-slot-share-per-job	In STRESS mode, it is the maximum share of a cluster's reduce slots capacity that can be counted towards a job's incomplete reduce tasks in overload calculation. The default value is 0.1.

that they would get submitted into the same queues as that of trace. But all the users would not have account on benchmark cluster. Hence a number of testing user accounts is created. Each user account in the trace is associated with a testing user in round-robin fashion.

The configuration parameters that affect the emulation of users and queues is described in Table 13.

Table 13. Configuration Parameters for Emulation of Users and Queues

Sl. No.	Parameter	Description
1.	gridmix.job-submission.use-queue-in-trace	It is a flag indicating whether the emulation can use the same set of queues as that of trace. The default value is FALSE.
2.	gridmix.job-submission.default-queue	It specifies the default queue to which all jobs should be submitted. If it is not specified, the GridMix uses the default queue for submitting user on the cluster.
3.	gridmix.user.resolve.class	It specifies which UserResolver implementation is to be used. There are three UserResolver implementations. They are: • *org.apache.hadoop.mapred.gridmix.* *EchoUserResolver* – submits a job as the user who submitted the original job. Here all the users in the production cluster must have account in the benchmark cluster also. • *org.apache.hadoop.mapred.gridmix.* *SubmitterUserResolver* –suubmits all jobs as current GridMix user. All users in the trace are mapped to the current GridMix user and submit the job. • *org.apache.hadoop.mapred.gridmix.* *RoundRobinUserResolver* –maps ttrace users to test users in a round-robin fashion. Here a number of testing user accounts is created and it is mapped to each unique user in trace. The default value is: *org.apache.hadoop.mapred.gridmix. SubmitterUserResolver*

Specifying Users List

If *RoundRobinUserResolver* is used, it is mandatory that the list of users has to be specified in a file called "user-list file". This can be specified using –users option. The "user-list-file" has one user per line as follows:

```
User1
User2
User3
```

The above file has 3 users. Each unique user in the trace has to be associated with the above users in a round-robin fashion. If trace users are Truser1, Truser2, Truser3, Truser4 and Truser5, then they can be mapped as follows:

```
Truser1→ User1
Truser2→ Use2
Truser3→ User3
Truser4→ User1
Truser5→ User2
```

For backward compatibility, each line in the above file can contain group name at the end as follows:

```
Username[, group]
The GridMix will not process the group name.
```

Emulating Distributed Cache Load

For LOADJOB type of jobs, the GridMix automatically emulates Distributed Cache load. For implementing this, the necessary Distributed Cache files are precreated for all simulated jobs. These cache files are created using a separate MapReduce job. The emulation of Disttributed Cache files can be controlled using gridmix.distributed-cache-emulation.enable. If it is set to False, the emulation of Distributed Cache cannot be done. But the generation of Distributed Cache by GridMix is controlled by -generate option. Both the generation of Distributed Cache and emulation of Distributed Cache will be disabled if:

- If the input comes from standard input stream instead of files.
- <iopath> indicated is on local file system.
- The distributed cache directory (<iopath>/distributedCache) and any of its ascendant directories do not have execution permission for others.

Configuration of Simulated Jobs

The simulated jobs can be mapped back to the jobs in the input trace by using GridMix. The corresponding configuration parameters are:

1. *gridmix.job.original-job-id*: The job id of the original cluster's job corresponding to the simulated job
2. *gridmix.job.original-job-name*: The job name of the original cluster's job corresponding to the simulated job

Emulating Compression/Decompression

The GridMix supports compression and decompression of both input and output of MapReduce jobs at constant compression ratio. The compression emulation is enabled by setting *gridmix.compression-emulation .enable* to True. The compression emulation is enabled for LOADJOB type jobs by default. The configuration parameter *gridmix.min.file.size* should be set to smaller value (approximately 10% of *gridmix.gen.bytes.per.file*) for enabling the GridMix to emulate compression correctly.

A typical MapReduce job deals with compression/decompression as follows:

1. **Job Input Data Compression:** If compression emulation is enabled, the GridMix generates compressible input data. The GridMix uses *mapreduce.input.fileinputformat.inputdir* to determine if the original job uses compressed input or not. If the input files of the original job are compressed, then the GridMix uses decompressor to read the input; otherwise it does not use decompressor.

2. **Intermediate Data Compression and Decompression:** If the original job has map output as compression enabled, the GridMix also compresses the Map output for the simulated job. Then the corresponding simulated reducer uses decompression.

3. **Job Output Data Compression:** If the original job's output is compressed, then the GridMix also compresses the job output of simulated job.

Emulating High-Ram Jobs

A MapReduce job can be defined as High-Ram job. The High-Ram job occupies more fraction of memory for processes. Emulating the High-Ram jobs is more important because:

- **Impact on Scheduler:** The tasks from High-Ram jobs normally reserve and use more resources. Hence the scheduling of High-ram jobs has more impact on overall scheduling.
- **Impact on Node:** High-Ram jobs occupy more memory. Hence NodeManagers have to do some extra work for allocating extra resources. This has to be considered for emulating memory.

The High-Ram emulation can be disabled by setting the parameter *gridmix. highram-emulation.enable* to False.

Emulating Resource Usages

The MapReduce tasks use resources such as CPU, physical memory, virtual memory, JVM heap, etc. during its entire lifetime. The MapReduce records the usage of all these resources using its task counters. The GridMix can use these statistics to emulate the resources usage. The GridMix also emulates the resources usage during the entire lifetime of simulated tasks. It emulates the resources only for LOADJOB type jobs. Each resource must have an emulator associated with it to implement emulation. Each resource also should implement *org.apache.hadoop.mapred.gridmix.emulators.resourceusage. ReourceUsageEmulatorPlugin* interface. The resource emulators in GridMix are plugins that are configurable. The users can configure multiple emulator plugins by providing comma separated values for *gridmix.emulators.resource-usage.plugins* parameter.

There are two types of resource usages emulators. They are:

1. **Cumulative CPU Usage Emulator:** The GridMix takes the cumulative CPU usage value provided by Rumen and tries to have the same value for simulated jobs. The emulation of Cumulative CPU usage can be enabled by adding the plugin *org.apache.hadoop.mapred.gridmix. emulators.resourceusage.CumulativeCpuUsageEmulatorPlugin* to the list of emulator plugins configured for *gridmix.emulators.resource-usage. plugins* parameter. This emulator emulates only at specific progress boundaries of the job. This interval can be configured using *gridmix. emulators.resource-usage.cpu.emulation-interval*. The default value is $10\% = 0.1$.

2. **Total Heap Usage Emulator:** The GridMix takes the Total heap usage value provided by Rumen and tries to have the same value for simulated jobs. The emulation of Toatl heap usage can be enabled by adding the plugin *org.apache.hadoop.mapred.gridmix.emulators.resourceusage. TotalHeapUsageEmulatorPlugin* to the list of emulator plugins configured for *gridmix.emulators.resource-usage.plugins* parameter. This emulator also emulates only at specific progress boundaries of the job. This interval can be configured using *gridmix.emulators.resource-usage.heap.emulation-interval*. The default value is $10\% = 0.1$.

Limitations of GridMix

The GridMix evaluates only MapReduce and HDFS performance and not the layers on top of them. The following characteristics of job load cannot be captured in job traces and hence cannot be reproduced in GridMix:

1. **Filesystem Properties:** The following properties are not matched:
   a. Block size
   b. Name space hierarchies

c. Any property of input, intermediate and output data other than bytes/records consumed and emitted from a task

Hence the most heavily used parts of the systems such as Text processing, streaming, etc, cannot be tested.

2. **I/O Rates:** The rate at which records are consumed/emitted is assumed to be limited only by the speed of the reader/writer and constant throughout the task.
3. **Memory Profile:** There is no data on memory usage over time even though maximum heap size is available.
4. **Skew:** The records are assumed to be more regular. Each map also produce a proportional percentage of data for each reduce. A job with unbalanced input (skew) will be flattened.
5. **Job Failure:** The user code is assumed to be correct and hence there is no job failure.
6. **Job Independence:** Each job is independent. Hence a job will run even though the other job does not run.

YARN SCHEDULER LOAD SIMULATOR (SLS)

In an operating system point of view, the definition of scheduling is process that handles the assignment of a running process to the CPU and removal of it for another process on the basis of a particular strategy and it is termed as a resource manager. Process scheduling is a challenge in a Multiprogramming and multi user environment. This scheduling process becomes still complex when it is to be deployed in distributed computing environment due to various factors such as heterogeneous resources, varying latency etc. Scheduling is one of the optimization techniques since it involves different requirements for the resources with different types of available requirements. Hadoop provides set of library classes for doing it.

Yarn scheduler Load Simulator has features such as FIFO, and Fair Scheduler and supports various optimization techniques for different types of workload. Metrics are required to characterize a particular scheduling technique. Evaluating the scheduling algorithm in the real time working environment is not feasible due to the requirements of large types of resources with different working scenarios. Hence, the required environment will be simulated and deployed in the real time. SLS is a tool which can simulate cluster and the variety of loads for working with different types of computing environment. This tool will be highly useful for the researcher to explore the possibilities of working with different environment. SLS has class ResourceManager simulating the NodeManagers(NM) and ApplicationMasters(AM) and handles the events by generated them (i.e NM and AM events). This simulator assumes that the networking factors are omitted (which is always the characteristics of the simulator).

The size and type of the resources in the cluster and the workload will be stored in the configuration file. Some of the metrics used are:

- Resource usage for the cluster
- Queue Usage
- Job turnaround time
- Throughput
- Fairness
- Capacity
- Time cost of the scheduler

The simulator has two major parts such as:

1. Yarn Resource Manager
   a. Scheduler Wrapper
      i. Real Scheduler
2. Simulator.
   a. Nodes
   b. Jobs

Everything in the real time environment system can be visualized in terms of Input-Process-Output (I-P-O) .

The Figure 1 shows the architecture of a general system. The system can be visualized in terms of a collection of subsystems interacting with each

Figure 1. Architecture of general system

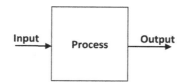

other in a simple/complex way. In the simulation point of view each system/ subsystem input, process, output and the associated events have to be simulated. As far as the Hadoop is concerned, the main parts are NameNode(NM) and ApplicationNode(AM). The various specification associated with NM/AM has to be configured. In SLS the simulator keeps sending its heartbeats (main events) to the Yarn Resource Manager. The scheduler's behaviors have to be logged for further analysis. The system consists of many subsystems and hence the behaviors are centered on: (1) when a job arrives into a system/ subsystem; (2) when it leaves the system/subsystem; (3) size of the time, and; (4) status of completion. If all these events are logged, a wonderful statistical analysis of the system can be made. This behavior enables the computation of the turnaround time, throughput, delay etc.

The simulator has different use cases such as: Engineering aspects (correctness, cost, validation, scalability), Quality assurance (cluster and workload profile), Solution(usage point of view such as SLA etc).

In SLS, the directory sls has the following four sub directories:

1. **Bin:** Has the running scripts of the simulator
2. **Html:** Director has all the html/css/js files
3. **Sample-conf:** Specifies the simulator configuration
4. **Sample-data:** Has the rumen trace used to generate the inputs for the simulator

Configuring the Simulator

The configuration of the simulator is done in the file 'sls-runner.xml'. The various parameters for SLS configuration are shown in the Table 14.

Running the Simulator

The simulator supports two types of input files:

1. Rumen traces
2. Own input traces

The script to start the simulator is *slsrun.sh*.
The command for starting the simulator with the options is as follows:

Table 14. SLS configuration parameters

SL. No.	Parameter	Description
1.	yarn.sls.runner.pool.size	The simulator uses a thread pool to simulate the NM and AM running, and this parameter specifies the number of threads in the pool
2.	yarn.sls.nm.memory.mb	The total memory for each NMSimulator
3.	yarn.sls.nm.vcores	The total vCores for each NMSimulator.
4.	yarn.sls.nm.heartbeat.interval.ms	The heartbeat interval for each NMSimulator
5.	yarn.sls.am.heartbeat.interval.ms	The heartbeat interval for each AMSimulator
6.	yarn.sls.am.type.mapreduce	The AMSimulator implementation for MapReduce-like applications. Users can specify implementations for other type of applications
7.	yarn.sls.container.memory.mb	The memory required for each container simulator.
8.	yarn.sls.container.vcores	The vCores required for each container simulator
9.	yarn.sls.runner.metrics.switch	The simulator introduces Metrics to measure the behaviors of critical components and operations. This field specifies whether we open (ON) or close (OFF) the Metrics running.
10.	yarn.sls.metrics.web.address.port	The port used by simulator to provide real-time tracking. The default value is 10001
11.	org.apache.hadoop.yarn.server.resourcemanager.scheduler.fifo.FifoScheduler	The implementation of scheduler metrics of Fifo Scheduler
12.	org.apache.hadoop.yarn.server.resourcemanager.scheduler.fair.FairScheduler	The implementation of scheduler metrics of Fair Scheduler
13.	org.apache.hadoop.yarn.server.resourcemanager.scheduler.capacity.CapacityScheduler	The implementation of scheduler metrics of implementation of Capacity Scheduler

```
$ cd $HADOOP_ROOT/share/hadoop/tools/sls
$ bin/slsrun.sh
  --input-rumen |--input-sls=<TRACE_FILE1,TRACE_FILE2,...>
  --output-dir=<SLS_SIMULATION_OUTPUT_DIRECTORY> [--nodes=<SLS_
NODES_FILE>]
    [--track-jobs=<JOBID1,JOBID2,...>] [--print-simulation]
```

The various options for running slsrun.sh are described in Table 15.

Rumen2sls Tool

The syntax for rumen2sls tool is as follows:

```
$ bin/rumen2sls.sh
  --rumen-file=<RUMEN_FILE>
```

Table 15. Options for slsrun

Sl. No.	Option	Description
1.	--input-rumen	It indicates that the input is Rumen trace files. The input can be multiple files separated by comma. The example trace is available in $HADOOP_ROOT/share/hadoop/tools/sls/sample-data/2jobs2min-rumen-jh.json
2.	--input-sls	It indicates that the simulator is using its own file in JSON format. Also there is a tool "*rumen2sls.sh*" to convert Rumen traces to sls traces.
3.	--output-dir	It indicates the output directory for generated logs and metrics.
4.	--nodes	It indicates the cluster topology. By default, the simulator will use the topology indicated in the input JSON file. The users can indicate a new topology using this parameter.
5.	--track-jobs	It indicates the list of comma separated jobs that would be tracked during simulation.
6.	--print-simulation	It indicates whether to print the following information before simulation: • Number of nodes, applications and tasks • Information for each application

```
--output-dir=<SLS_OUTPUT_DIRECTORY>
  [--output-prefix=<SLS_FILE_PREFIX>]
```

The various options for rumen2sls are explained in Table 16.

Example for SLS JSON Input File

The following example shows the format of sls json input file which contains two jobs. The first job has 3 map tasks and the second job has 2 map tasks.

Table 16. Parameters for rumen2sls

Sl. No.	Option	Description
1.	--rumen-file	It indicates the input file which is a Rumen trace file. The example trace file is available in the directory sample-data.
2.	--output-dir	It indicates the output directory where sls trace files would be written. Two files are generated in this output directory: 1. Trace file including all job and task information 2. File showing Topology information
3.	--output-prefix	It indicates the prefix of generated files. The default value is '*sls*'. The two generated files are *sls-jobs.json* and *sls-nodes.json*.

```json
{
  "am.type": "mapreduce",
  "job.start.ms": 0,
  "job.end.ms": 67875,
  "job.queue.name": "sls_new_queue_1",
  "job.id": "id_1",
  "job.user": "default",
  "job.tasks": [ {
    "container.host": "/default-rack/node1",
    "container.start.ms": 5554,
    "container.end.ms": 57000,
    "container.priority": 20,
    "container.type": "map"
  }, {
    "container.host": "/default-rack/node3",
    "container.start.ms": 6665,
    "container.end.ms": 21593,
    "container.priority": 20,
    "container.type": "map"
  }, {
    "container.host": "/default-rack/node2",
    "container.start.ms": 34770,
    "container.end.ms": 45613,
    "container.priority": 20,
    "container.type": "map"
  } ]
}
{
  "am.type": "mapreduce",
  "job.start.ms": 95204,
  "job.end.ms": 207256,
  "job.queue.name": "sls_new_queue_2",
  "job.id": "id_2",
  "job.user": "default",
  "job.tasks": [ {
    "container.host": "/default-rack/node1",
    "container.start.ms": 221822,
    "container.end.ms": 333985,
    "container.priority": 20,
    "container.type": "map"
  }, {
    "container.host": "/default-rack/node2",
    "container.start.ms": 221788,
    "container.end.ms": 331377,
    "container.priority": 20,
    "container.type": "map"
  } ]
}
```

Example for Input Topology File

The following example shows an input topology file which as 2 nodes organized in a rack.

```
{
  "rack": "rack-1",
  "nodes": [ {
    "node": "node1"
  }, {
    "node": "node2"
    }]
}
```

Measuring Metrics

The YARN Scheduler Load Simulator has Metrics to measure the behaviors of running applications, containers, cluster available resources, scheduler operation time cost, etc. If the option *yarn.sls.runner.metrics.switch* is set to ON, the Metrics will run. The Metrics will output its logs in –output-dir directory indicated by user. Then the user can track these information during simulator running and even after running.

Real-Time Tracking

The SLS simulator provides an interface for tracking its running. The users should go to *http://host:port/simulate* to track the whole running. A particular job or queue can be tracked using *http://host:port/track*. Here *host* is the place where simulator is run. The port is the value configured by *yarn.sls.metrics. web.address.port*. The default port value is 10001. The tracking shows the following charts in the webpage:

- Number of running applications Vs time
- Number of running containers Vs time
- Allocated memory in the cluster Vs time
- Available memory in the cluster Vs time
- Allocated memory for each queue Vs time
- Scheduler allocate & handle operations timecost Vs time

- JVM memory usage Vs time
- Resource usage for each queue Vs time
- Resource usage for each job Vs time

Offline Analysis

After the simulation is over, all logs are stored in the output directory indicated by – -*output-dir* option in *$HADOOP_ROOT/share/hadoop/tools/sls/bin/ slsrun.sh*. The log contains the following files/folder:

- ***Realtimetrack.json* File:** Records all real time tracking logs every 1 second
- ***Jobruntime.csv* File:** Records start time and end time for all jobs
- ***Metrics* Folder:** Records the logs generated by Metrics

Hence the users can view all logs and charts in the off-line mode also. For viewing in offline mode, the *realtimetrack.json* must be uploaded in: *$HADOOP_ROOT/share/hadoop/tools/sls/html/showSimulationTrace. html*. For browser security problems, both *realtimetrack.json* and *showSimulationTrace.html* must be in the same directory.

RESEARCH ISSUES WITH HADOOP TOOLS

All the entities in the Internet world produces large volume of unstructured and structured data from the sources such as Emails, web logs, social media like Twitter, Facebook etc. By means of deploying the Hadoop and its associated tools, the major obstacles with processing Big Data like capturing, storing, searching, sharing and analysis could be overcome. With the help of big data analytics, many enterprises are able to improve customer retention, help with product development and gain competitive advantage, speed and reduce complexity. E-commerce companies study traffic on web sites or navigation patterns to determine probable views, interests and dislikes of a person or a group as a whole depending on the previous purchases. In this paper, we compare some typically used data analytic tools. The discussion on the use of Hadoop and tools was presented by Mrunal Sogodekar et.al (2016).

Trust Odia (2014) reviewed some tools for migrating from traditional databases to the big data platform and thus suggests a model, based on the review. Also they related the business intelligence to be achieved by the use of Hadoop tools.

The issues with the traditional data management, warehousing and analysis systems were addressed by Shankar Ganesh Manikandan (2014) to analyze this data and elaborated the benefits of using Hadoop and HDFS by Apache for storing and managing Big Data. They emphasize the Map Reduce concept which is a Minimization technique making use of file indexing with mapping, sorting, shuffling and finally reducing. The study of Map Reduce techniques is studied in their paper which was implemented for Big Data analysis using HDFS

Chatuporn Vorapongkitipun (2014) addresses the issues related to handling of large number of small files by the name node as NameNode stores the entire metadata of HDFS in its main memory. A mechanism based on Hadoop Archive (HAR), was introduced by them to improve the memory utilization for metadata and enhance the efficiency of accessing small files in HDFS. Also they extended the HAR capabilities to allow additional files to be inserted into the existing archive files and they have the claimed the access efficiencies.

The researchers introduced the concept of Big Data and Hadoop to handle this. The business people makes use of for their applications. However, the effectiveness of the using the environment like Hadoop is to be studied. Hence it becomes crucial for both research and industry communities. Such bench marking details were proposed by Rui Han et.al (2015). Generating such kind of big data with implementation specific and with 4V properties demands workloads. However, most of the existing big data benchmarks are focusing on specific problems.

CONCLUSION

Hadoop provides a number of tools to archive and analyze the data. The usage of each tool has to be justified. The additional tools provided by the Hadoop distribution are provided in this chapter with an explanation. Appropriate examples to demonstrate the working with Hadoop Streaming concept are given. Also the Yarn Scheduler Load Simulator (SLS) was described in this chapter. The usage and the research issues associated with Hadoop tools were also addressed.

REFERENCES

Han, R., Jia, Z., Gao, W., Tian, X., & Wang, L. (2015). *Benchmarking Big Data Systems: State-of-the-Art and Future Directions, Technical Report. ICT.* ACS.

Manikandan, S. G., & Ravi, S. (2014). *Big Data Analysis Using Apache Hadoop.* 2014 International Conference on IT Convergence and Security (ICITCS), Beijing, China.

Odia, T., Misra, S., & Adewumi, A. (2014). Evaluation of hadoop/mapreduce framework migration tools. *Asia-Pacific World Congress on Computer Science and Engineering.* 10.1109/APWCCSE.2014.7053870

Sogodekar, M., Pandey, S., Tupkari, I., & Manekar, A. (2016). Big data analytics: hadoop and tools. *2016 IEEE Bombay Section Symposium (IBSS).* 10.1109/IBSS.2016.7940204

Vorapongkitipun, C., & Nupairoj, N. (2014). Improving performance of small-file accessing in Hadoop. *11th International Joint Conference on Computer Science and Software Engineering.* 10.1109/JCSSE.2014.6841867

Chapter 10
Hadoop Auth

ABSTRACT

One of the factors for the reliability of the services is authentication, which decides who can access what services. Since big data offers a wide variety of services, authentication becomes one of the main criteria for consideration. This chapter outlines the features of the security services in terms of the requirements and the issues in the business services. This chapter also gives a little background about the services in the cloud and the interaction between clients and services in the cloud, emphasizing the security services. The authentication procedure with the authentication protocol, Kerberos SPNEGO, which is offered as a security service in Hadoop, is introduced. The configuration details in a typical browser (Mozilla Firefox) are detailed. The usage of the Linux command curl is introduced in this chapter. The command to key distribution center "kinit" is outlined. Also, the procedure for accessing the server within the Java code is given. A section on server-side configuration speaks about the Maven repository, which holds all the necessary library Jar files organized as local, central, and remote. The explanation for the configuration is given with a typical XML file. Also, the usage of Simple Logging Facade for Java is introduced. The configuration has many parameters with its values and they are tabulated for better perception. The use of LDAP server, which is one of the lightweight directory access protocols, is introduced. Also, the provision for multi-scheme configuration is outlined with an example configuration file. The facilities available to provide advanced security features using signer secret provide are highlighted with appropriate examples for the parameter name and parameter value.

DOI: 10.4018/978-1-5225-3790-8.ch010

BACKGROUND

The word authentication refers to who can access a set of resources. The practice of accessing the critical resources started from the inception of the multiuser environment. Though it was made available even in the dumb terminals of the Unix operation system based environment, it was seriously viewed during usage with the client server based system. As the access to the various services was accounted for its usage, the authentication scheme took much importance. Recently, the cloud authentication scheme is still viewed seriously, since the exact place of our storage and the computing elements are not known to any of the users. Hence the authentication becomes one of the important issues in the bigger system.

INTRODUCTION TO SECURITY

Security is the only issue the business service providers and the clients hesitate to do during online access. Though the security mechanisms could be easily implemented recently, due to the availability of algorithm, codes, and tools, the security implementation in large sized data and distribution environment is still having challenges.

For any reliable communication between two entities, authentication plays major role as a security mechanism intended to verify identify of the entity on the information exchange. Both private and public key encryption methods could be used to provide the authentication as shown in Figure 1.

Figure 1a shows the passing of messages from sender to receiver with the usage of two different keys (asymmetric) where for every message communication, a pair of key has to be generated (public key, private key). If the sender encrypts the messages with his private key at the sender side, it should be decrypted by receiver using the public key. It could be done in other way also. The confidentiality of the messages is achieved if message is encrypted using public key and decrypted using private key leading to the confidentiality of the message i.e. the message can be decrypted only by the person having the private key of this message. If the message is encrypted by the private key and is to be decrypted by the receiver using the public key it is authentication of the person.

Figure 1. Principle of Authentication mechanisms using: (a) public key (b) private key

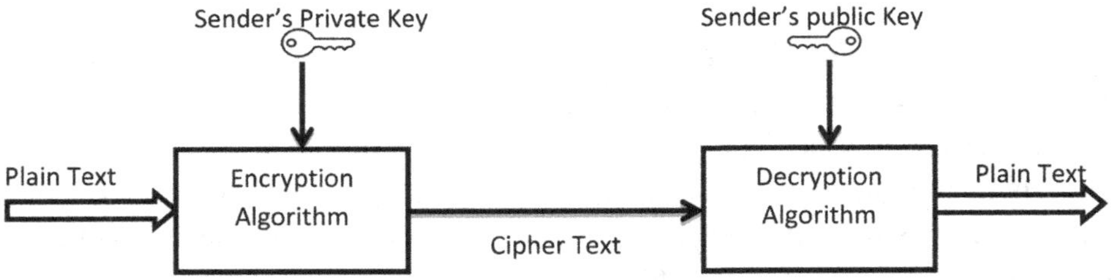

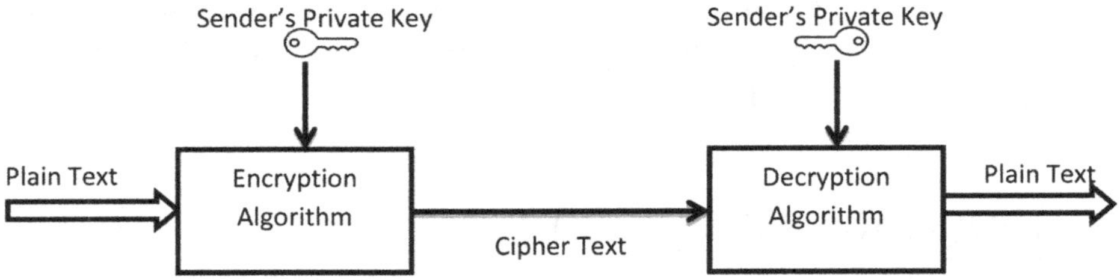

Authentication Services

It is to be ensured that the messages received from a source are coming from the intended source or not. It should not be altered in transit. Message authentication is a procedure that has to verify sequencing (checking for the sequence of messages) and timeliness (checking for the right order of the messages).

Though the authentication of the message is done, there are chances that the intruder in the network may damage the message in the transit. Hence a digital signature mechanism is followed. The message is added with the message authentication code and sent. The receiver having known the private key of message verifies it.

Message Authentication Code (MAC) is the plain text added with the secret code of fixed length message and this procedure is publicly known serving as the authenticator.

When sender Rama has a message to send to Sita, Rama calculates the MAC as a function of the message M and the key K, i.e., $MAC = C_K(M)$. The message (M) is added with the MAC and sent to Sita, where she uses

Figure 2. Public key based authentication

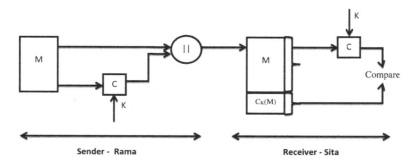

the private key to reconstruct MAC and verify with MAC sent by Rama and compared and validated. Using the hash function and the variable length of any message, a fixed sized message can be constructed which is the Digital Signature of the message. This digital signature ensures the right source and integrity of the message.

Figure 2 and Figure 3 shows the public key based authentication. Figure 4 shows it with the certification authorities involved.

Digital Certificate in Authentication

The sharing of the public key is done using digital certificates through the Certification Authority (CA).

In Hadoop environment, the Kerberos protocol is used. The following section outlines the Kerberos.

Figure 3. Public key based authentication with the entities involved

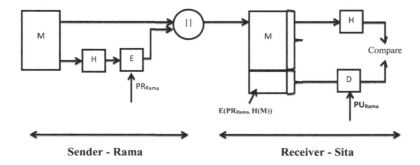

Figure 4. Public key based authentication with the entities and certification authority involved

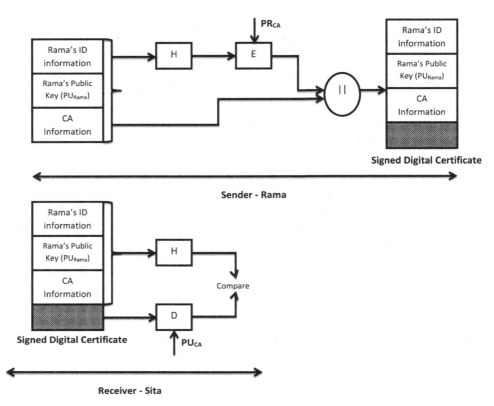

INTRODUCTION TO KERBEROS

Kerberos (https://www.kerberos.org/software/tutorial.html) is an authentication protocol where you want to protect data sent on an unsecured network. However the requirements are that authentication servers, application servers and client system should be free from vulnerabilities. Also it is expected that the password must be well protected i.e. it should not be transmitted over the untrusted network and should not be stored in plain format. The application server and clients should be mutually authenticated periodically to avoid unnecessary loss of information. Using the authentication and authorization a complete secure network connection could be established between server and client, by which the generation and exchange of secret key can be done for encryption of the data.

Realm refers to the boundary of authentication domain of the network. If the two objects belong to two different domains, the authentication called cross-authentication. The name of the realm is written in case sensitive form. However it is customary that the name of realm is given in upper case letters and will be reflecting the DNS name. For example the DNS of the particular entity is mepcoeng.ac.in, the realm name is given as MEPCOENG.AC.IN.

A user, service and host are the entities of a domain and are referred as Principal and it occupies an entry in the authentication server database. It is represented as entity@REALM. Depending on whether it is a user or service or host the complete name is given. Some of the valid Principal names are:

1. Imap/mbox.mepcoeng.ac.in@MEPCOENG.AC.IN
2. AdaLab22/ftp.mepcoeng.ac.in@MEPCOENG.AC.IN
3. Kmuni/admin@MEPCOENG.AC.IN

Ticket is the term used by the client, application server and authentication server. The ticket request is raised by the client and presented to the application server. The encrypted tickets (using the private key of the service) are issued by the authentication server to the application server for the clients. The content of the ticket is:

*   The name of the requester.
*   Name of the service.
*   IP address of the client in which the ticket will be used (optional in Kerberos 5). It could be multiple to be issued to clients under NAT or multihomed environment.
*   The date and time of the commencement of the validity.
*   Ticket's maximum duration of life time (generally 10 hours). The admin of the administration can have the control of whether to issue the ticket or not. However, once the token is issued, even the authentication server has no control over it.

Encryption

DES 56 bits version of private key encryption is used by Kerberos 4 which is redefined Kerberos 5 which does not predetermine the number or type of encryption methods and is negotiated among the types of encryption. However, the interoperability issues arise during communication between Unix implementation of Kerberos 5 and the Active Directory of Windows where

DES at 56 bits is common with Unix and Windows. This interoperability is well addressed by version 1.3 of MIT Kerberos 5, which has RC4-HMAC support, as is present in Windows (stronger than DES). Also the encryption standards such as triple DES (3DES), AES128 and AES256 are some of the improved encryption standards.

Kerberos protocol does not allow to store the unencrypted password, including in the authentication server database. Each encryption algorithm uses different length of key. Considering that each encryption algorithm uses its own key length, by using a special function called 'string2key' transforming unencrypted password into an encryption key. This is done for every change of password by the user or he/she enters it for authentication. The function string2key is based on hashing operation, which is irreversible. Some of the hashing algorithms are MD5 and CRC32.

Salt is the concept used in Kerberos 5. Salt is a string to be concatenated to the unencrypted password and is one of the arguments for the string2key function to obtain the key. Kerberos 5 uses the principal of the user as salt. For example:

```
K_kmuni = string2key (P_kmuni + "kmuni@MEPCOENG.AC.IN")
```

K_{kmuni} is the encryption key of the user kmuni and P_{kmuni} is the unencrypted password of the user.

The advantages of the salt are as follows:

- Though two principals have same unencrypted password, using salt produces two different keys. For example, kmuni@MEPCOENG.AC.IN and kmuni/admin@MEPCOENG.AC.IN (the same user with different roles) have two different keys.
- A user having two accounts in different realms, likely to have unencrypted password and with the presence of the salt, they will have two different keys and hence the compromise in one realm will not affect use in other realm since they two different keys in two realms.

In order to have compatibility with Kerberos 4 based authentication a null salt can be configured.

For every change of password by the user, or for the updation of the secret key by the administrator, a counter is used to update the current version of the key which is called key version number (kvno).

222

Key Distribution Center (KDC)

It consists of three parts as:

1. Database
2. Authentication Server (AS)
3. Ticket Granting Server (TGS)

Each entry by the principal in the database corresponds to either the user or service with the following information:

- The principal name
- The encryption key along with key version number
- The duration of the validity of the ticket for the principal
- The maximum duration by which a ticket associated to the principal can be renewed (only Kerberos 5)
- The flag or the attributes for representing the behaviour of the tickets
- The expiry date and time of the password
- The expiry date and time of the principal. There afterwards the tickets will not be issued.

To make robustness of the database, the entries in the data base are encrypted using the master key, which is associated with the principal.

The block diagram showing the process of request/reply pair among the application server, authentication server, and the clients are shown in Figure 5.

The client makes a request (AS_REQ) to the authentication server and the server replies with reply (AS_REP) which is the initial process expecting the password from the unauthenticated. Following this, the AS issues a special ticket known as the Ticket Granting Ticket (TGT), the principal associated with which is krbtgt/mepcoeng.ac.in@MEPCOENG.AC.IN. The valid users can use the TGT to obtain other service tickets, without having to re-enter their password by means of exchanging the messages TGS_REQ and TGS_REP. The Ticket Granting Server (TGS) sends service tickets to clients with a valid TGT with the guaranteed authenticity of the identity for getting the requested services on the application servers. The usages of TGT and TGS should be well distinguished.

The users and services share a secret with the KDC. For the user the key is derived from its password. For the services, the secret key is set by the administrator. These keys are used for long duration (long term key) over

Figure 5. Interaction among the client and server for the authentication purposes

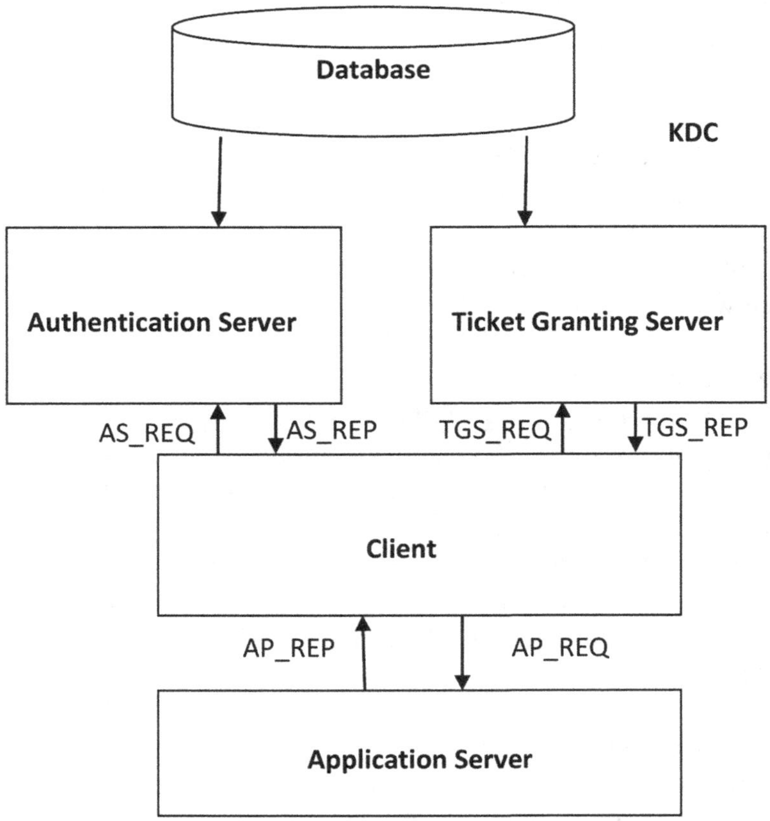

multiple sessions unless they voluntarily change. Also it is required to share a secret for the session during which they work, which is called the session key. This session key is generated by the KDC when a ticket is issued. This session key from the service is enveloped by the KDC in the ticket for user side which is encapsulated in an encrypted packet with the user long term key and hence this session key plays a major role in the authenticity of the user.

There are various ways of deriving the keys for the effective authentication. However due to finance specific applications and benefits out of the cracking the keys, the effectiveness of the authentication keeps demanding new techniques and this field becomes the scope for research. The different techniques like adding IP address (if it is fixed), various bio metric symbols are used for authentication.

ACCESSING HADOOP AUTH PROTECTED URL

This section explores the authentication facilities available in the Hadoop environment which is the major platform for the distribution computing purposes.

It is a Java library with collection of classes enabling the security features between the client and server using Kerberos SPNEGO authentication scheme. Kerberos is an authentication protocol, taking care of the security consideration between any communicating entities over a non-secure network by using secret-key cryptography. While Kerberos is an authentication protocol over computer network, Simple and Protected GSS-API Negotiation Mechanism (SPNEGO) is its extension over Internet using HTTP protocol. The working principle of SPNEGO is shown in Figure 6.

Steps for Site 1 to access web service from Site 3 are as follows: Here Site 1 is the client machine. Site 2 is the key distribution Centre and Site 3 is the machine with the web services to be accessed.

1. Site 1 logon to Site 2 using Kerberos Logon
2. Site 1 connects to site 3
3. Site 3 returns error (401)
4. Site 1 raises a ticket request
5. Site 1 contacts Site 2 with authentication with SPNEGO
6. Site 3 renders the service
7. Ticket verification is done between Site 3 and Site 2
8. The user name is supplied by Site to Site 3 for further access of services

It works for both web and non-web orientation services.

Figure 6. Authentication procedure with SPNEGO

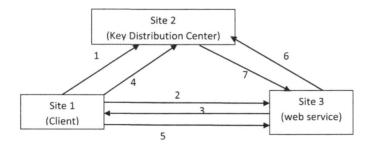

The protected resources are authenticated using Hadoop Auth. Once the authentication is done the client has the token signed. The client has the token with the details such as name, user principal, authentication type and expiration time and this token is available as a cookie in the client for accessing the protected resources till the HTTP cookie expires. The authentication scheme has multiple implementations. In order to work with this, the browser must support HTTP Kerberos SPNEGO.

To access an URL protected by Kerberos HTTP SPNEGO, use the following instructions for the browser you are using.

To configure Mozilla Firefox:

1.   Open the low level Firefox configuration page by loading the about:config page. A part of the response looks as shown in Figure 7.
2.   In the Search text box, enter network.negotiate-auth.trusted-uris.

A typical out of the browser screen will look as shown in Figure 8.

3.   Double-click the network.negotiate-auth.trusted-uris preference and enter the hostname or the domain of the web server that is protected by

Figure 7. Firefox configuration page

Preference Name	Status	Type	Value
accessibility.AOM.enabled	default	boolean	false
accessibility.accesskeycausesactivation	default	boolean	true
accessibility.blockautorefresh	default	boolean	false
accessibility.browsewithcaret	default	boolean	false
accessibility.browsewithcaret_shortcut.enabled	default	boolean	true
accessibility.delay_plugin_time	default	integer	10000
accessibility.delay_plugins	default	boolean	false

Figure 8. Search text box

Preference Name	Status	Type	Value
network.negotiate-auth.trusted-uris	default	string	

Kerberos HTTP SPNEGO. Separate multiple domains and hostnames with a comma.
4.   Click OK.

The sequence of screen shots is shown in Figure 9 to Figure 11.

Figure 9. Screen shot number 1

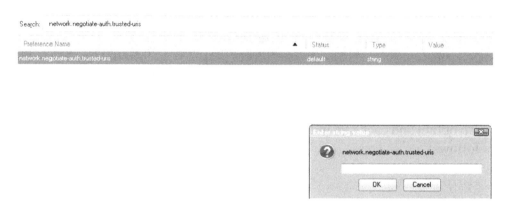

Figure 10. Screen shot number 2

Figure 11. Screen shot number 3

A slightly variation of this procedure is adapted for the setting with IE based browser and browser for Intranet.

Accessing Server

Accessing the Hadoop auth protected resources is done using the Curl command. The syntax is as follows:

```
$ curl -V
curl 7.15.5 (x86_64-redhat-linux-gnu) libcurl/7.15.5
OpenSSL/0.9.8b zlib/1.2.3 libidn/0.6.5
```

Protocols: tftp ftp telnet dict ldap http file https ftps
Features: GSS-Negotiate IDN IPv6 Largefile NTLM SSL libz
First login to the key distribution center and use curl.

To obtain and cache an initial ticket-granting ticket for principal, use kinit as follows:

```
$ kinit
```

Please enter the password for *user.*

For the complete reference to curl, please refer to man page of url.

For example the access to the web server, the command and its partial outputs are as follows:

```
-----------------------------------------------------------------
-----------
 [muni@mepcolinux:~]curl http://172.16.16.201:8080
<html>
<head>
<style type="text/css">
<!--
body {
        background-color: #C8F5F6;
}
-->
</style>
</head>
<body>
<head>
<meta http-equiv="Content-Type" content="text/html;
charset=iso-8859-1" />
<title>Welcome to Mepco Schlenk Engineering College, Sivakasi</
```

```
title>
<style type="text/css">
...................
</body>
</html>[muni@mepcolinux:~]
----------------------------------------------------------------
-----------
```

Accessing the server from the Java Code is as follows:

```
...
URL url = new URL("http://localhost:8080/hadoop-auth/kerberos/
who");
AuthenticatedURL.Token token = new AuthenticatedURL.Token();
...
HttpURLConnection conn = new AuthenticatedURL().
openConnection(url, token);
...
conn = new AuthenticatedURL().openConnection(url, token);
...
```

The AuthenticationFilter filter is Hadoop Auth's server side component, which must be configured before starting its use. For example: The Hadoop Auth and dependent JAR files must be in the web application classpath (commonly the WEB-INF/lib directory).

Maven Repository means a place or folder, where the Project Jars, Library Jars, Plugins, are stored and used by Maven. They are categorized into three parts. They are:

1. **Local:** Available as local repository
2. **Central:** Available as collection from all the developers
3. **Remote:** Available in the remote location customized by the deveoper

CONFIGURATION

Hadoop Auth uses Simple Logging Facade for Java (SLF4J-API) for logging. Depending on the types of logging, the appropriate Jar files must be available for rendering of the web services. The authentication related configuration has to be done at the server side.

Some of the configuration parameters are:

- Type
- Signature.secret.file
- Token.validity
- Cookie.domain
- Cookie.path
- Signer.secret.provider

In order to use this configured parameters, the key distribution centre must be started and running. In order to use Kerberos SPNEGO as the authentication mechanism, the authentication filter must be configured with the following init parameters:

- Type
- Kerberos.principal
- Kerberos.keytab

A typical example file (xml) for the configuration is as follows:

```
<web-app version="2.5" xmlns="http://java.sun.com/xml/ns/
javaee">
        ...
    <filter>
    <filter-name>kerberosFilter</filter-name>
    <filter-class>
        org.apache.hadoop.security.authentication.server.
AuthenticationFilter
    </filter-class>
    <init-param>
            <param-name>type</param-name>
        <param-value>kerberos</param-value>
    </init-param>
        ........   ...........   ..........
    <init-param>
        <param-name>kerberos.keytab</param-name>
        <param-value>/tmp/auth.keytab</param-value>
    </init-param>
```

The param-name and param-value are placed in Table 1 for better understanding.

```
    </filter>
    <filter-mapping>
            <filter-name>kerberosFilter</filter-name>
```

Table 1.

Param-Name	Param-Value
type	kerberos
token.validity	30
cookie.domain	foo.com
cookie.path	/
kerberos.principal	HTTP/localhost@LOCALHOST
kerberos.keytab	/tmp/auth.keytab

```
        <url-pattern>/kerberos/*</url-pattern>
    </filter-mapping>
</web-app>
```

AltKerberos Configuration

```
<web-app version="2.5" xmlns="http://java.sun.com/xml/ns/
javaee">
        ...
   <filter>
      <filter-name>kerberosFilter</filter-name>
      <filter-class>
         org.apache.hadoop.security.authentication.server.
AuthenticationFilter
      </filter-class>

   </filter>
   <filter-mapping>
      <filter-name>kerberosFilter</filter-name>
      <url-pattern>/kerberos/*</url-pattern>
```

Table 2.

Param-Name	Param-Value
type	org.my.subclass.of.AltKerberosAuthenticationHandler
alt-kerberos.non-browser.user-agents	java,curl,wget,perl
token.validity	30
cookie.domain	.foo.com
cookie.path	/
kerberos.principal	HTTP/localhost@LOCALHOST
kerberos.keytab	/tmp/auth.keytab

```
    </filter-mapping>
</web>
```

LDAP Server Configuration

LDAP service is one of the authenticating services. It is a Light weight Directory Access Protocol. The typical parameters and its values are shown in the Table 3.

```
<web-app version="2.5" xmlns="http://java.sun.com/xml/ns/
javaee">
<filter>
    <filter-name>authFilter</filter-name>
    <filter-class>
      org.apache.hadoop.security.authentication.server.
AuthenticationFilter
    </filter-class>

</filter>
    <filter-mapping>
        <filter-name>authFilter</filter-name>
        <url-pattern>/ldap/*</url-pattern>
    </filter-mapping>
</web-app>
```

Multi Scheme Configuration

In a similar manner, a combination of many authentication schemes can be used in Hadoop. The typical configuration parameters are:

- Type
- Multi-scheme-auth-handler.schemes
- Multi-scheme-auth-handler.schemes.<scheme-name>.handler

Table 3.

Param-Name	Param-Value
type	ldap
ldap.providerurl	ldap://ldap-server-host:8920
ldap.basedn	ou=users,dc=example,dc=com
ldap.enablestarttls	true

The configuration properties are set as follows:

```
<web-app version="2.5" xmlns="http://java.sun.com/xml/ns/
javaee">
        ...
    <filter>
      <filter-name>authFilter</filter-name>
      <filter-class>
        org.apache.hadoop.security.authentication.server.
AuthenticationFilter
      </filter-class>

</filter>
        <filter-mapping>
            <filter-name>authFilter</filter-name>
            <url-pattern>/multi-scheme/*</url-pattern>
        </filter-mapping>
        ...
</web-app>
```

SignerSecretProvider Configuration

It is used to provide advanced behaviors for the secret used for signing the HTTP cookies.

The configuration properties are:

Table 4.

Param-Name	Param-Value
type	multi-scheme
multi-scheme-auth-handler.schemes	basic,negotiate
multi-scheme-auth-handler.basic.handler	ldap
multi-scheme-auth-handler.negotiate. handler	kerberos
ldap.providerurl	ldap://ldap-server-host:8920
ldap.basedn	ou=users,dc=example,dc=com
ldap.enablestarttls	true
token.validity	30
cookie.domain	.foo.com
cookie.path	/
kerberos.principal	HTTP/localhost@LOCALHOST
kerberos.keytab	/tmp/auth.keytab

- Signer.secret.provider
- Signature.secret.file
- Token.validity

The properties specific to zookeeper (centralized service for maintaining configuration information, naming, providing distributed synchronization, and providing group services) implementation are as follows:

- Signer.secret.provider.zookeeper.connection.string
- Signer.secret.provider.zookeeper.path
- Signer.secret.provider.zookeeper.auth.type
- Signer.secret.provider.zookeeper.kerberos.keytab
- Signer.secret.provider.zookeeper.kerberos.principal
- Signer.secret.provider.zookeeper.disconnect.on.shutdown

The typical parameters are specified as shown in Tables 5-7.

Table 5. Parameter setting: Example 1

Param-Name	Param-Value
signer.secret.provide	file
signature.secret.file	/myapp/secret_file

Table 6. Parameter setting: Example 2

Param-Name	Param-Value
signer.secret.provider	random
token.validity	30

Table 7. Parameter setting: Example 2

Param-Name	Param-Value
signer.secret.provider	zookeeper
token.validity	30
signer.secret.provider.zookeeper.connection.string	/myapp/secrets
signer.secret.provider.zookeeper.kerberos.keytab	/tmp/auth.keytab
signer.secret.provider.zookeeper.kerberos.principal	HTTP/localhost@LOCALHOST

RESEARCH ISSUES IN AUTHENTICATION

Due to the advent of the cloud and distributed computing environment, there is need for the multi user authentication, which in cloud can be achieved by groups, Role based access structure, tree structure etc. A group can have multiple members and it is managed by a group manager. Group manager is responsible to perform operations like adding new members into groups and removing some of them from the group based on the user request. The group members of group can upload files and share them to other members and also perform operations on them. Similarly, in role based access method, each user is assigned with particular role and the accesses to files are restricted based on the user roles. In tree structure, user accounts are maintained in a tree manner and all the users are placed in a leaf node and intermediate nodes are used to store the key information.

The work proposed by Jian Shen et.al, (2018) consists of number of groups and each of them having separate group manager (Shen, Zhou, Chen, Li & Susilo, 2018). Before registering the cloud server checks if the new user is revoked user or not by checking the revocation list. Revoked user means, he cannot register as a new one. He should send unrevoked request to cloud server to activate his account. Once the registration process is completed, the user will be allocated to specific group based on the interest while he was registering. Each group consists of common key (CK) and group private and public key pairs. CK will get updated in a time based manner and the group keys will get updated while any users leave/join. These updates are done by the key server.

Initially any user wants to store data into cloud; he should encrypt the data using the cryptographic key. This will help to protect the data which are shared within the group. Once the encryption gets completed user can set the File access list by adding the users those who can access the file. This will add more security to the file. Once all the process gets completed the encrypted file is sent to group manager and the manager add the group signature (σ) using the group key and store the file into cloud server. If any user wants to access the file in the cloud, he should login into the cloud and search for the particular files. The group manager checks permission for particular user by checking the file access list. If they don't have access to particular file means, the user has to request the data owner to update the access list. Users can leave from the group at any time. If any users leave from the group, their credentials are moved into revocation list and all access permission provide for the specific user in each File Access list will get erased. It will help to achieve forward secrecy.

Kumar, Kumar, and Pandey (2017) propose on cluster tree structure to manage the multiple users in cloud efficiently to handle the user keys. Moreover, this scheme is very scalable and can handle the joining or leaving request of members in the batches efficiently. In this scheme the key server needs to perform only one multiplication operation upon batch of users joining and needs to perform only one division operation upon batch of existing members leave the group. The system consists of key server (KS), sender, group members.

The Centralized Group key Distribution (CGKD) method consists of five phases. First phase is known as key server initialization phase. Second phase is called member initial join phase where member computes secret and private key. The third phase is called key update phase. The fourth phase is the key recovery phase which deals with the recovery of group key. The fifth phase is called member leave phase where the key server performs necessary operation to recompute and distribute the group key.

In cluster tree structure the members are divided into small number of groups called clusters. The first level of the tree represents the Key server. The second level represents the middle level nodes where the key server stores the temporary variables like subgroup key encryption key. The third level consists of members, where the members are grouped into clusters. When a batch of members wants to join the group then a new cluster for this batch is created and a new middle level node is created to connect them. Similarly, whenever a batch of members leave the group then complete cluster of that batch is removed.

Xuanxia et al. presented their work where they designed a credentials based access control method which is also known as Attribute based access control. The system model consists of cloud server, data owner and data sharer. The cloud server delivers the cloud storage based on the user credentials. Data owner is a registered cloud server to store the files into cloud and share the data with other users by giving their credentials to them. Based on the credentials the users are limited to access the resource. The authorization credentials consist of seven items namely $I_1, I_2, I_3, I_4, I_5, I_6, I_7$. I_1 defines the full name of the files. $I_2 I_3 I_4$ describe the validity period, credential number, credential issuer ID. I_5 denotes the signature of the credential owner. I_6 denotes the verification code and which is verified by the cloud server, whether the credential is used by the owner or not. I_7 is the binding code and which is used to verify the integrity of the credentials. Any user can access the encrypted file listed in

I_1 by showing their identity to cloud server. Based on the encrypted file and its binding code the user can reconstruct the file key and decrypt the data and use them (Yao, Liu, Ning, Yang & Xiang, n.d.).

Lan Zhou et.al used a role based access control (RBAC) mechanism, which can simplify the security in large scale system. The roles are used to provide set of permissions to users. Instead of assigning permission to each user, here roles are assigned to set of users and permissions are assigned to roles to reduce the time. Only users that have specific role can access the specific data. Here they implement Role based access structure in hierarchical structure. For example, role R2 inherits from R3 and R4, and R1 inherits from R2 means user who assign with role R1 can eligible for all the remaining roles (Zhou, Varadharajan, & Hitchens, 2015).

To achieve efficient RBAC they propose two techniques namely Owner-Role RBAC Trust Model and Role-User RBAC Trust Model. Owner-Role model consists of three entities namely owner, user, role. Owner is the entity who is the owner of the data and stores the data into cloud in encrypted form. Users are denoted as consumers who wish to access the file stored in the cloud. Role is used to associate users with access permissions to owner data. Trust models are used to evaluate the Owner-Role model. For example, interaction trust model evaluates only authenticated users in the predecessor roles of the role have accessed the data. Role-User RBAC model is used for analyzing the behavior of the user, it is important that only the members with good behavior can only get a membership. They also presented a trust model to evaluate trust of the user that, which user belongs to which role as well as the new user who wants to join the role. The trust models used by them are Trust vectors, Trust records, direct trust, Recommendation trust, combination trust.

Identity based encryption was presented by Jianghong Wei el (Wei, Liu, & Hu, n.d.). Identity access management is defined as right user access the right resources for the right reason at right time. They proposed a Revocable-Storage Identity Based Encryption (RS-IBE) to achieve the integrity by avoiding unauthorized users accessing the data and also achieve forward and backward secrecy. The term forward secrecy defines that, when the user's authority is expired, then he should not access the file in future. Similarly, backward secrecy means, user who registered as a new cannot access the files which was previously shared without the knowledge of data owner. Here they use two binary trees. One is used to store and manage the identity and another one is used to manage the time period or validity of the encryption. The RS-IBE scheme for data sharing works as follows: At first the data provider decides the number of users who can access the data. Then the data owner encrypts the data based on the user identities and shares the data into cloud. The members who have the permissions to access the file can download and decrypt them. However, for unauthorized members the data are not available for them. In some case, if anyone's authorization gets expired means, the data owner once again decrypts the data and then re-encrypts the data based on the identity of the user. However, this brings a computation and communication complexity. One method to avoid the problem is for the cloud server to directly re-encrypt the data without decrypting it, but it also introduces cipher text extension.

CONCLUSION

In this chapter, various authentication schemes in the Hadoop distributed computing environment are outlined preceded by an Introduction to security mechanism and the Kerberos protocol. It is left to the designer choice to choose the appropriate authentication scheme. In order to select the right authentication scheme, it is mandatory to go through the white paper of each authentication scheme to analyze the strength and weakness of each scheme. The trade off must be made between the strength of the authentication scheme, the cost of implementation and the seriousness of the applications.

REFERENCES

Kumar, Kumar, & Pandey. (2017). A computationally efficient centralized group key distribution protocol for secure multicast communications based upon RSA public key cryptosystem. *Journal of King Saud University - Computer and Information Sciences.* doi: 10.1016/j.jksuci.2017.12.014

Shen, J., Zhou, T., Chen, X., Li, J., & Susilo, W. (2018, April). Anonymous and Traceable Group Data Sharing in Cloud Computing. *IEEE Transactions on Information Forensics and Security, 13*(4), 912–925. doi:10.1109/TIFS.2017.2774439

Wei, J., Liu, W., & Hu, X. (n.d.). Secure Data Sharing in Cloud Computing Using Revocable-Storage Identity-Based Encryption. *IEEE Transactions on Cloud Computing.* Retrieved from https://www.kerberos.org/software/tutorial.html

Yao, Liu, Ning, Yang, & Xiang. (n.d.). Anonymous Credential-Based Access Control Scheme for Clouds. *IEEE Cloud Computing*. doi: 10.1109/MCC.2015.79

Zhou, Varadharajan, & Hitchens. (n.d.). Trust Enhanced Cryptographic Role-based Access Control for Secure Cloud Data Storage. *IEEE Transactions on Information Forensics and Security*. doi:10.1109/TIFS.2015.2455952

About the Authors

T. Revathi has completed her B.E. Degree in Electrical & Electronics Engineering from Madurai Kamaraj University, Madurai, India in the year 1986. Immediately she started her career as Lecturer in Mepco Schlenk Engineering College, Sivakasi. She completed her Master degree in Computer Science and Engineering from Bharathiar University, Coimbatore in the year 1995. Her research work is in the field of Computer Networks and she obtained Ph.D. in the year 2008 from Manonmainam Sundaranar University, Tirunelveli. Currently she is working as Senior Professor & Head in Information Technology Department of Mepco Schlenk Engineering College, Sivakasi. She has more than 32 years of teaching experience. She has published 83 papers in various International & National journals & conferences. Her research interests include Big data analytics, Streaming analytics, and Sensor networks.

Muneeswaran Karuppiah received the Bachelor of Engineering degree in Electronics and Communication Engineering from Madurai Kamarajar University, Tamilnadu, India in 1984 and the Master of Engineering in Computer Science and Engineering from Bharathiyar University, Tamilnadu, India, in 1990. In 2006, he received the Ph.D. degree in Computer Science and Engineering from M.S. University, Tamilnadu, India. He is in teaching and research for the past 34 years and 17 years respectively and currently, he is working as Senior Professor in Computer Science and Engineering Department at Mepco Schlenk Engineering College, Tamilnadu. His research interests are image analysis, machine learning techniques, and Data Analytics. He has authored or co-authored about 125 publications in journal/conference level and one book on Compiler Design with Oxford University.

About the Authors

M. Blessa Binolin Pepsi, M.E. (CS), B.tech (IT), Senior Assistant Professor, currently working in the department of Information Technology, Mepco Schlenk Engineering College, Sivakasi has work experience of 5 years since 2013. Authoress had published 8 papers in International Journals and 7 papers in various conferences. Authoress is the recipient of Venus International Award for Young Women in Engineering. Authoress's research interest includes big data and machine learning. Had guided nearly 15 UG and PG scholars in this research area to develop projects connected with recent era.

Index

W

Web Data Analytics 8
workspaces 6

Y

Yahoo 34, 36
YARN (Yet Another Resource Negotiator)
    39-40, 45-46, 51, 55, 57-58, 62, 64, 78,
90-94, 100-101, 105-107, 114, 117-
118, 122, 147-148, 155, 159, 166-167,
181, 206, 208, 212, 214

Z

zettabytes 1, 90

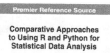

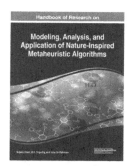

Ensure Quality Research is Introduced to the Academic Community

Become an IGI Global Reviewer for Authored Book Projects

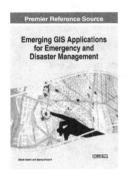   

The overall success of an authored book project is dependent on quality and timely reviews.

In this competitive age of scholarly publishing, constructive and timely feedback significantly expedites the turnaround time of manuscripts from submission to acceptance, allowing the publication and discovery of forward-thinking research at a much more expeditious rate. Several IGI Global authored book projects are currently seeking highly qualified experts in the field to fill vacancies on their respective editorial review boards:

Applications may be sent to:
development@igi-global.com

Applicants must have a doctorate (or an equivalent degree) as well as publishing and reviewing experience. Reviewers are asked to write reviews in a timely, collegial, and constructive manner. All reviewers will begin their role on an ad-hoc basis for a period of one year, and upon successful completion of this term can be considered for full editorial review board status, with the potential for a subsequent promotion to Associate Editor.

If you have a colleague that may be interested in this opportunity, we encourage you to share this information with them.

Printed in the United States
By Bookmasters